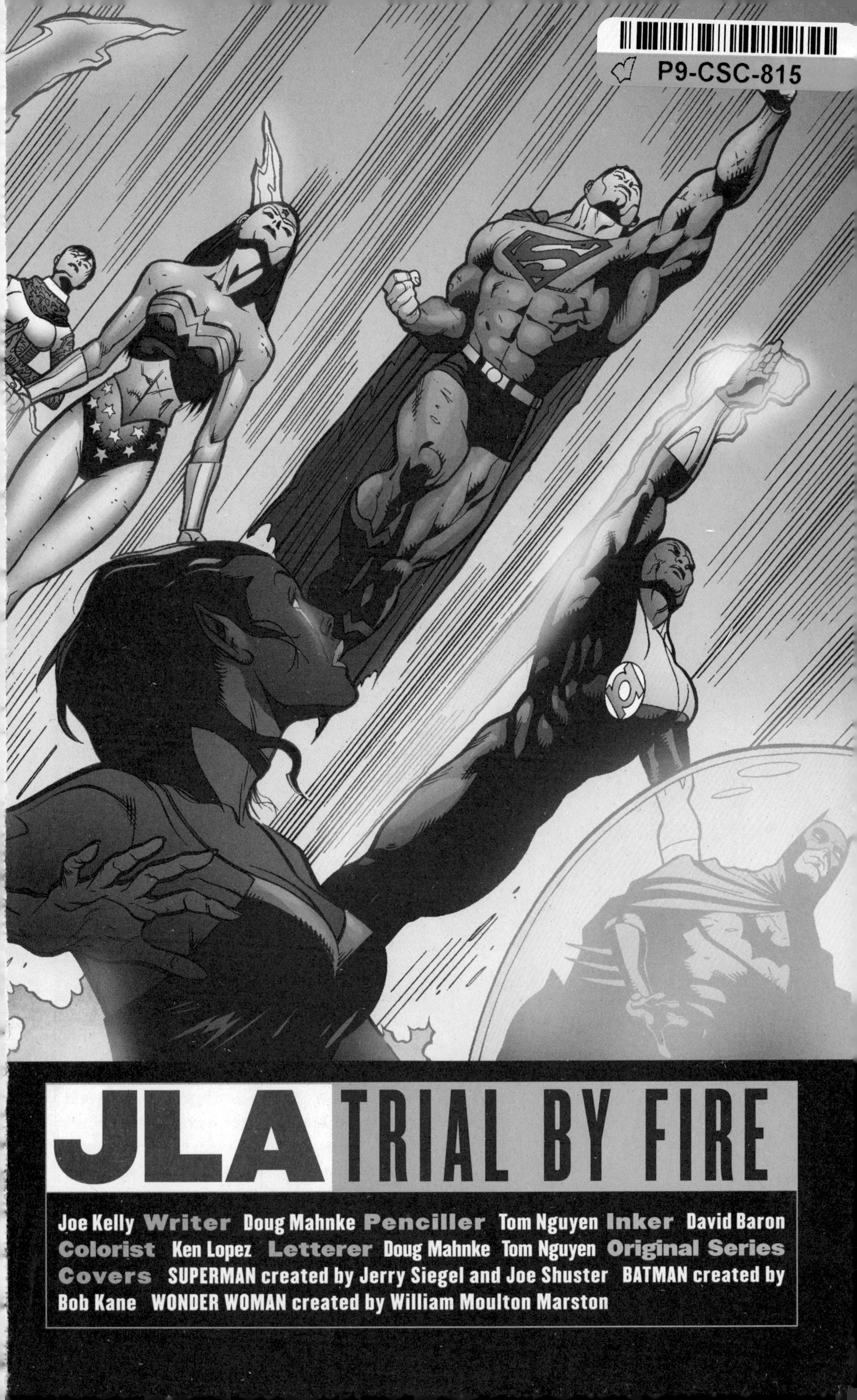

JLA TRIAL BY FIRE

Joe Kelly **Writer** Doug Mahnke **Penciller** Tom Nguyen **Inker** David Baron **Colorist** Ken Lopez **Letterer** Doug Mahnke Tom Nguyen **Original Series Covers** SUPERMAN created by Jerry Siegel and Joe Shuster BATMAN created by Bob Kane WONDER WOMAN created by William Moulton Marston

Dan DiDio	VP-Editorial
Mike Carlin	Editor-original series
Valerie D'Orazio	Assistant Editor-original series
Robert Greenberger	Senior Editor-collected edition
Robbin Brosterman	Senior Art Director
Paul Levitz	President & Publisher
Georg Brewer	VP-Design & Retail Product Development
Richard Bruning	Senior VP-Creative Director
Patrick Caldon	Senior VP-Finance & Operations
Chris Caramalis	VP-Finance
Terri Cunningham	VP-Managing Editor
Alison Gill	VP-Manufacturing
Rich Johnson	VP-Book Trade Sales
Hank Kanalz	VP-General Manager, WildStorm
Lillian Laserson	Senior VP & General Counsel
Jim Lee	Editorial Director-WildStorm
David McKillips	VP- Advertising & Custom Publishing
John Nee	VP-Business Development
Gregory Noveck	Senior VP-Creative Affairs
Cheryl Rubin	Senior VP-Brand Management
Bob Wayne	VP-Sales & Marketing

JLA

The Justice League of America is Earth's first and last line of defense, a pantheon of super-powered protectors watching over the Earth from a fortress on the Moon.

Superman: The last son of the doomed planet Krypton, Kal-El uses his incredible powers of flight, super-strength, and invulnerability to fight for truth and justice on his adopted planet, Earth. When not protecting the planet, he is *Daily Planet* reporter Clark Kent, married to fellow journalist Lois Lane.

Batman: Dedicated to ridding the world of crime since the brutal murder of his parents, billionaire Bruce Wayne dons the cape and cowl of the Dark Knight to battle evil from the shadows of Gotham City.

Wonder Woman: Born an Amazonian princess, Diana was chosen to serve as her people's ambassador of peace in the World of Man. Armed with the Lasso of Truth and indestructible bracelets, she directs her gods-given abilities of strength and speed toward the betterment of mankind.

The Flash: A member of the Teen Titans when he was known as Kid Flash, Wally West now takes the place of the fallen Flash, Barry Allen, as the speedster of the Justice League.

Green Lantern: John Stewart didn't necessarily want to be a hero. As an architect he had a good career going, and he saw the role of Green Lantern as a distraction. In time he knew the tremendous satisfaction that came with using the ring responsibly, but after his actions led to the destruction of the planet Xanshi his spirit was crushed, and he suffered a series of ordeals that left him physically crippled as well. Recently John regained the use of his limbs, and he is now coming to terms with the traumatic events of his past.

Martian Manhunter: The most dedicated member of the Justice League, J'onn J'onzz has been present for every one of the team's many incarnations. His strength rivals that of Earth's mightiest heroes, and his shape-shifting abilities allow him to pass anonymously among our planet's populace. Currently on a leave of absence, J'onn works to overcome his fear of fire.

The Atom: One of the first heroes to join after the League's founding, Ray Palmer is a scientist who harnessed the properties of a white dwarf star. This led to the creation of unique size and weight controls that enable him to reduce his physical form to that of an atom, or even smaller. Forgoing the world of heroics for research and teaching, the Atom remains available as a reserve member. He has been helping Firestorm to master his power.

Firestorm: High school student Ronnie Raymond and nuclear physicist Martin Stein were both present when an explosion occurred at a nuclear reactor. Fused into one being, they found that they had the power to rearrange the atomic structure of inorganic matter, and eventually joined the Justice League. Stein has since disappeared, and Raymond, now struggling with college, is in sole control of the power of Firestorm — as far as we know.

Major Disaster: Small-time thief Paul Booker originally used various scientific devices to create large-scale disasters that would serve as distractions for his robberies. Eventually, Booker internalized the power in the devices and he began a career as a super-criminal. After several defeats (and a short stint with a previous incarnation of the League and the Suicide Squad), Booker found himself struggling with his evil nature once again — only to be inspired by Superman to righteousness.

Manitou Raven: An Apache American from 3000 years ago with uncanny magical powers, he is the newest member of the JLA. With his wife Dawn, he is adjusting to his new century and his role as earthly champion, and is still learning about his teammates.

Faith: Very little is known about the woman called Faith that isn't highly classified. Previously in the employ of an unidentified government Black Ops team, the exact nature of her job is unknown. However, nicknamed the "Fat Lady" by her teammates, one can infer that Faith is traditionally called in to finish what others have started. Faith claims to have met Batman during a past mission, during which they spent some time together. Apparently, it was enough time for her to earn Batman's trust, as he recommended her for JLA membership.

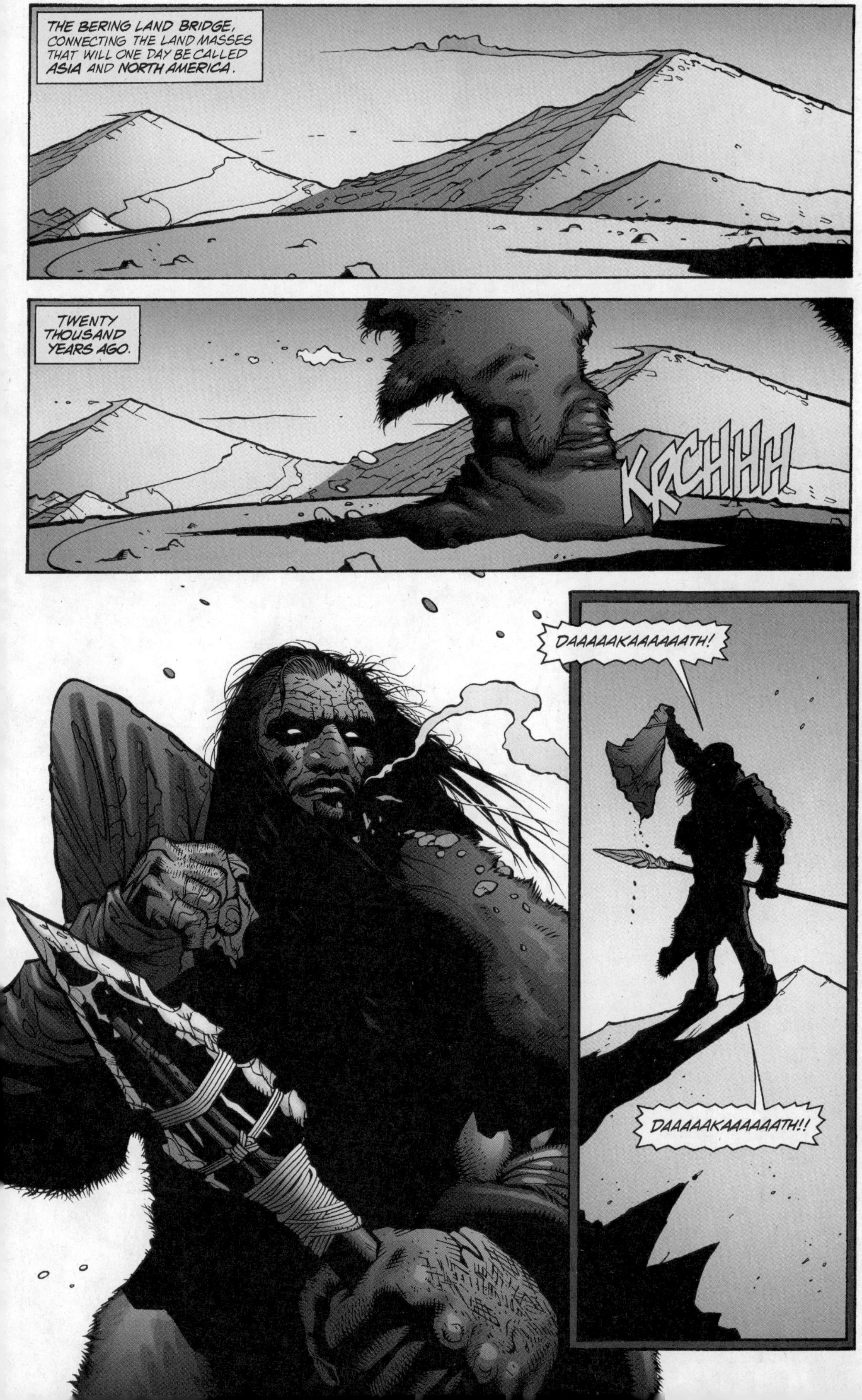
THE BERING LAND BRIDGE, CONNECTING THE LAND MASSES THAT WILL ONE DAY BE CALLED ASIA AND NORTH AMERICA.
TWENTY THOUSAND YEARS AGO.
KRCHHH
DAAAAAKAAAAAATH!
DAAAAAKAAAAAATH!!

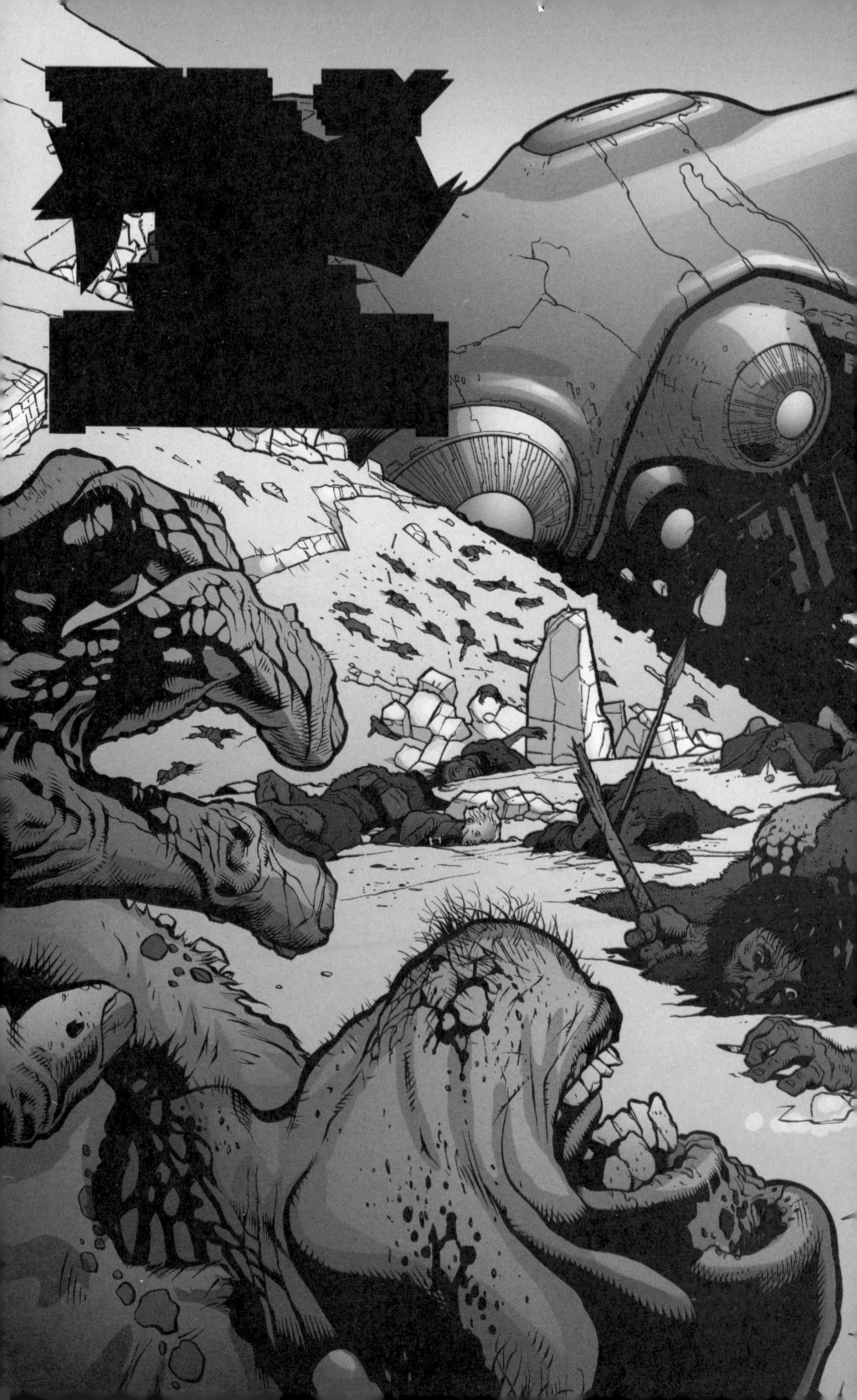
[redacted]

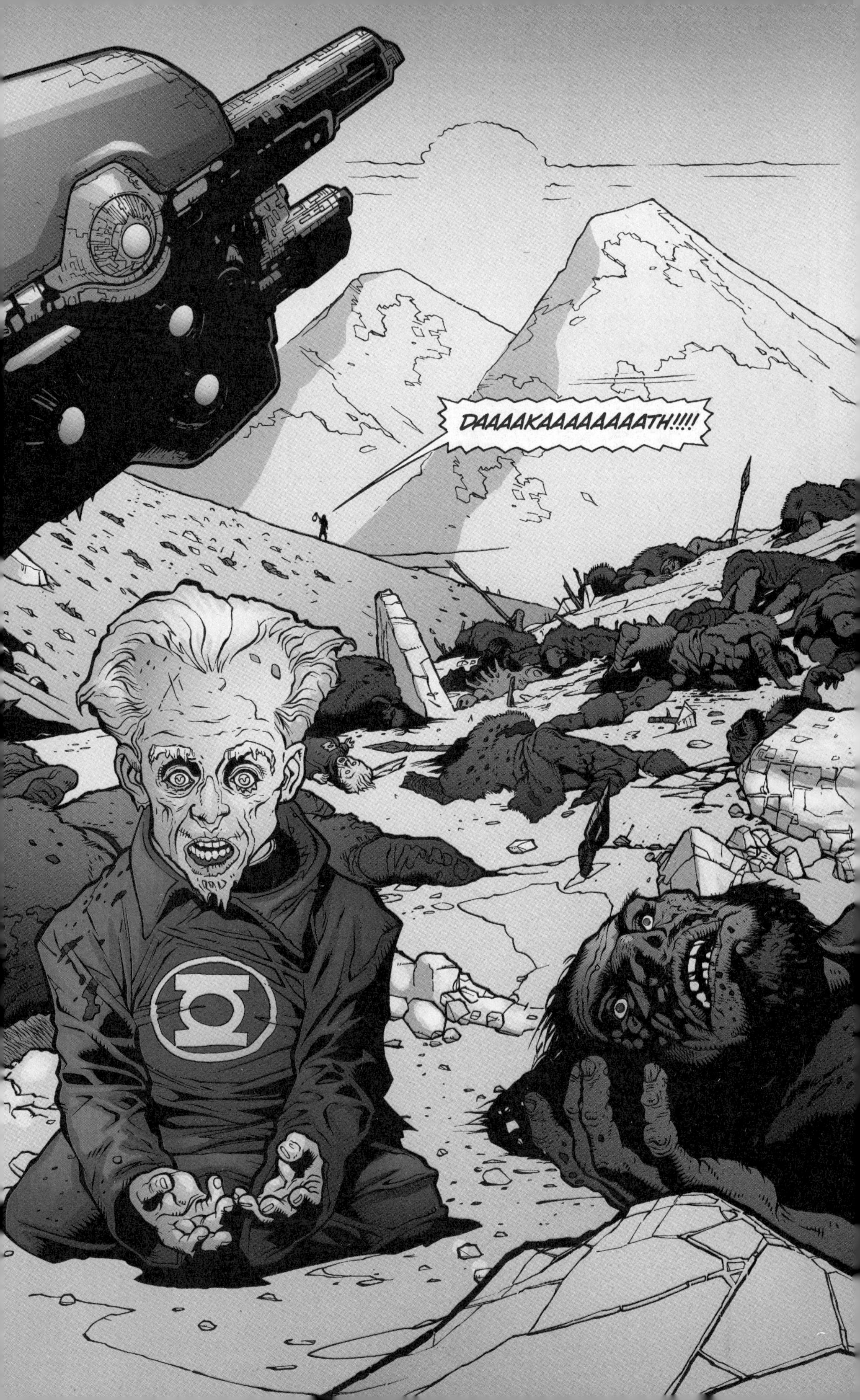
DAAAAKAAAAAAAATH!!!!!

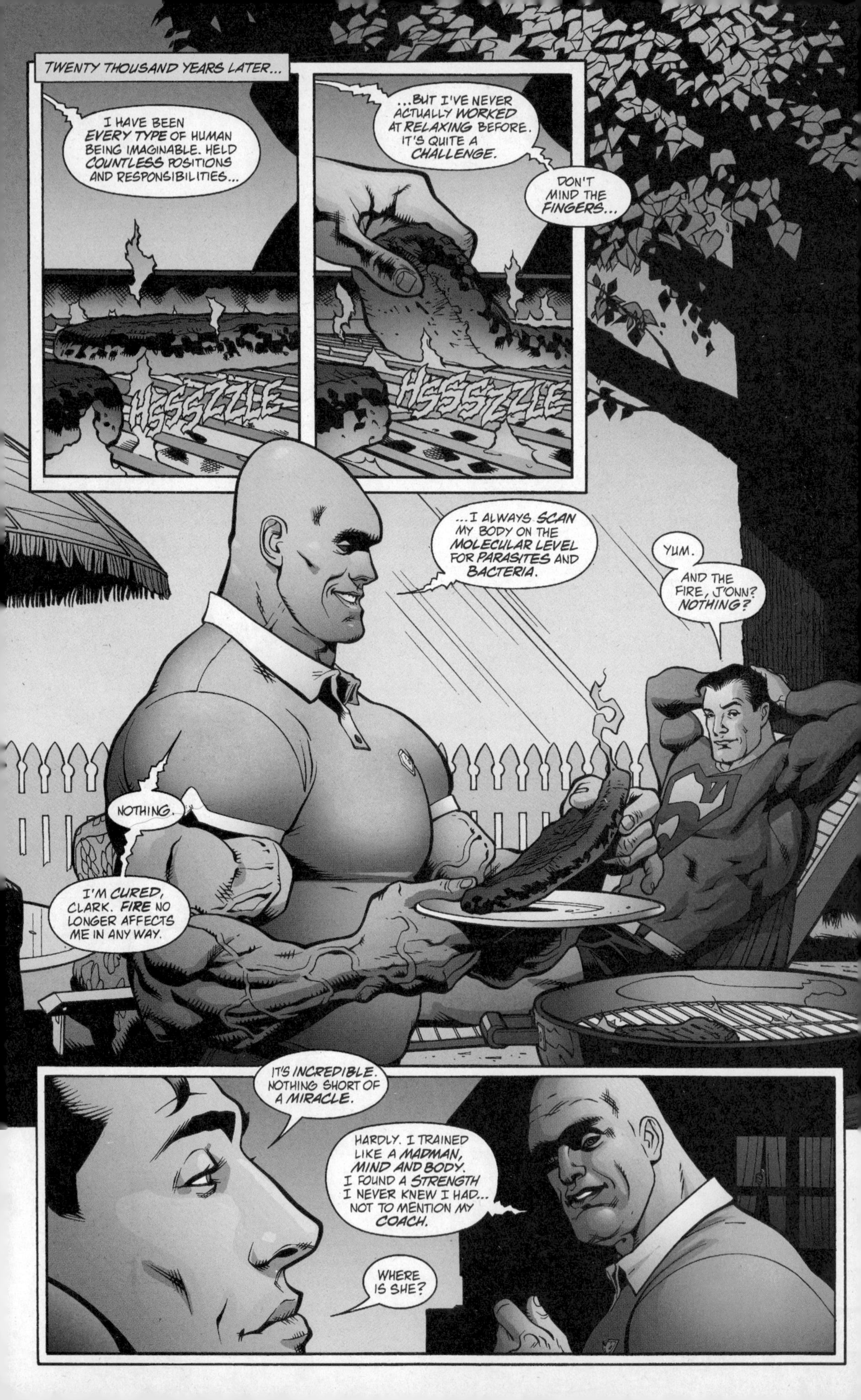
TWENTY THOUSAND YEARS LATER...
I HAVE BEEN EVERY TYPE OF HUMAN BEING IMAGINABLE. HELD COUNTLESS POSITIONS AND RESPONSIBILITIES...
HSSSZZLE
...BUT I'VE NEVER ACTUALLY WORKED AT RELAXING BEFORE. IT'S QUITE A CHALLENGE.
DON'T MIND THE FINGERS...
HSSSZZLE
...I ALWAYS SCAN MY BODY ON THE MOLECULAR LEVEL FOR PARASITES AND BACTERIA.
YUM.
AND THE FIRE, J'ONN? NOTHING?
NOTHING.
I'M CURED, CLARK. FIRE NO LONGER AFFECTS ME IN ANY WAY.
IT'S INCREDIBLE. NOTHING SHORT OF A MIRACLE.
HARDLY. I TRAINED LIKE A MADMAN, MIND AND BODY. I FOUND A STRENGTH I NEVER KNEW I HAD... NOT TO MENTION MY COACH.
WHERE IS SHE?

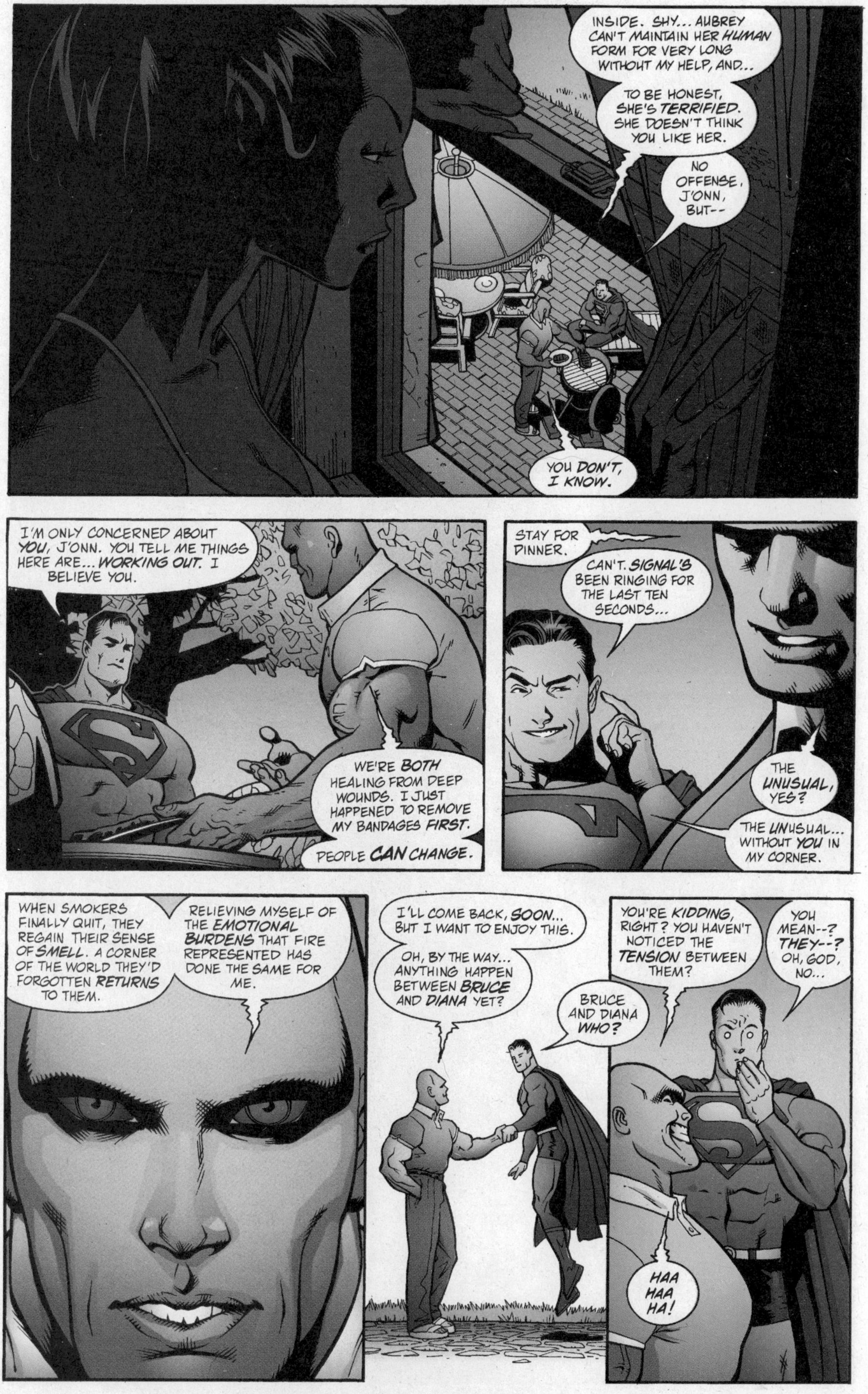
INSIDE. SHY... AUBREY CAN'T MAINTAIN HER HUMAN FORM FOR VERY LONG WITHOUT MY HELP, AND...
TO BE HONEST, SHE'S TERRIFIED. SHE DOESN'T THINK YOU LIKE HER.
NO OFFENSE, J'ONN, BUT--
YOU DON'T, I KNOW.
I'M ONLY CONCERNED ABOUT YOU, J'ONN. YOU TELL ME THINGS HERE ARE... WORKING OUT. I BELIEVE YOU.
WE'RE BOTH HEALING FROM DEEP WOUNDS. I JUST HAPPENED TO REMOVE MY BANDAGES FIRST.
PEOPLE CAN CHANGE.
STAY FOR DINNER.
CAN'T. SIGNAL'S BEEN RINGING FOR THE LAST TEN SECONDS...
THE UNUSUAL, YES?
THE UNUSUAL... WITHOUT YOU IN MY CORNER.
WHEN SMOKERS FINALLY QUIT, THEY REGAIN THEIR SENSE OF SMELL. A CORNER OF THE WORLD THEY'D FORGOTTEN RETURNS TO THEM.
RELIEVING MYSELF OF THE EMOTIONAL BURDENS THAT FIRE REPRESENTED HAS DONE THE SAME FOR ME.
I'LL COME BACK, SOON... BUT I WANT TO ENJOY THIS.
OH, BY THE WAY... ANYTHING HAPPEN BETWEEN BRUCE AND DIANA YET?
BRUCE AND DIANA WHO?
YOU'RE KIDDING, RIGHT? YOU HAVEN'T NOTICED THE TENSION BETWEEN THEM?
YOU MEAN--? THEY--? OH, GOD, NO...
HAA HAA HA!

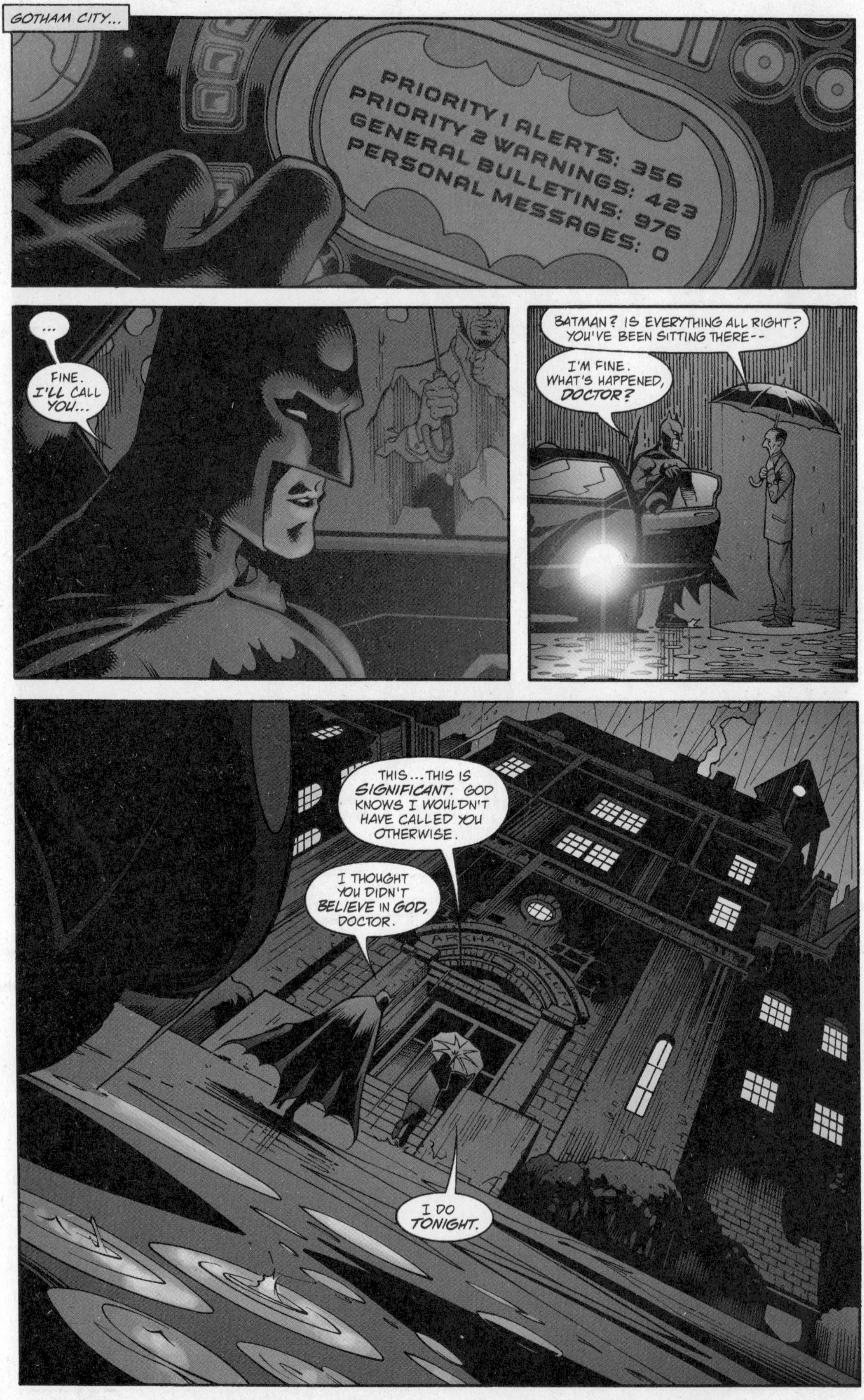
GOTHAM CITY...
PRIORITY 1 ALERTS: 356
PRIORITY 2 WARNINGS: 423
GENERAL BULLETINS: 976
PERSONAL MESSAGES: 0
...
FINE. I'LL CALL YOU...
BATMAN? IS EVERYTHING ALL RIGHT? YOU'VE BEEN SITTING THERE--
I'M FINE. WHAT'S HAPPENED, DOCTOR?
THIS...THIS IS SIGNIFICANT. GOD KNOWS I WOULDN'T HAVE CALLED YOU OTHERWISE.
I THOUGHT YOU DIDN'T BELIEVE IN GOD, DOCTOR.
I DO TONIGHT.

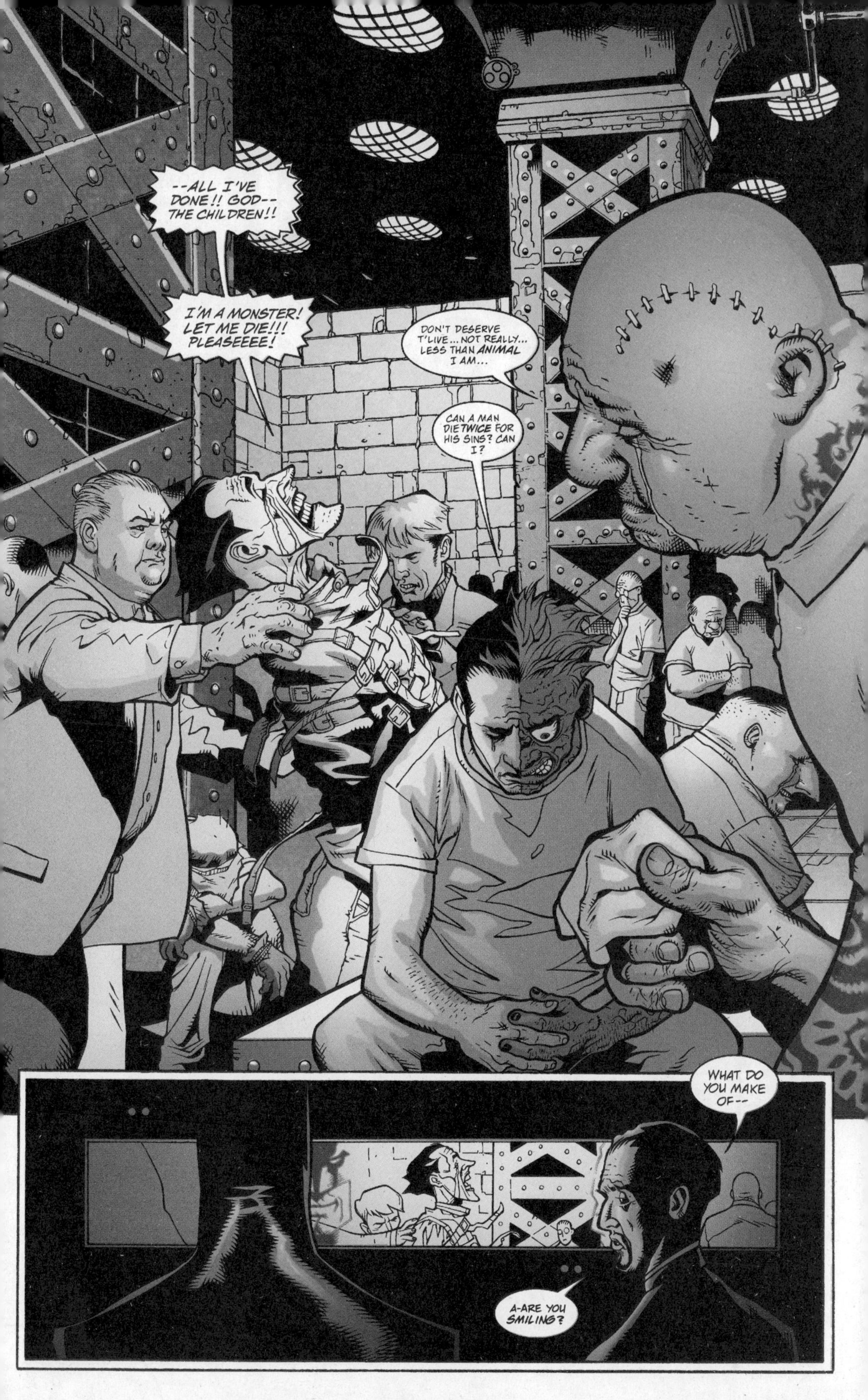
--ALL I'VE DONE!! GOD-- THE CHILDREN!!
I'M A MONSTER! LET ME DIE!!! PLEASEEEE!
DON'T DESERVE T'LIVE... NOT REALLY... LESS THAN ANIMAL I AM...
CAN A MAN DIE TWICE FOR HIS SINS? CAN I?
WHAT DO YOU MAKE OF--
A-ARE YOU SMILING?

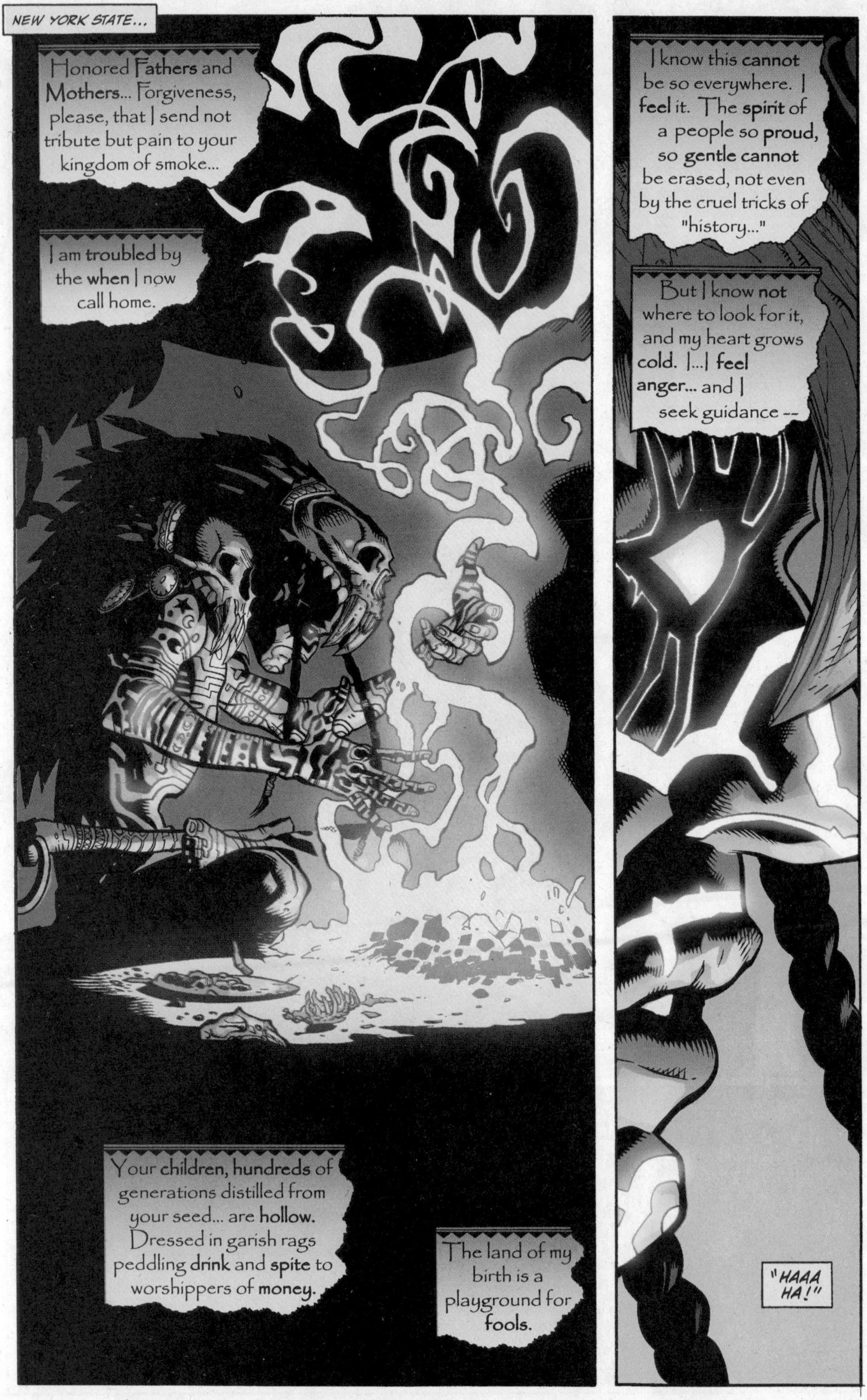
NEW YORK STATE...
Honored Fathers and Mothers... Forgiveness, please, that I send not tribute but pain to your kingdom of smoke...
I am troubled by the when I now call home.
Your children, hundreds of generations distilled from your seed... are hollow. Dressed in garish rags peddling drink and spite to worshippers of money.
The land of my birth is a playground for fools.
I know this cannot be so everywhere. I feel it. The spirit of a people so proud, so gentle cannot be erased, not even by the cruel tricks of "history..."
But I know not where to look for it, and my heart grows cold. I...I feel anger... and I seek guidance --
"HAAA HA!"

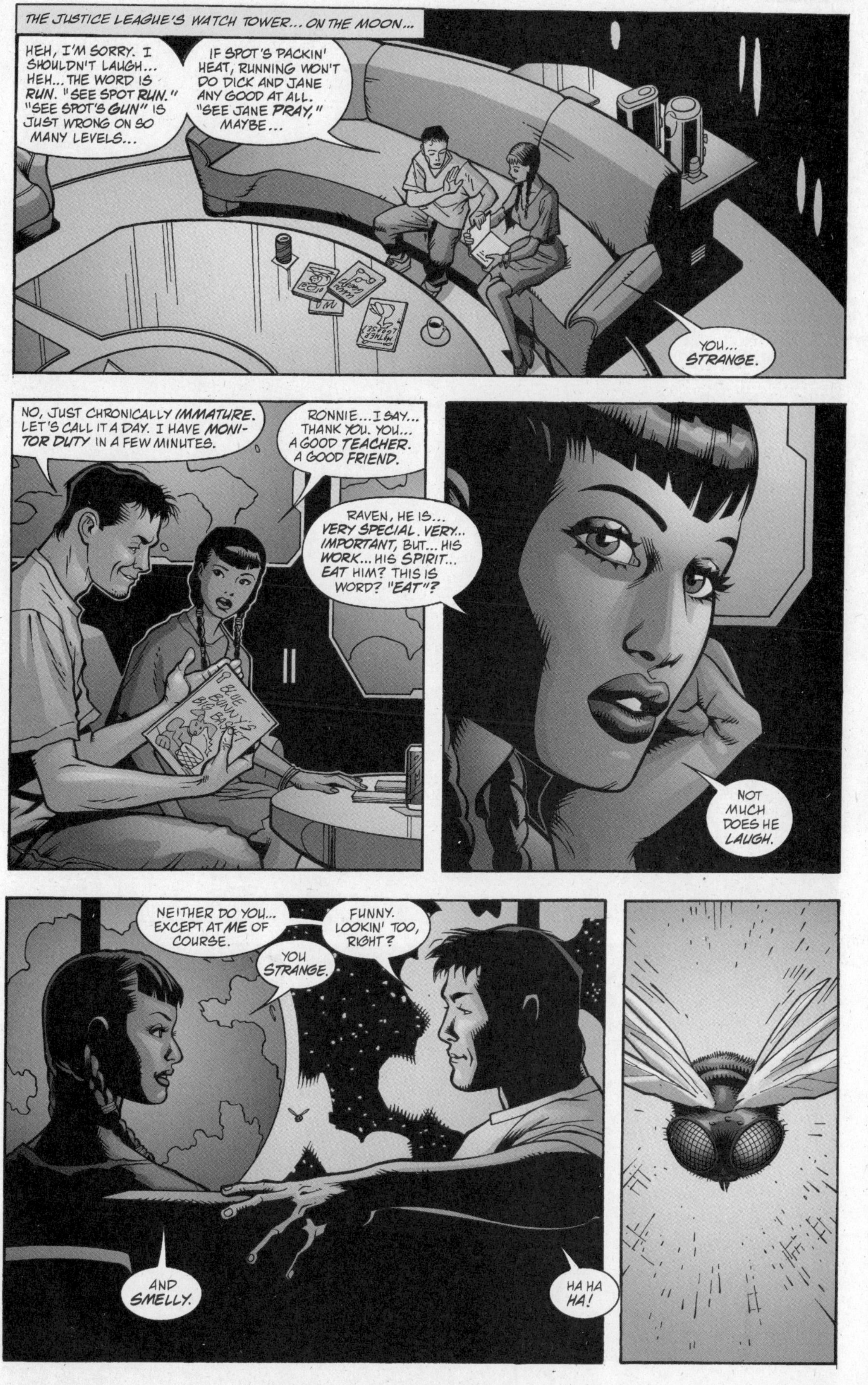
THE JUSTICE LEAGUE'S WATCH TOWER... ON THE MOON...
HEH, I'M SORRY. I SHOULDN'T LAUGH... HEH... THE WORD IS *RUN*. "SEE SPOT *RUN*." "SEE SPOT'S *GUN*" IS JUST WRONG ON SO MANY LEVELS...
IF SPOT'S PACKIN' HEAT, RUNNING WON'T DO DICK AND JANE ANY GOOD AT ALL. "SEE JANE *PRAY*," MAYBE...
YOU... *STRANGE*.
NO, JUST CHRONICALLY *IMMATURE*. LET'S CALL IT A DAY. I HAVE *MONITOR DUTY* IN A FEW MINUTES.
RONNIE... I SAY... THANK *YOU*. YOU... A GOOD *TEACHER*. A GOOD *FRIEND*.
RAVEN, HE IS... *VERY SPECIAL*. *VERY*... *IMPORTANT*, BUT... HIS *WORK*... HIS *SPIRIT*... *EAT* HIM? THIS IS WORD? *"EAT"*?
BLUE BUNNY'S BIG BASKET
NOT MUCH DOES HE *LAUGH*.
NEITHER DO YOU... EXCEPT AT *ME* OF COURSE.
FUNNY. LOOKIN' TOO, RIGHT?
YOU *STRANGE*.
AND *SMELLY*.
HA HA *HA!*

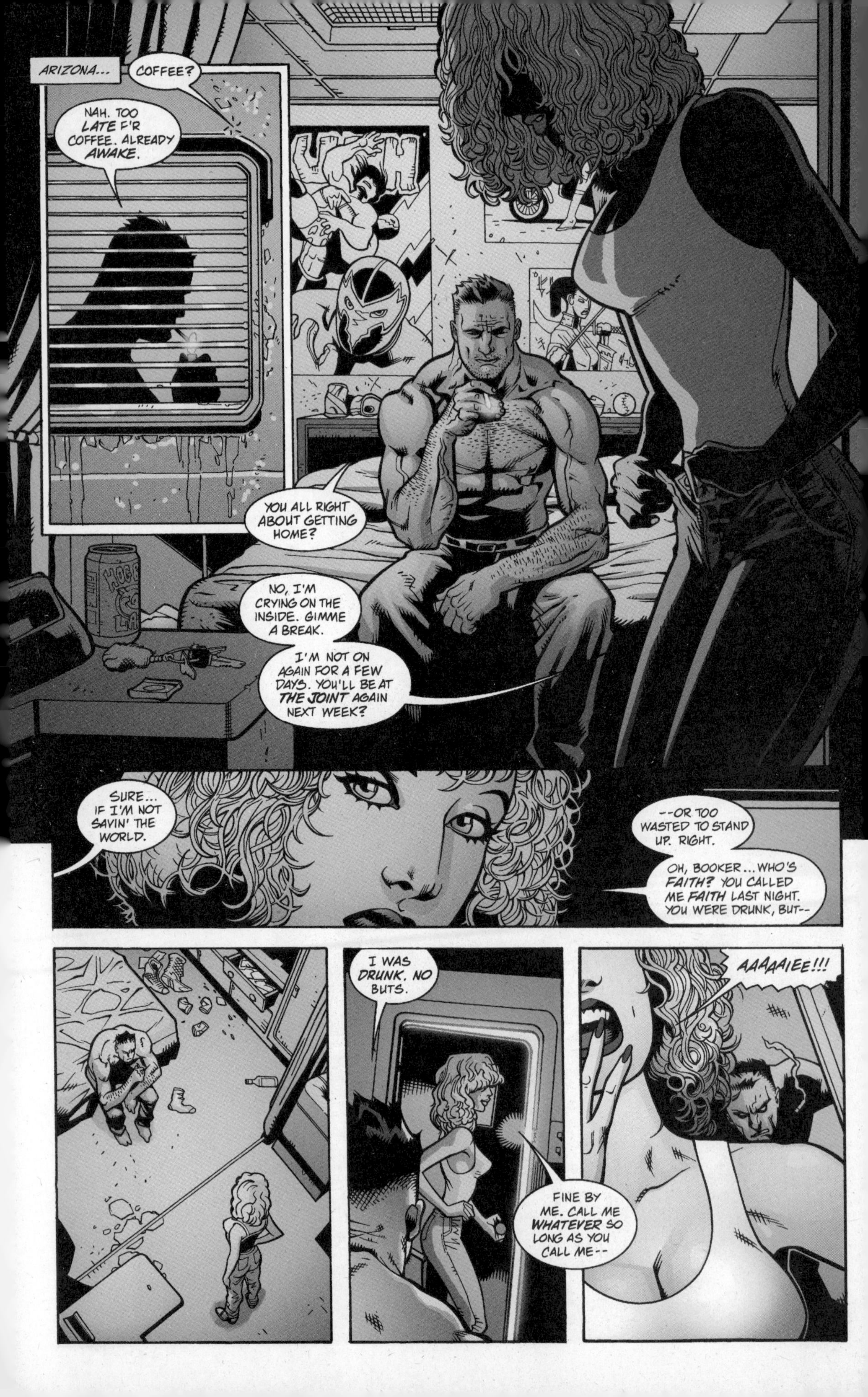
ARIZONA...
COFFEE?
NAH. TOO LATE F'R COFFEE. ALREADY AWAKE.
YOU ALL RIGHT ABOUT GETTING HOME?
NO, I'M CRYING ON THE INSIDE. GIMME A BREAK.
I'M NOT ON AGAIN FOR A FEW DAYS. YOU'LL BE AT THE JOINT AGAIN NEXT WEEK?
SURE... IF I'M NOT SAVIN' THE WORLD.
--OR TOO WASTED TO STAND UP. RIGHT.
OH, BOOKER... WHO'S FAITH? YOU CALLED ME FAITH LAST NIGHT. YOU WERE DRUNK, BUT--
I WAS DRUNK. NO BUTS.
FINE BY ME. CALL ME WHATEVER SO LONG AS YOU CALL ME--
AAAAAIEE!!!

GET DOWN! GET THE HELL DOWN!!!
WHAT THE @&#%$ ARE YOU PEOPLE--?
OH, DAMN.
C-COVER MY EYES... PLEASE...
GOD, PLEASE... CAN'T CLOSE THEM. C-CAN'T--
I CAN'T SEE. ARE MY EYES STILL OPEN... I CAN'T SEE.

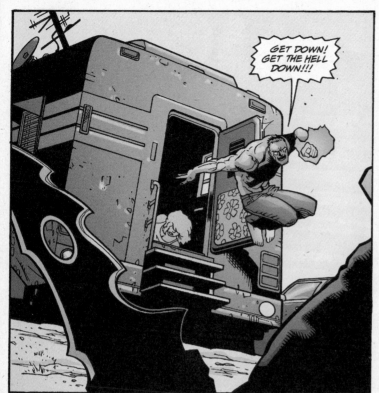

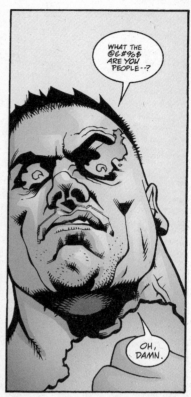

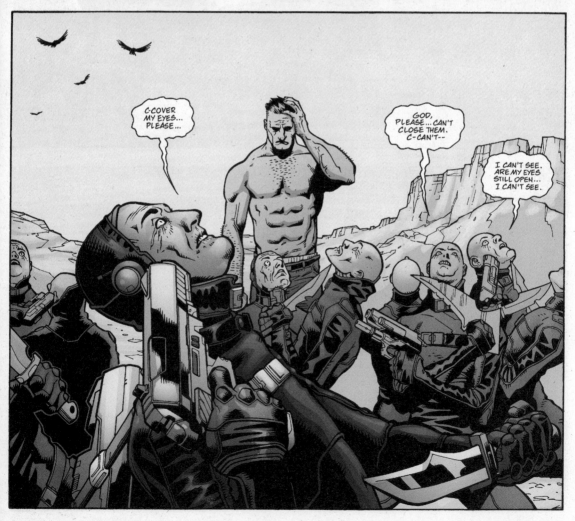

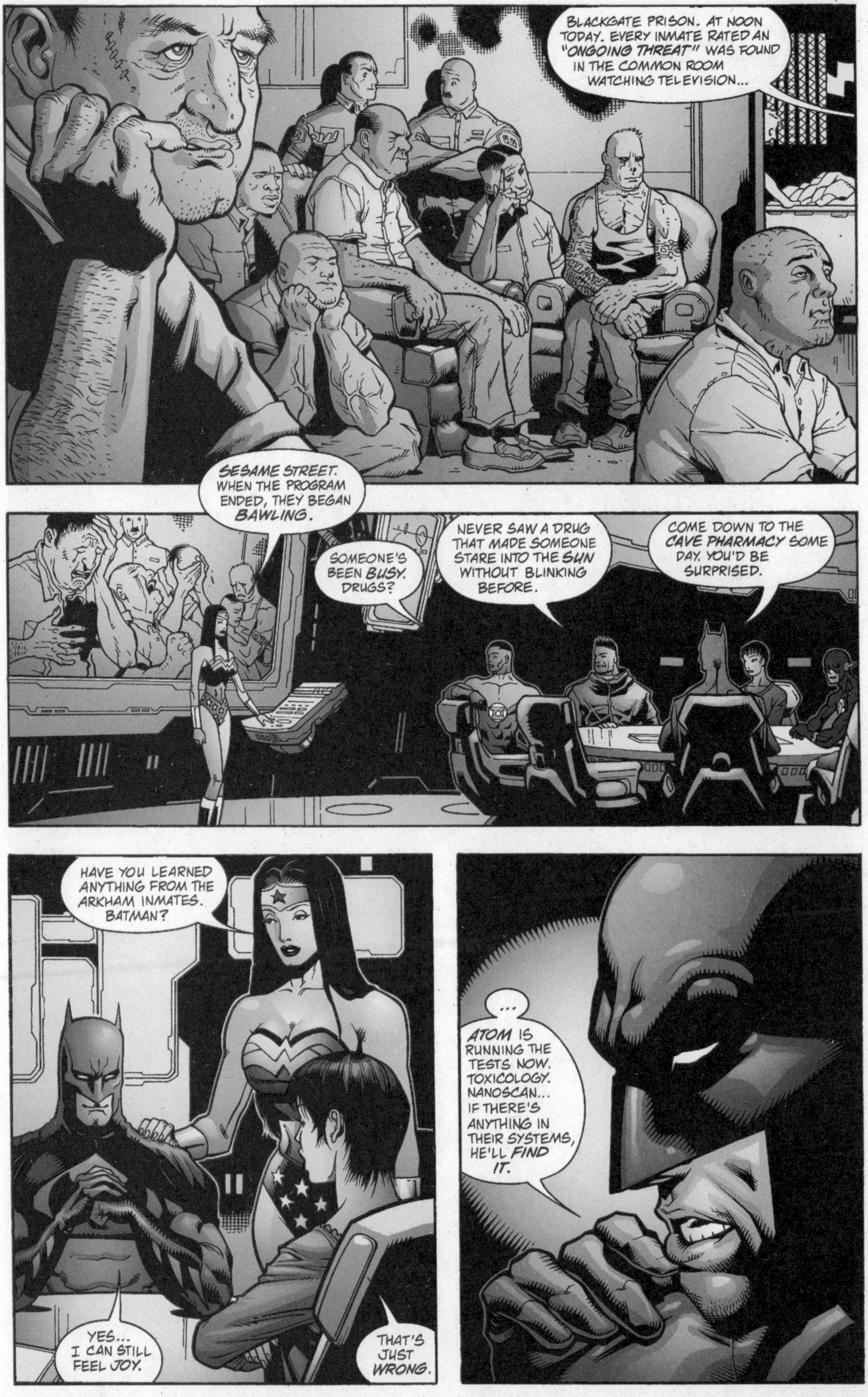
BLACKGATE PRISON. AT NOON TODAY. EVERY INMATE RATED AN "ONGOING THREAT" WAS FOUND IN THE COMMON ROOM WATCHING TELEVISION...
SESAME STREET. WHEN THE PROGRAM ENDED, THEY BEGAN BAWLING.
SOMEONE'S BEEN BUSY. DRUGS?
NEVER SAW A DRUG THAT MADE SOMEONE STARE INTO THE SUN WITHOUT BLINKING BEFORE.
COME DOWN TO THE CAVE PHARMACY SOME DAY. YOU'D BE SURPRISED.
HAVE YOU LEARNED ANYTHING FROM THE ARKHAM INMATES. BATMAN?
YES... I CAN STILL FEEL JOY.
THAT'S JUST WRONG.
...
ATOM IS RUNNING THE TESTS NOW. TOXICOLOGY. NANOSCAN... IF THERE'S ANYTHING IN THEIR SYSTEMS, HE'LL FIND IT.

IF I HAVE THE TIMELINE RIGHT, IT'S BEEN *EXACTLY* A DAY SINCE THE FIRST STRIKE.

WHOEVER HIT THESE GUYS, FOR BETTER OR WORSE, COVERED A FEW THOUSAND MILES IN A COUPLE OF HOURS, *AND* TOOK THEM DOWN WITHOUT A SCRATCH.

I'M THINKING *TELEPATH.*

OR A CREW ATTACKING *SIMULTANEOUSLY.* BUT *WHY?* TO ELIMINATE THE COMPETITION--?

OR TO DO THE WORLD A BIG *FAVOR?*

AND WHO *WERE* THOSE GUYS ANYWAY, BOOKER?

≶UH≶

EX-*"ASSOCIATES"* ≶AHEM≶ FROM BACK IN THE DAYS. NO BIG.

"NO *BIG"?*

DID I *STUTTER?*

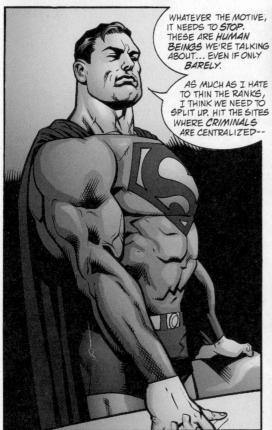

WHATEVER THE MOTIVE, IT NEEDS TO *STOP.* THESE ARE *HUMAN BEINGS* WE'RE TALKING ABOUT... EVEN IF ONLY *BARELY.*

AS MUCH AS I HATE TO THIN THE RANKS, I THINK WE NEED TO SPLIT UP. HIT THE SITES WHERE *CRIMINALS* ARE CENTRALIZED--

BDEET

BDEET

I GOT IT!

UMMM...

WHO HASN'T HAD THEIR HELPING OF *IRONY* TODAY?

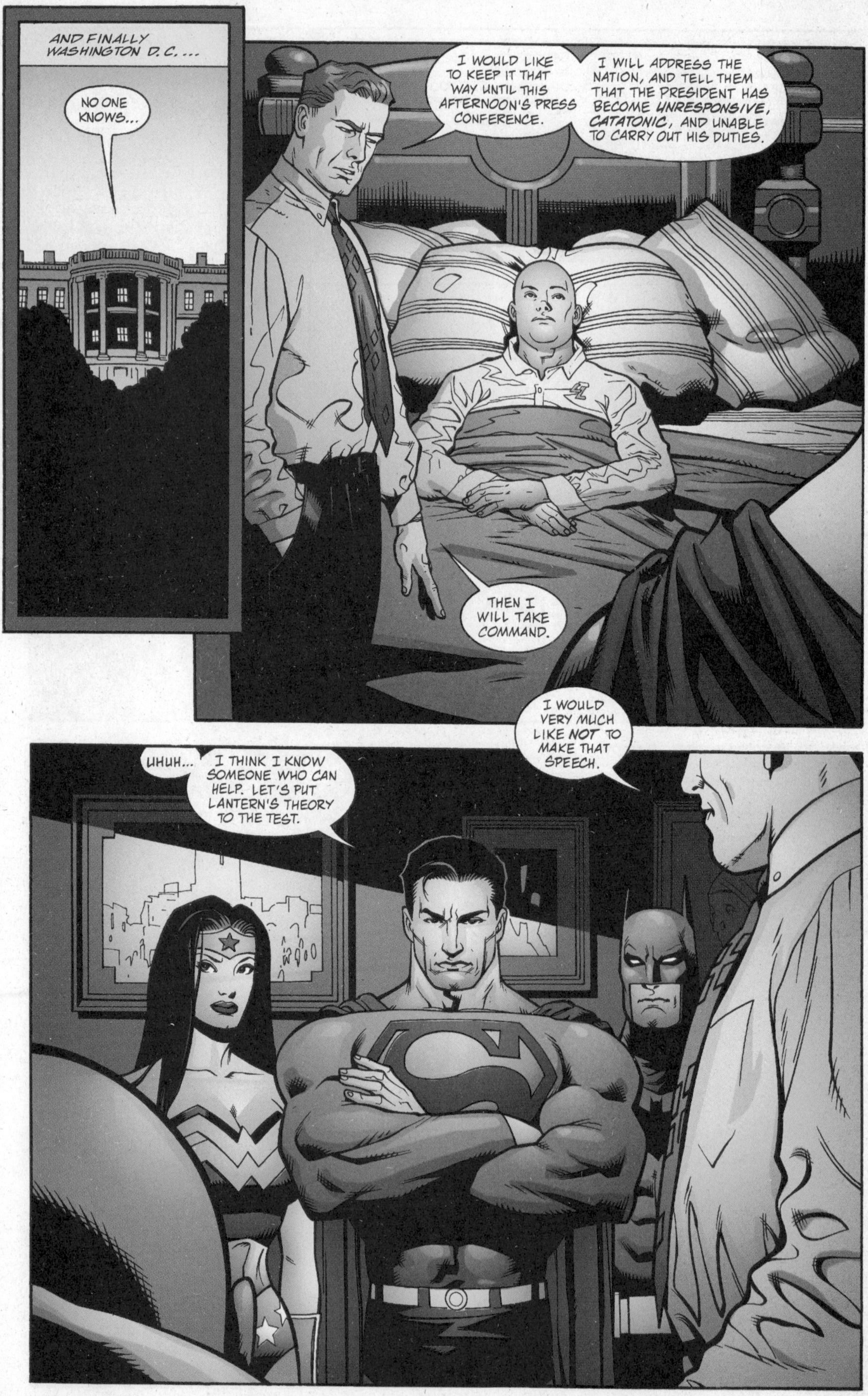
AND FINALLY WASHINGTON D.C. ...
NO ONE KNOWS...
I WOULD LIKE TO KEEP IT THAT WAY UNTIL THIS AFTERNOON'S PRESS CONFERENCE.
I WILL ADDRESS THE NATION, AND TELL THEM THAT THE PRESIDENT HAS BECOME UNRESPONSIVE, CATATONIC, AND UNABLE TO CARRY OUT HIS DUTIES.
THEN I WILL TAKE COMMAND.
I WOULD VERY MUCH LIKE NOT TO MAKE THAT SPEECH.
UHUH...
I THINK I KNOW SOMEONE WHO CAN HELP. LET'S PUT LANTERN'S THEORY TO THE TEST.

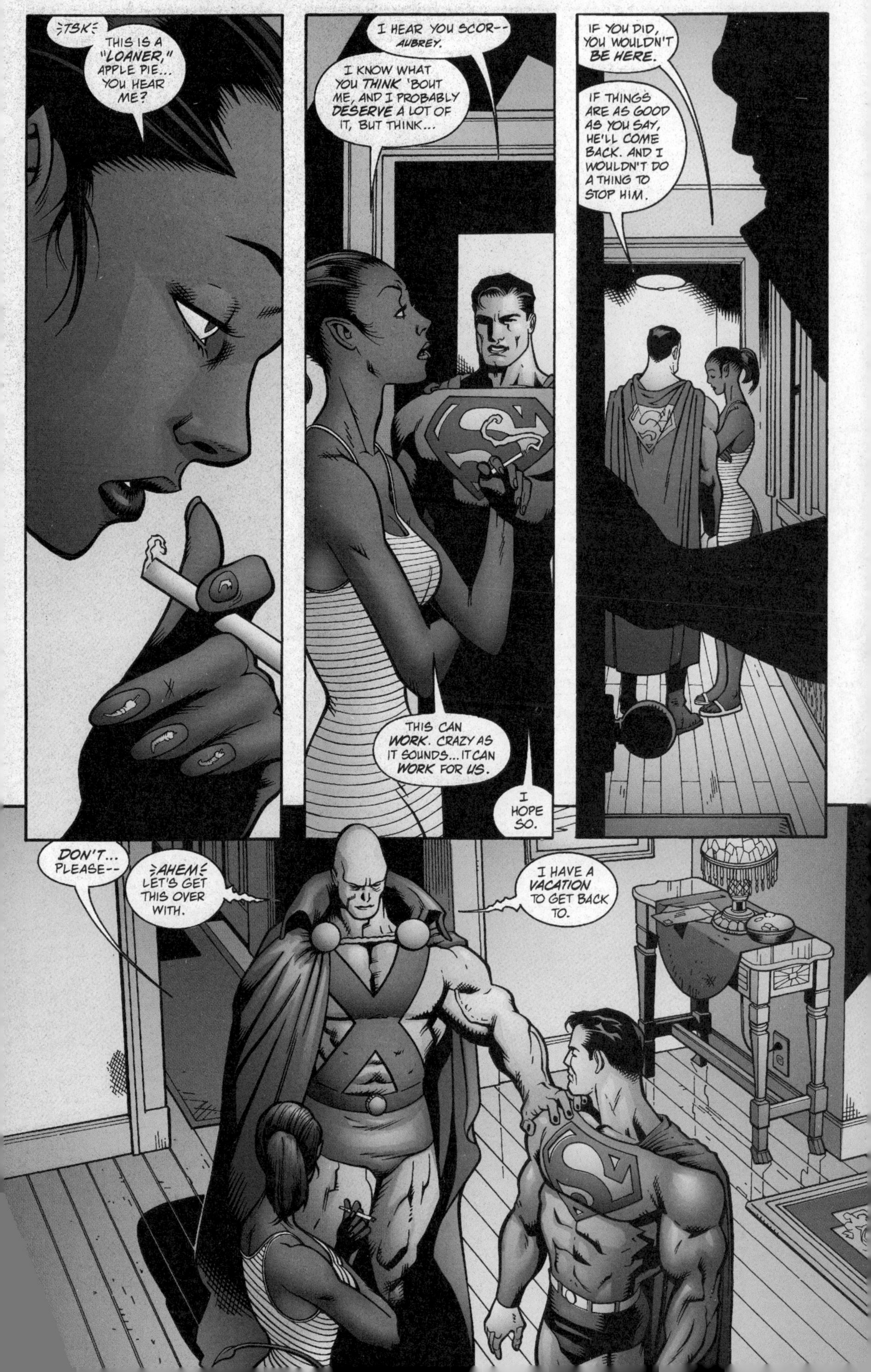
TSK
THIS IS A "LOANER," APPLE PIE... YOU HEAR ME?
I HEAR YOU SCOR-- AUBREY.
I KNOW WHAT YOU THINK 'BOUT ME, AND I PROBABLY DESERVE A LOT OF IT, BUT THINK...
THIS CAN WORK. CRAZY AS IT SOUNDS... IT CAN WORK FOR US.
I HOPE SO.
IF YOU DID, YOU WOULDN'T BE HERE.
IF THINGS ARE AS GOOD AS YOU SAY, HE'LL COME BACK. AND I WOULDN'T DO A THING TO STOP HIM.
DON'T... PLEASE--
AHEM
LET'S GET THIS OVER WITH.
I HAVE A VACATION TO GET BACK TO.

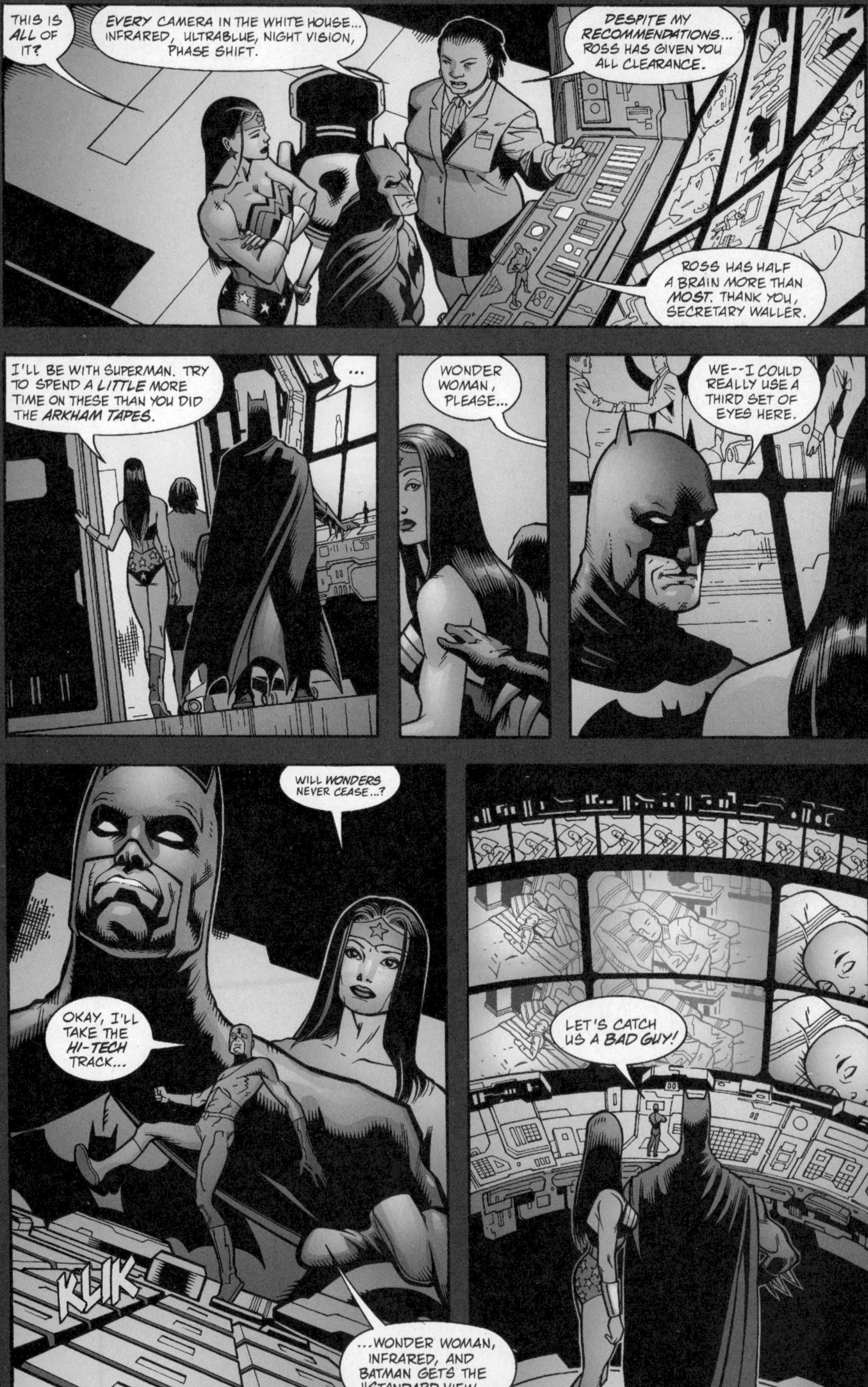
THIS IS ALL OF IT?
EVERY CAMERA IN THE WHITE HOUSE... INFRARED, ULTRABLUE, NIGHT VISION, PHASE SHIFT.
DESPITE MY RECOMMENDATIONS... ROSS HAS GIVEN YOU ALL CLEARANCE.
ROSS HAS HALF A BRAIN MORE THAN MOST. THANK YOU, SECRETARY WALLER.
I'LL BE WITH SUPERMAN. TRY TO SPEND A LITTLE MORE TIME ON THESE THAN YOU DID THE ARKHAM TAPES.
...
WONDER WOMAN, PLEASE...
WE--I COULD REALLY USE A THIRD SET OF EYES HERE.
WILL WONDERS NEVER CEASE...?
OKAY, I'LL TAKE THE HI-TECH TRACK...
KLIK
...WONDER WOMAN, INFRARED, AND BATMAN GETS THE "STANDARD VIEW.
LET'S CATCH US A BAD GUY!

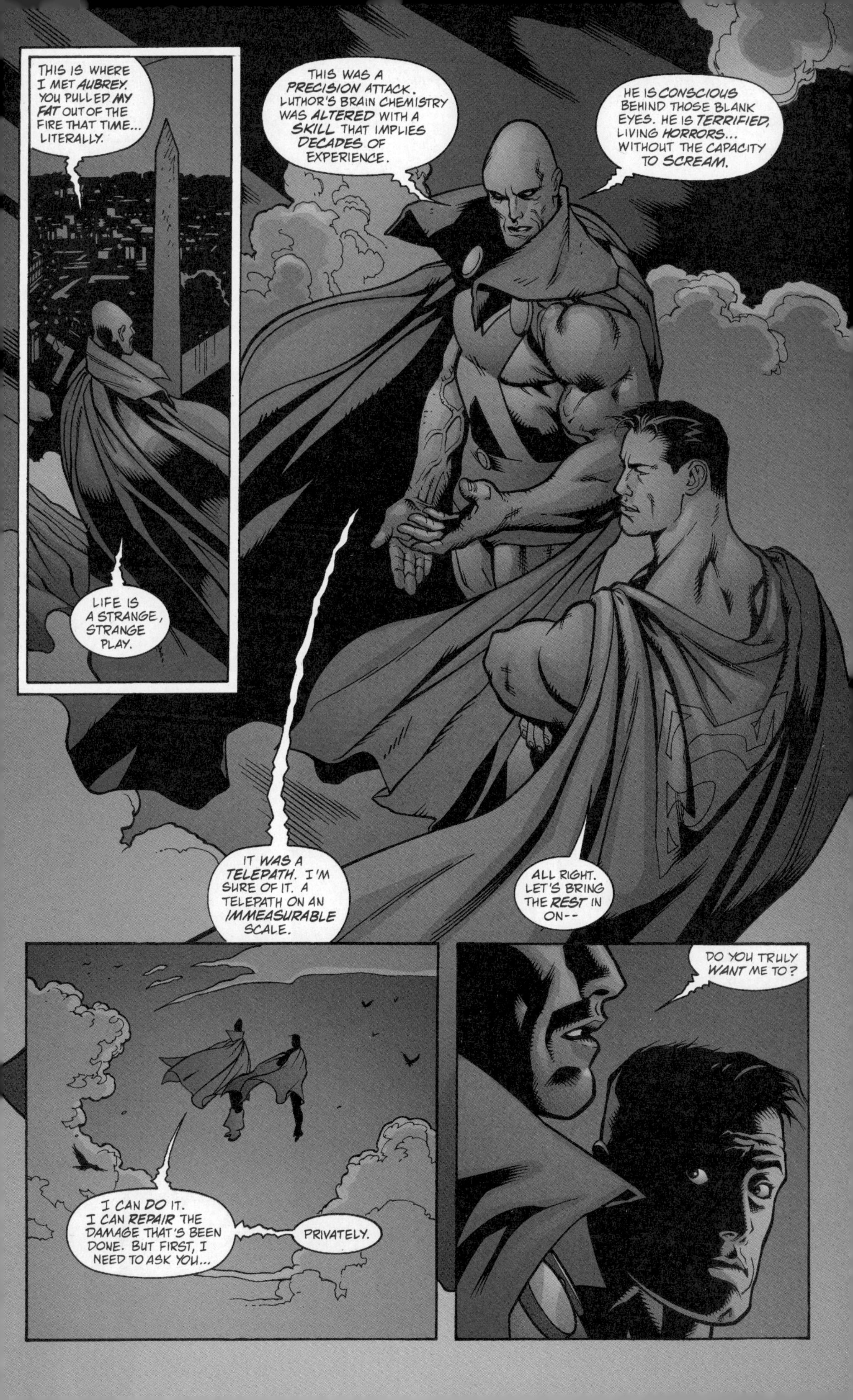
THIS IS WHERE I MET AUBREY. YOU PULLED MY FAT OUT OF THE FIRE THAT TIME... LITERALLY.
LIFE IS A STRANGE, STRANGE PLAY.
THIS WAS A PRECISION ATTACK. LUTHOR'S BRAIN CHEMISTRY WAS ALTERED WITH A SKILL THAT IMPLIES DECADES OF EXPERIENCE.
HE IS CONSCIOUS BEHIND THOSE BLANK EYES. HE IS TERRIFIED, LIVING HORRORS... WITHOUT THE CAPACITY TO SCREAM.
IT WAS A TELEPATH. I'M SURE OF IT. A TELEPATH ON AN IMMEASURABLE SCALE.
ALL RIGHT. LET'S BRING THE REST IN ON--
I CAN DO IT. I CAN REPAIR THE DAMAGE THAT'S BEEN DONE. BUT FIRST, I NEED TO ASK YOU...
PRIVATELY.
DO YOU TRULY WANT ME TO?

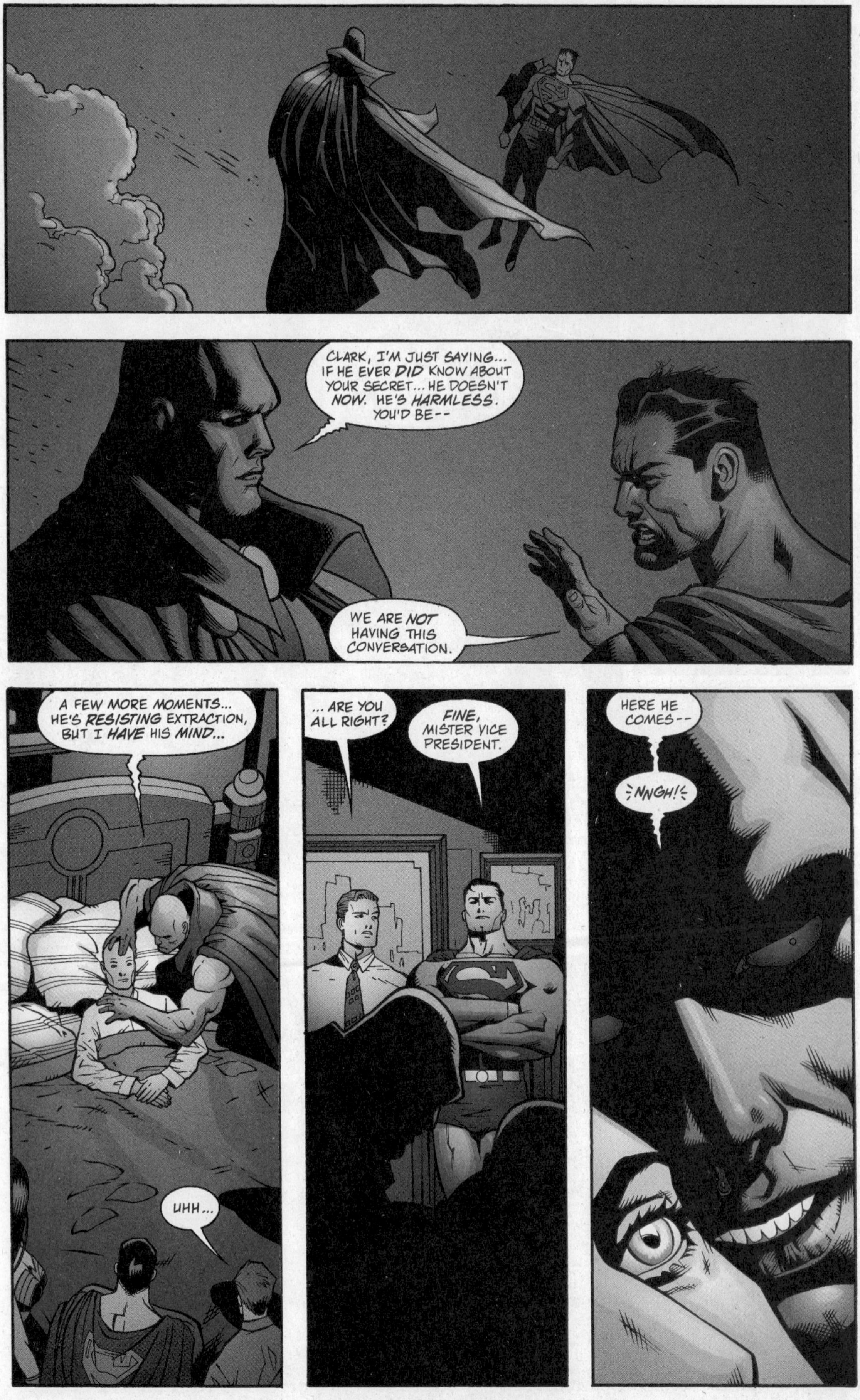
CLARK, I'M JUST SAYING... IF HE EVER DID KNOW ABOUT YOUR SECRET... HE DOESN'T NOW. HE'S HARMLESS. YOU'D BE--
WE ARE NOT HAVING THIS CONVERSATION.
A FEW MORE MOMENTS... HE'S RESISTING EXTRACTION, BUT I HAVE HIS MIND...
UHH...
...ARE YOU ALL RIGHT?
FINE, MISTER VICE PRESIDENT.
HERE HE COMES--
NNGH!

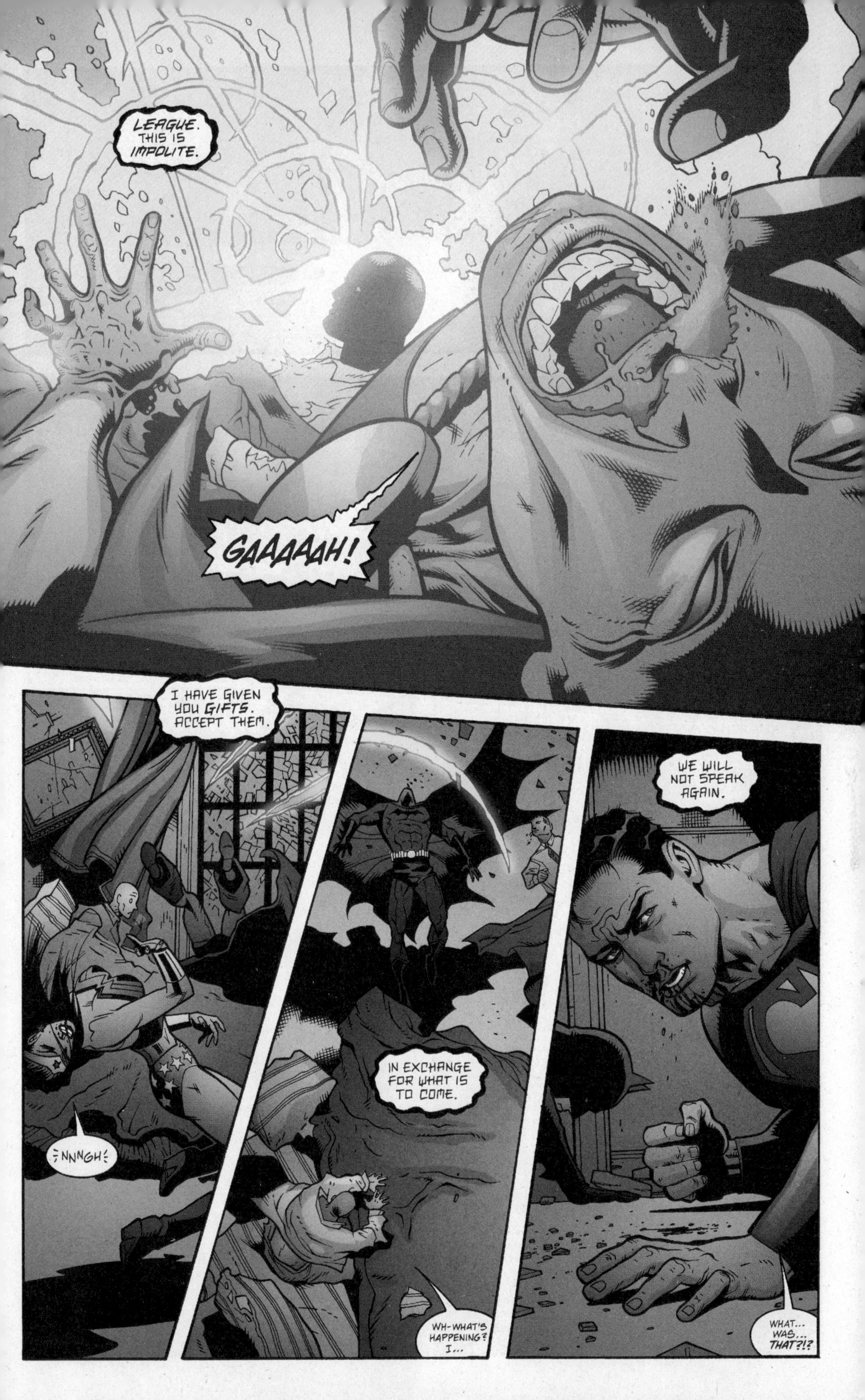
LEAGUE. THIS IS IMPOLITE.
GAAAAAH!
I HAVE GIVEN YOU GIFTS. ACCEPT THEM.
NNNGH!
IN EXCHANGE FOR WHAT IS TO COME.
WH-WHAT'S HAPPENING? I...
WE WILL NOT SPEAK AGAIN.
WHAT... WAS... THAT?!?

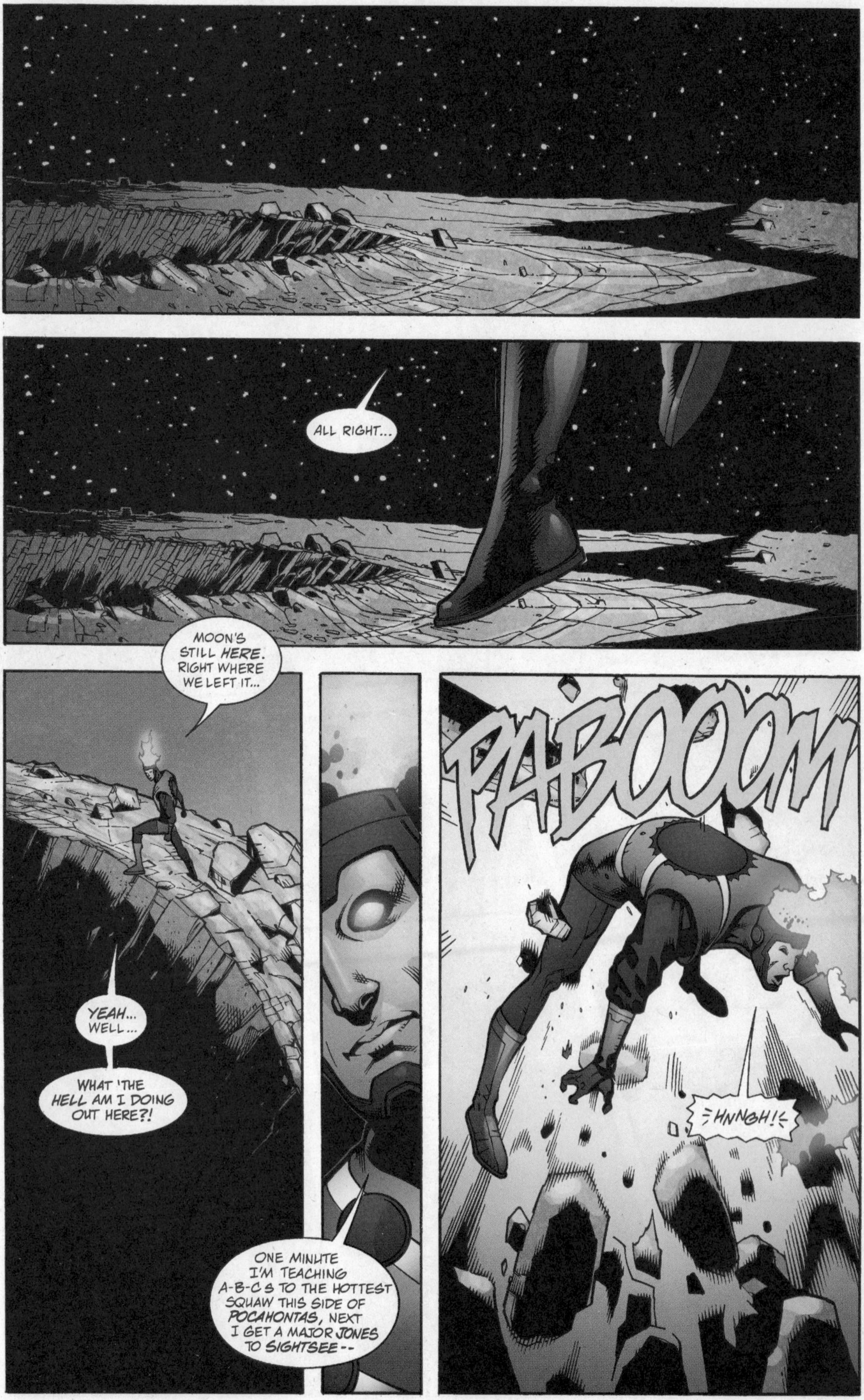
ALL RIGHT...
MOON'S STILL HERE. RIGHT WHERE WE LEFT IT...
YEAH... WELL...
WHAT 'THE HELL AM I DOING OUT HERE?!
ONE MINUTE I'M TEACHING A-B-C S TO THE HOTTEST SQUAW THIS SIDE OF POCAHONTAS, NEXT I GET A MAJOR JONES TO SIGHTSEE--
PABOOOM
HNNGH!

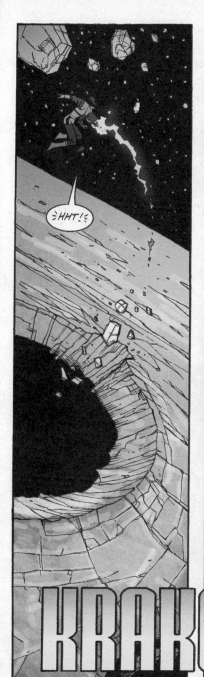

≤HHT!≥

KRAKOOM!

GYEAAAAAH!!!

NO!

NOOOO!

≤URRKT≥

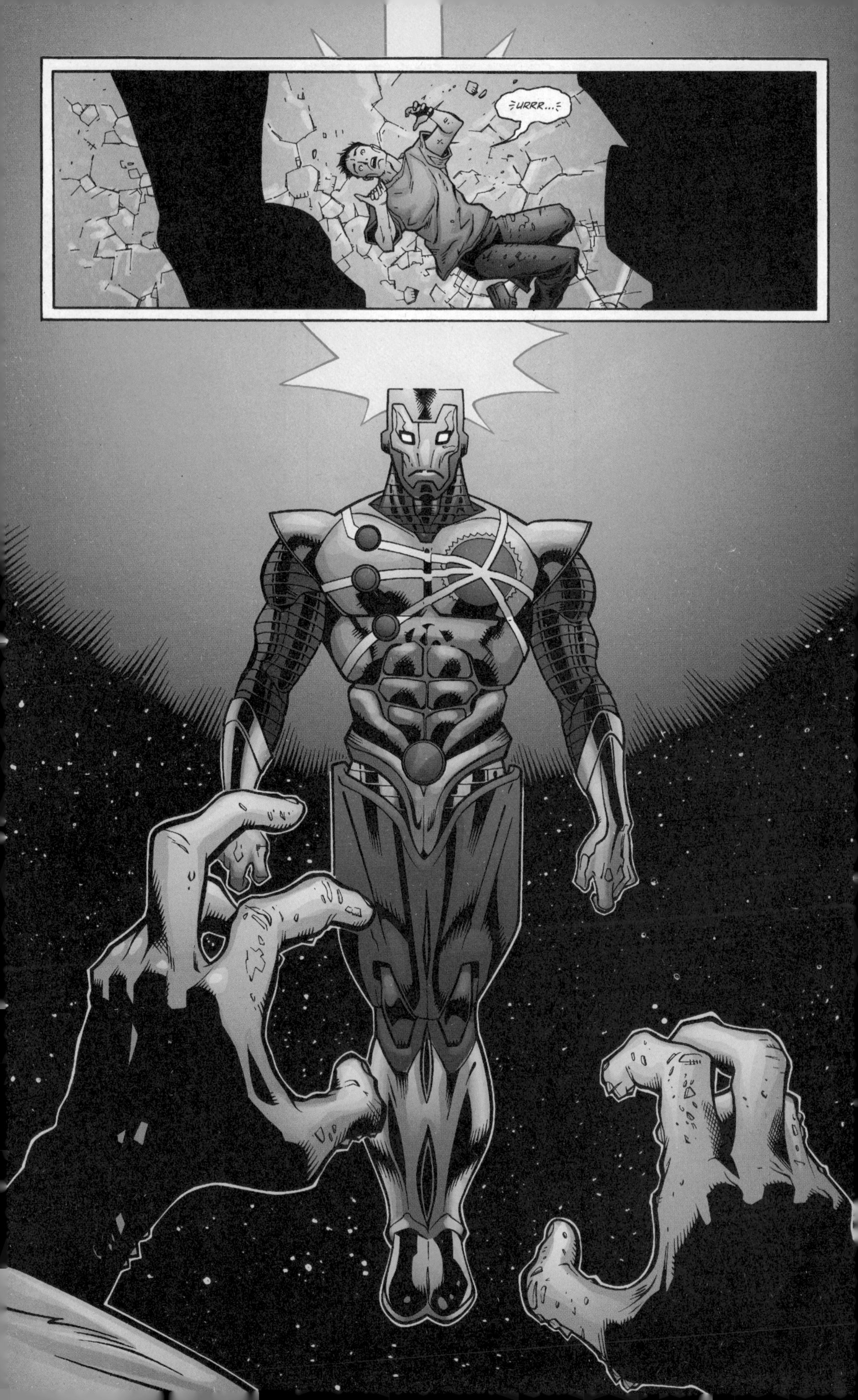
URRR...

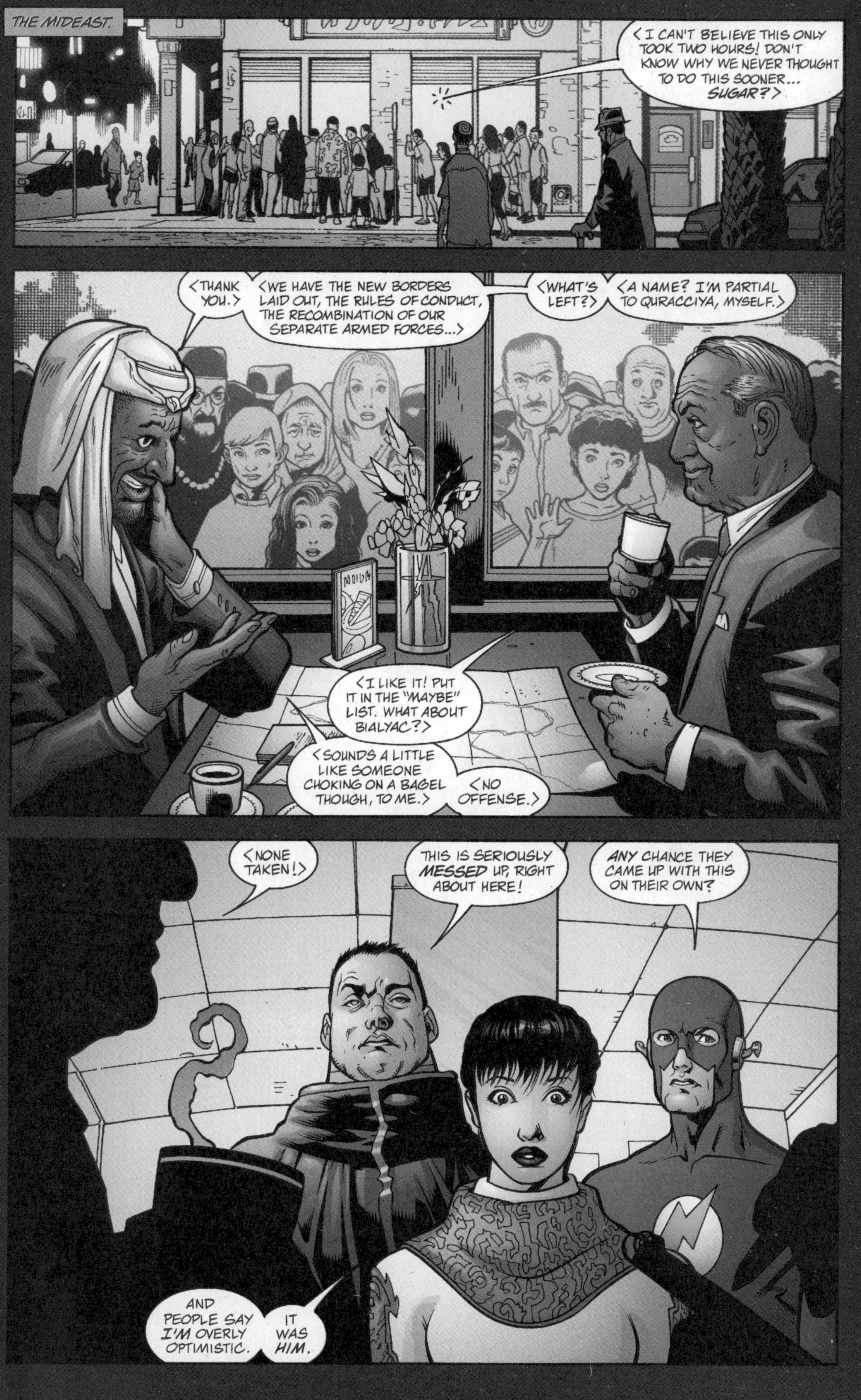
THE MIDEAST.
<I CAN'T BELIEVE THIS ONLY TOOK TWO HOURS! DON'T KNOW WHY WE NEVER THOUGHT TO DO THIS SOONER... SUGAR?>
<THANK YOU.>
<WE HAVE THE NEW BORDERS LAID OUT, THE RULES OF CONDUCT, THE RECOMBINATION OF OUR SEPARATE ARMED FORCES...>
<WHAT'S LEFT?>
<A NAME? I'M PARTIAL TO QURACCIYA, MYSELF.>
<I LIKE IT! PUT IT IN THE "MAYBE" LIST. WHAT ABOUT BIALYAC?>
<SOUNDS A LITTLE LIKE SOMEONE CHOKING ON A BAGEL THOUGH, TO ME.>
<NO OFFENSE.>
<NONE TAKEN!>
THIS IS SERIOUSLY MESSED UP, RIGHT ABOUT HERE!
ANY CHANCE THEY CAME UP WITH THIS ON THEIR OWN?
AND PEOPLE SAY I'M OVERLY OPTIMISTIC.
IT WAS HIM.

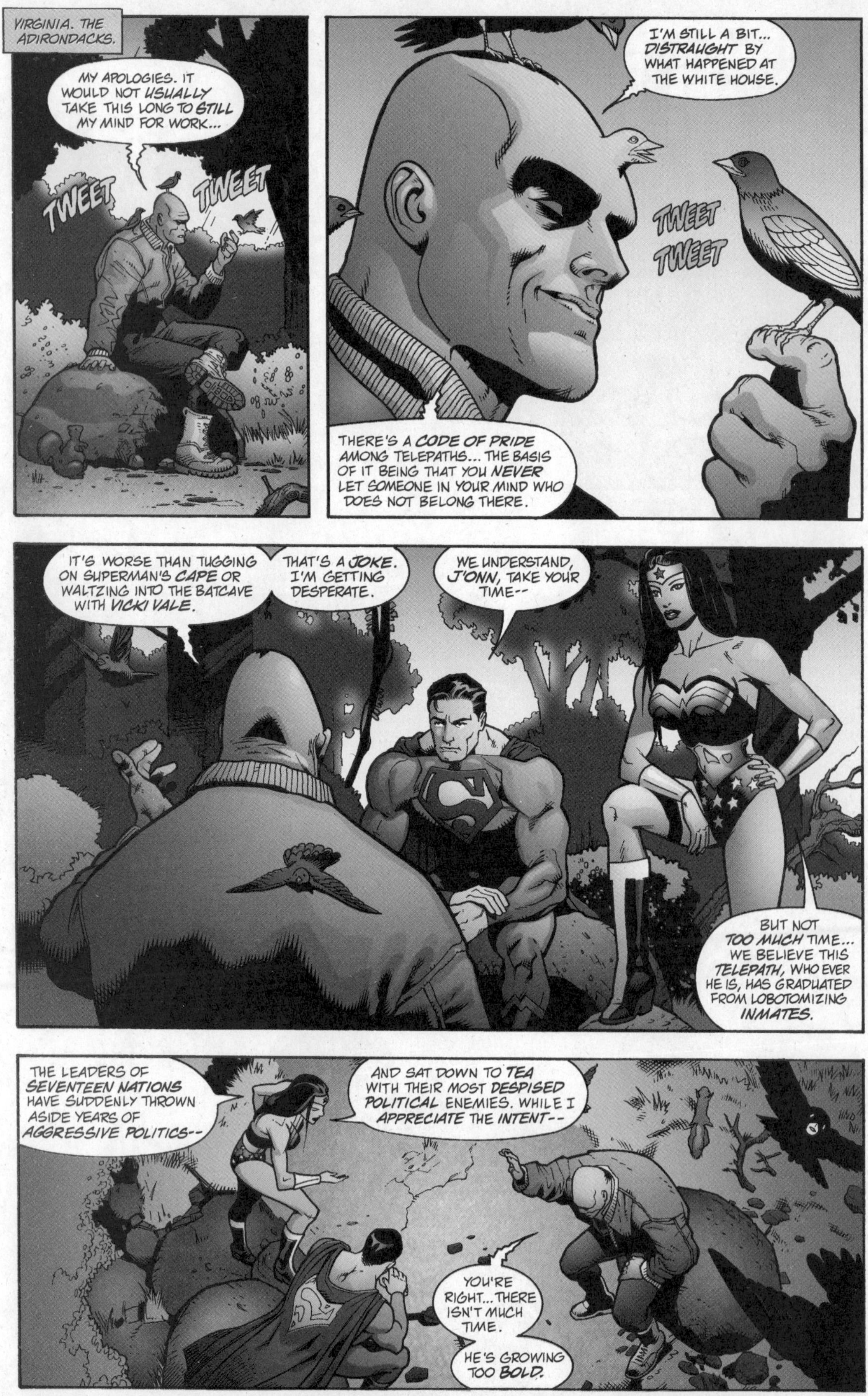
VIRGINIA. THE ADIRONDACKS.
MY APOLOGIES. IT WOULD NOT USUALLY TAKE THIS LONG TO STILL MY MIND FOR WORK...
TWEET
TWEET
I'M STILL A BIT... DISTRAUGHT BY WHAT HAPPENED AT THE WHITE HOUSE.
TWEET
TWEET
THERE'S A CODE OF PRIDE AMONG TELEPATHS... THE BASIS OF IT BEING THAT YOU NEVER LET SOMEONE IN YOUR MIND WHO DOES NOT BELONG THERE.
IT'S WORSE THAN TUGGING ON SUPERMAN'S CAPE OR WALTZING INTO THE BATCAVE WITH VICKI VALE.
THAT'S A JOKE. I'M GETTING DESPERATE.
WE UNDERSTAND, J'ONN, TAKE YOUR TIME--
BUT NOT TOO MUCH TIME... WE BELIEVE THIS TELEPATH, WHO EVER HE IS, HAS GRADUATED FROM LOBOTOMIZING INMATES.
THE LEADERS OF SEVENTEEN NATIONS HAVE SUDDENLY THROWN ASIDE YEARS OF AGGRESSIVE POLITICS--
AND SAT DOWN TO TEA WITH THEIR MOST DESPISED POLITICAL ENEMIES. WHILE I APPRECIATE THE INTENT--
YOU'RE RIGHT... THERE ISN'T MUCH TIME.
HE'S GROWING TOO BOLD.

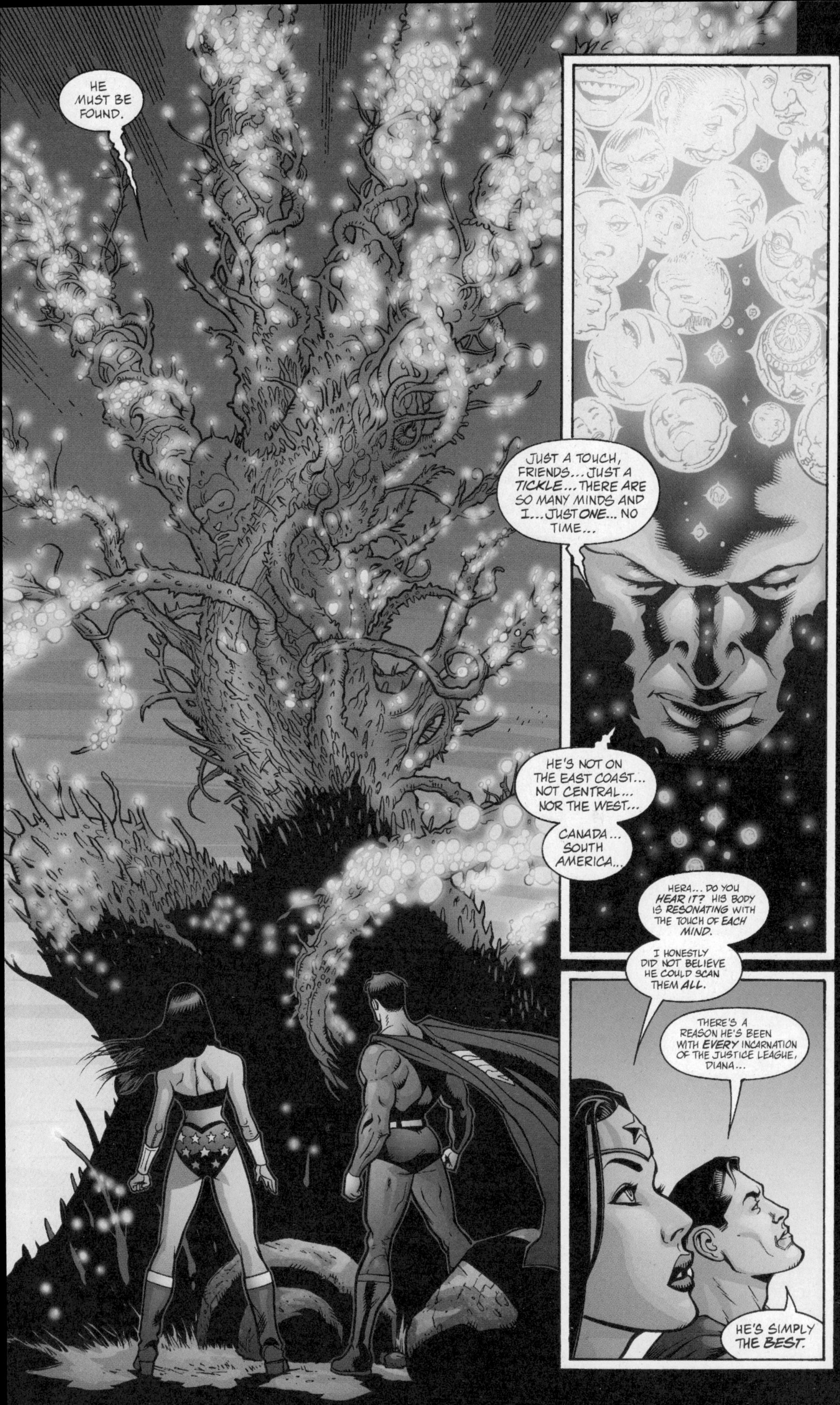

HE MUST BE FOUND.
JUST A TOUCH, FRIENDS... JUST A TICKLE... THERE ARE SO MANY MINDS AND I... JUST ONE... NO TIME...
HE'S NOT ON THE EAST COAST... NOT CENTRAL... NOR THE WEST...
CANADA... SOUTH AMERICA...
HERA... DO YOU HEAR IT? HIS BODY IS RESONATING WITH THE TOUCH OF EACH MIND.
I HONESTLY DID NOT BELIEVE HE COULD SCAN THEM ALL.
THERE'S A REASON HE'S BEEN WITH EVERY INCARNATION OF THE JUSTICE LEAGUE, DIANA...
HE'S SIMPLY THE BEST.

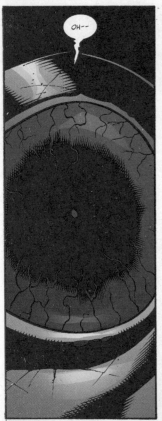

OH--

≈NNNGHHHH!≈

KRRAKKT

CACHOOOOOM!

ARE YOU ALL RIGHT? DID HE ATTACK YOU?

N-NO... NOT...

NOTHING... I--I FOUND NOTHING.

TAKE ME HOME, PLEASE. TAKE ME TO AUBREY.

J'ONN? PLEASE, TALK TO US. WHAT DID YOU SEE?

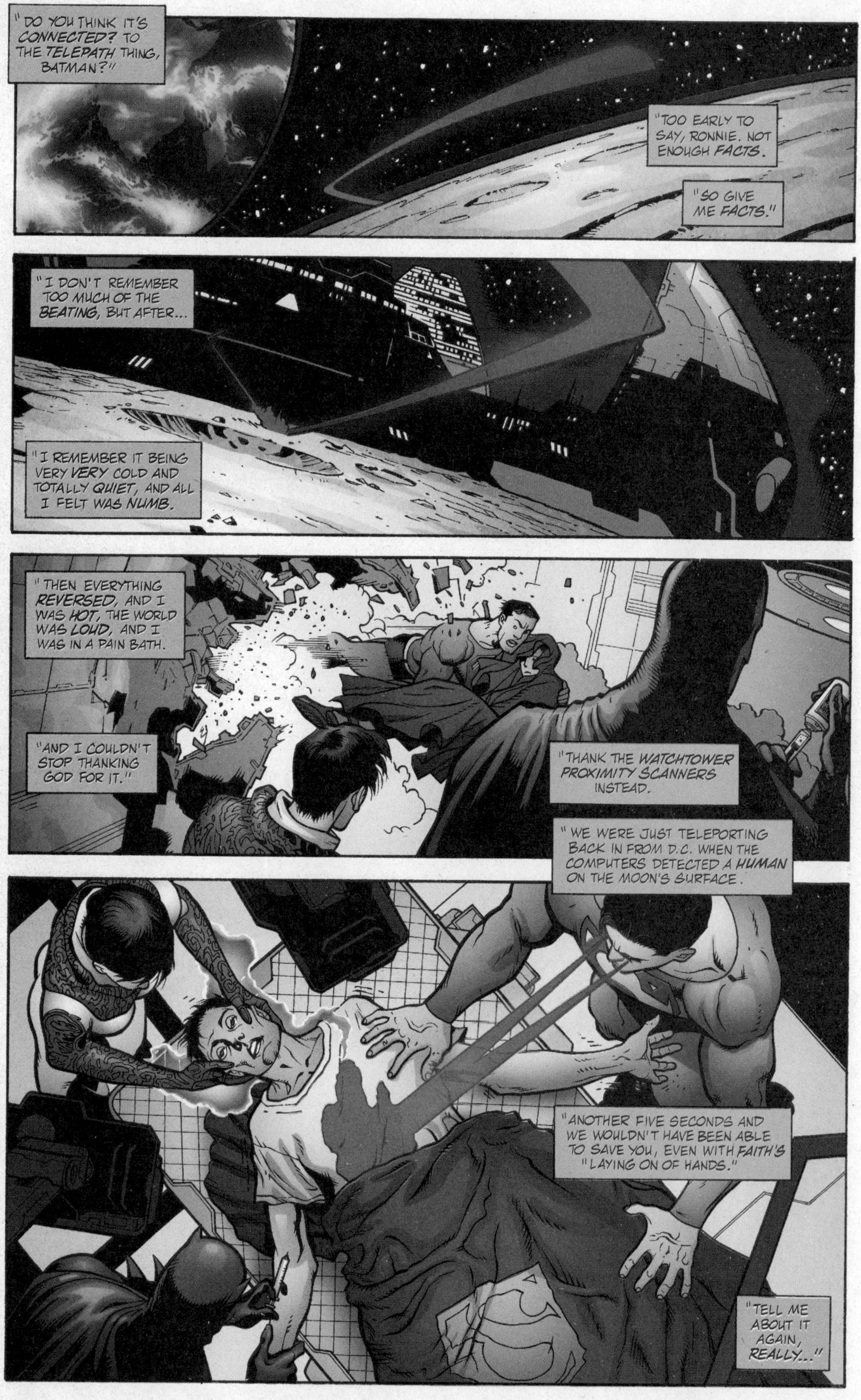
"DO YOU THINK IT'S CONNECTED? TO THE TELEPATH THING, BATMAN?"
"TOO EARLY TO SAY, RONNIE. NOT ENOUGH FACTS.
"SO GIVE ME FACTS."
"I DON'T REMEMBER TOO MUCH OF THE BEATING, BUT AFTER...
"I REMEMBER IT BEING VERY VERY COLD AND TOTALLY QUIET, AND ALL I FELT WAS NUMB.
"THEN EVERYTHING REVERSED, AND I WAS HOT, THE WORLD WAS LOUD, AND I WAS IN A PAIN BATH.
"AND I COULDN'T STOP THANKING GOD FOR IT."
"THANK THE WATCHTOWER PROXIMITY SCANNERS INSTEAD.
"WE WERE JUST TELEPORTING BACK IN FROM D.C. WHEN THE COMPUTERS DETECTED A HUMAN ON THE MOON'S SURFACE.
"ANOTHER FIVE SECONDS AND WE WOULDN'T HAVE BEEN ABLE TO SAVE YOU, EVEN WITH FAITH'S "LAYING ON OF HANDS."
"TELL ME ABOUT IT AGAIN, REALLY..."

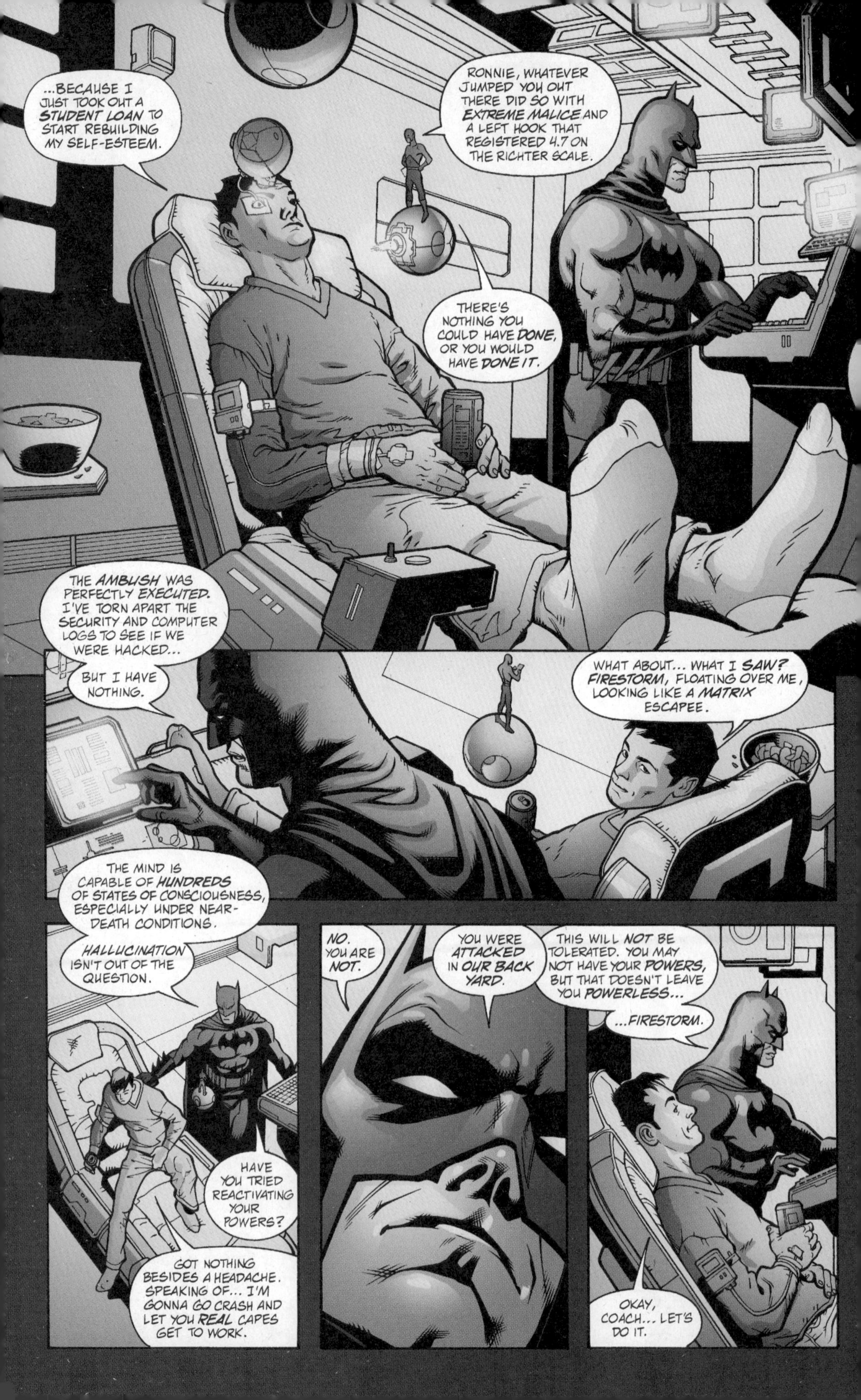
...BECAUSE I JUST TOOK OUT A STUDENT LOAN TO START REBUILDING MY SELF-ESTEEM.
RONNIE, WHATEVER JUMPED YOU OUT THERE DID SO WITH EXTREME MALICE AND A LEFT HOOK THAT REGISTERED 4.7 ON THE RICHTER SCALE.
THERE'S NOTHING YOU COULD HAVE DONE, OR YOU WOULD HAVE DONE IT.
THE AMBUSH WAS PERFECTLY EXECUTED. I'VE TORN APART THE SECURITY AND COMPUTER LOGS TO SEE IF WE WERE HACKED...
BUT I HAVE NOTHING.
WHAT ABOUT... WHAT I SAW? FIRESTORM, FLOATING OVER ME, LOOKING LIKE A MATRIX ESCAPEE.
THE MIND IS CAPABLE OF HUNDREDS OF STATES OF CONSCIOUSNESS, ESPECIALLY UNDER NEAR-DEATH CONDITIONS.
HALLUCINATION ISN'T OUT OF THE QUESTION.
HAVE YOU TRIED REACTIVATING YOUR POWERS?
GOT NOTHING BESIDES A HEADACHE. SPEAKING OF... I'M GONNA GO CRASH AND LET YOU REAL CAPES GET TO WORK.
NO. YOU ARE NOT.
YOU WERE ATTACKED IN OUR BACK YARD.
THIS WILL NOT BE TOLERATED. YOU MAY NOT HAVE YOUR POWERS, BUT THAT DOESN'T LEAVE YOU POWERLESS...
...FIRESTORM.
OKAY, COACH... LET'S DO IT.

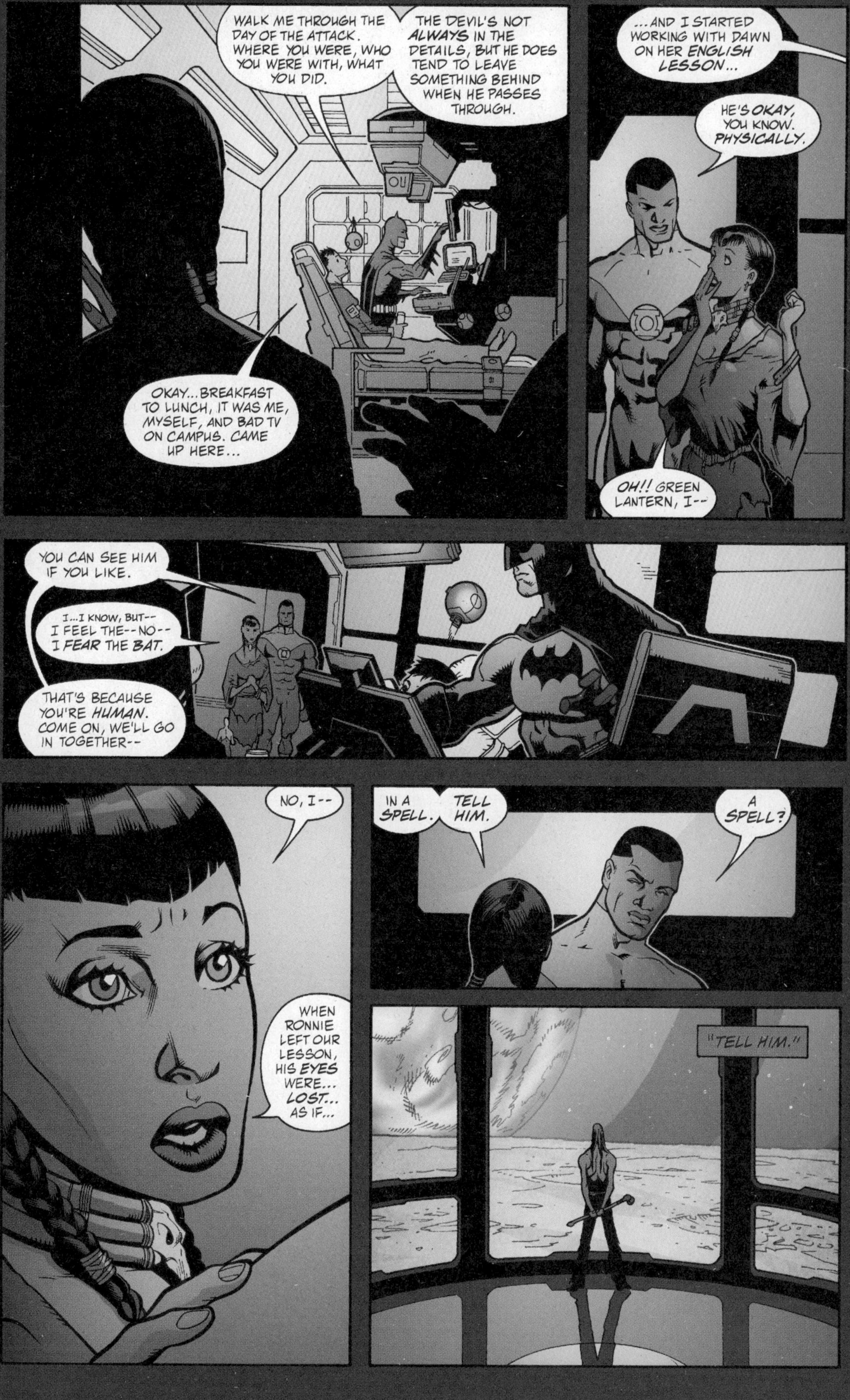
WALK ME THROUGH THE DAY OF THE ATTACK. WHERE YOU WERE, WHO YOU WERE WITH, WHAT YOU DID.
THE DEVIL'S NOT ALWAYS IN THE DETAILS, BUT HE DOES TEND TO LEAVE SOMETHING BEHIND WHEN HE PASSES THROUGH.
OKAY... BREAKFAST TO LUNCH, IT WAS ME, MYSELF, AND BAD TV ON CAMPUS. CAME UP HERE...
...AND I STARTED WORKING WITH DAWN ON HER ENGLISH LESSON...
HE'S OKAY, YOU KNOW. PHYSICALLY.
OH!! GREEN LANTERN, I--
YOU CAN SEE HIM IF YOU LIKE.
I...I KNOW, BUT-- I FEEL THE--NO-- I FEAR THE BAT.
THAT'S BECAUSE YOU'RE HUMAN. COME ON, WE'LL GO IN TOGETHER--
NO, I--
WHEN RONNIE LEFT OUR LESSON, HIS EYES WERE... LOST... AS IF...
IN A SPELL.
TELL HIM.
A SPELL?
"TELL HIM."

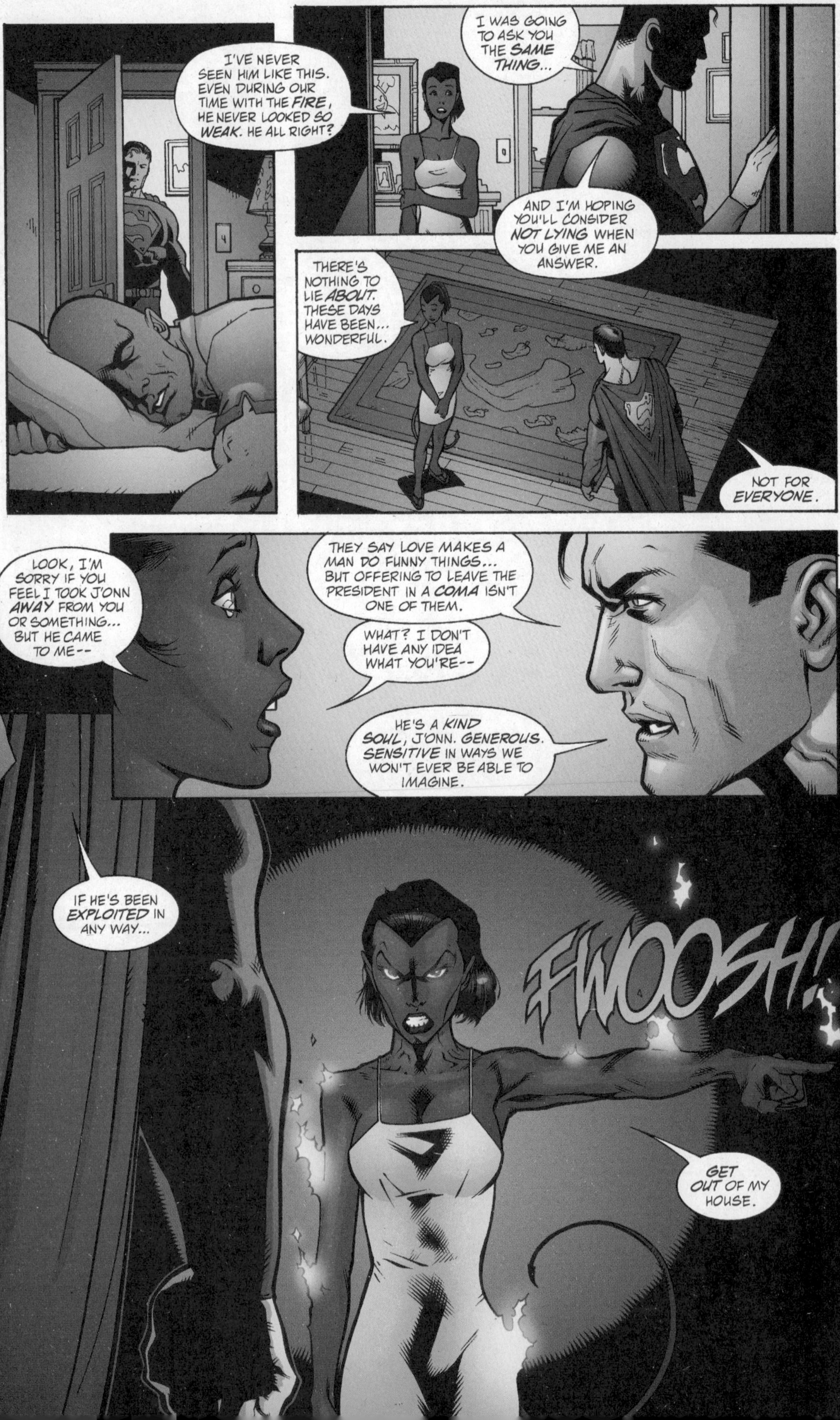
I'VE NEVER SEEN HIM LIKE THIS. EVEN DURING OUR TIME WITH THE FIRE, HE NEVER LOOKED SO WEAK. HE ALL RIGHT?
I WAS GOING TO ASK YOU THE SAME THING...
AND I'M HOPING YOU'LL CONSIDER NOT LYING WHEN YOU GIVE ME AN ANSWER.
THERE'S NOTHING TO LIE ABOUT. THESE DAYS HAVE BEEN... WONDERFUL.
NOT FOR EVERYONE.
LOOK, I'M SORRY IF YOU FEEL I TOOK J'ONN AWAY FROM YOU OR SOMETHING... BUT HE CAME TO ME--
THEY SAY LOVE MAKES A MAN DO FUNNY THINGS... BUT OFFERING TO LEAVE THE PRESIDENT IN A COMA ISN'T ONE OF THEM.
WHAT? I DON'T HAVE ANY IDEA WHAT YOU'RE--
HE'S A KIND SOUL, J'ONN. GENEROUS. SENSITIVE IN WAYS WE WON'T EVER BE ABLE TO IMAGINE.
IF HE'S BEEN EXPLOITED IN ANY WAY...
FWOOSH!
GET OUT OF MY HOUSE.

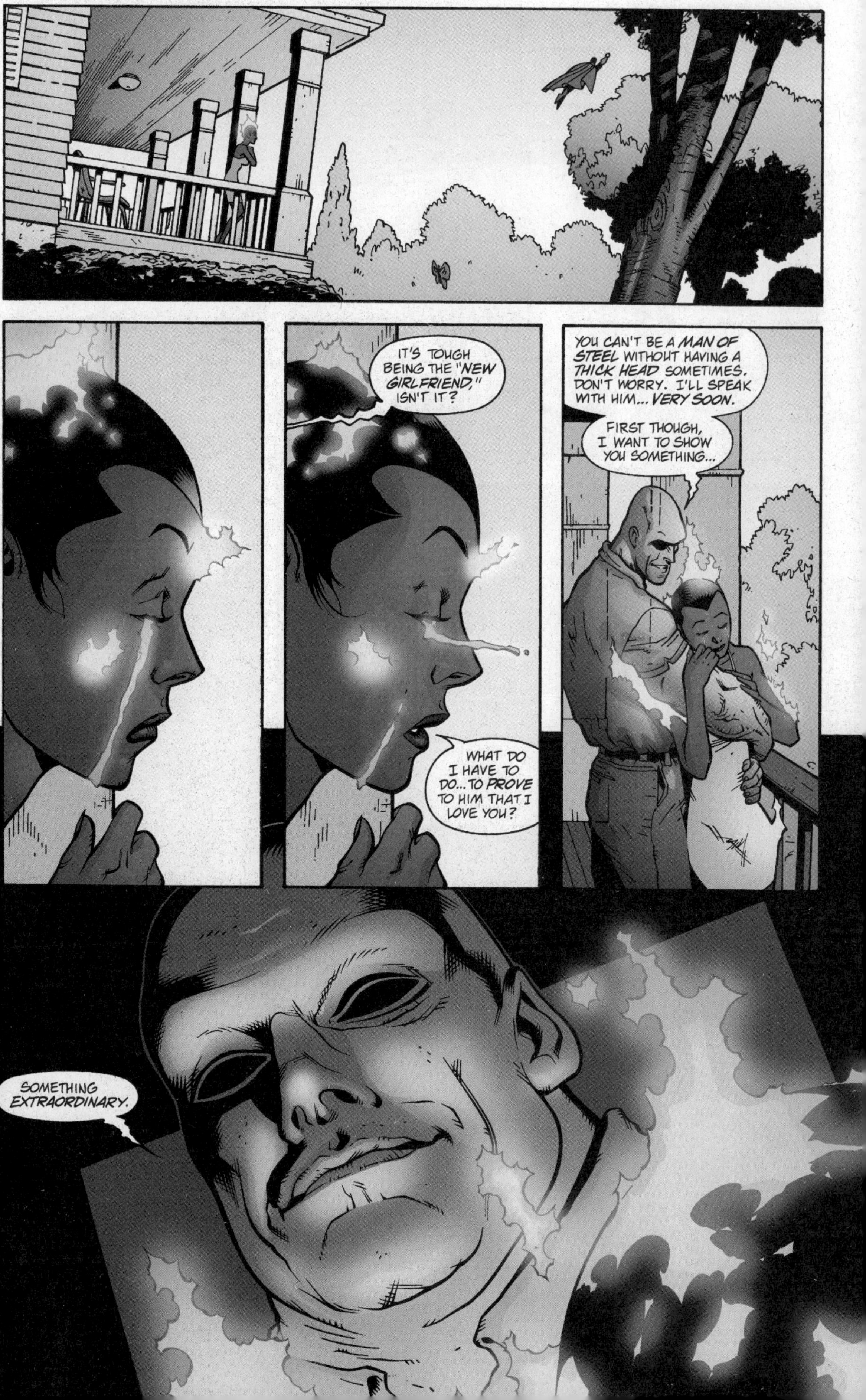
IT'S TOUGH BEING THE "NEW GIRLFRIEND," ISN'T IT?
WHAT DO I HAVE TO DO... TO PROVE TO HIM THAT I LOVE YOU?
YOU CAN'T BE A MAN OF STEEL WITHOUT HAVING A THICK HEAD SOMETIMES. DON'T WORRY. I'LL SPEAK WITH HIM... VERY SOON.
FIRST THOUGH, I WANT TO SHOW YOU SOMETHING...
SOMETHING EXTRAORDINARY.

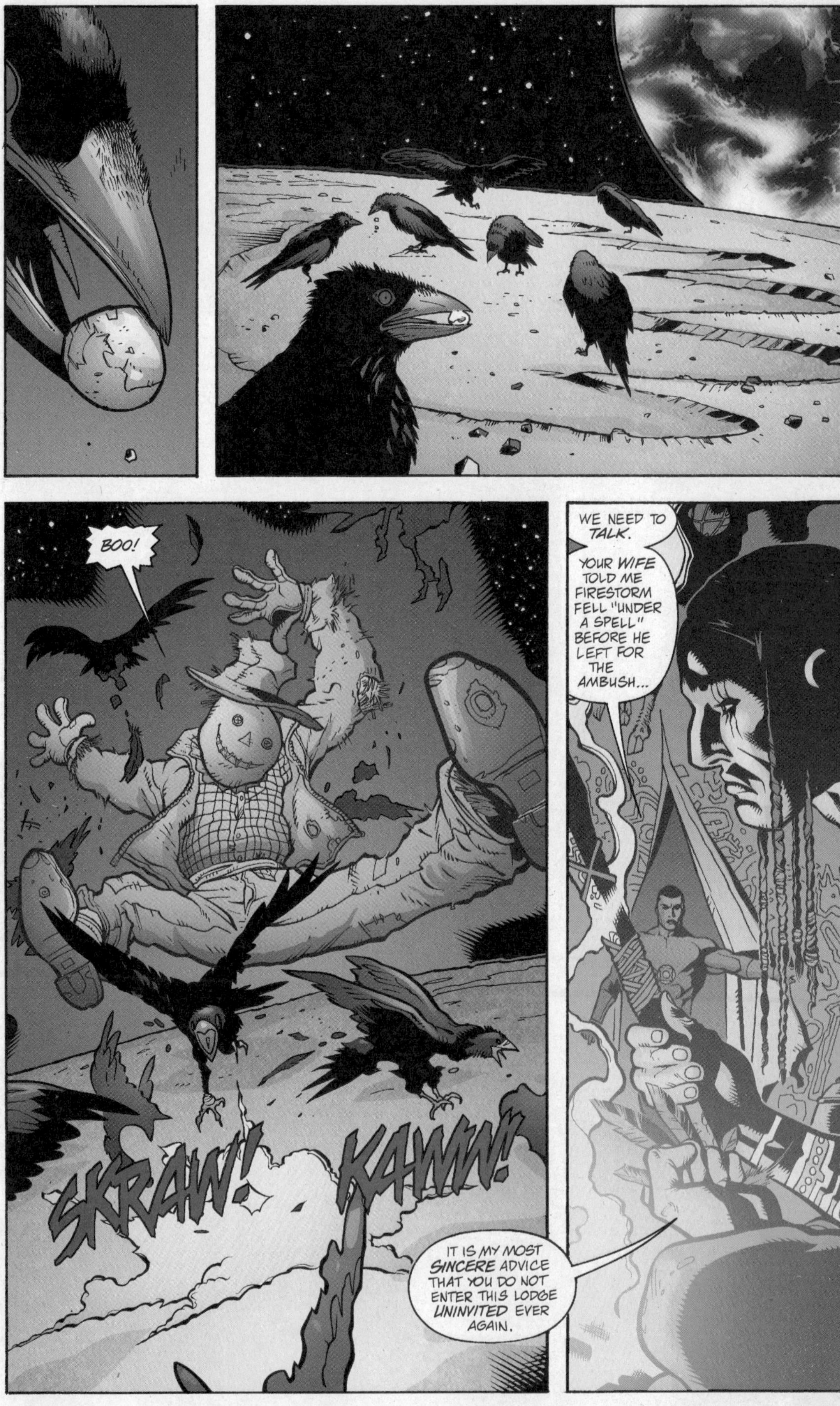

BOO!
SKRAW!
KAWW!
WE NEED TO TALK.
YOUR WIFE TOLD ME FIRESTORM FELL "UNDER A SPELL" BEFORE HE LEFT FOR THE AMBUSH...
IT IS MY MOST SINCERE ADVICE THAT YOU DO NOT ENTER THIS LODGE UNINVITED EVER AGAIN.

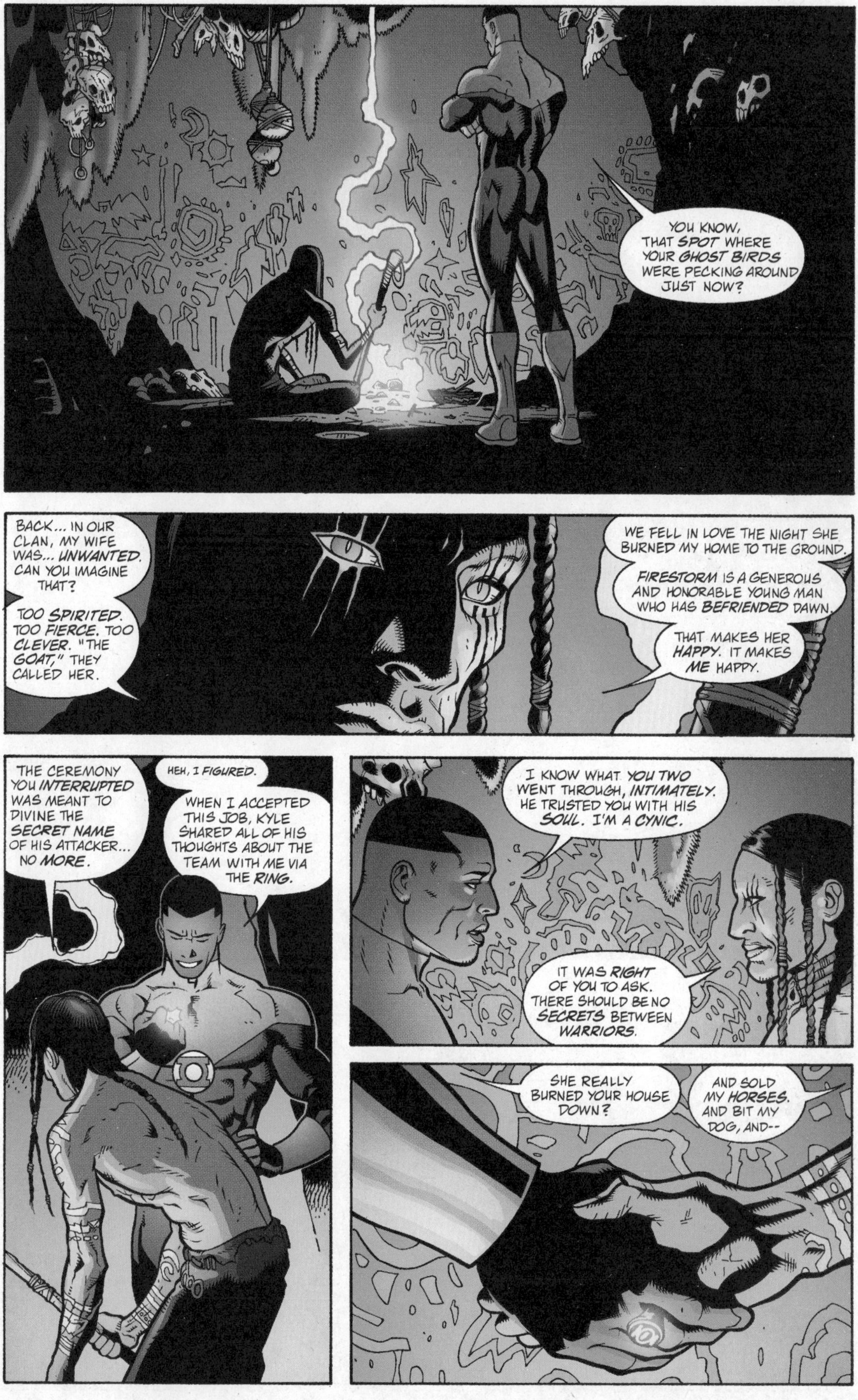
YOU KNOW, THAT SPOT WHERE YOUR GHOST BIRDS WERE PECKING AROUND JUST NOW?
BACK... IN OUR CLAN, MY WIFE WAS... UNWANTED. CAN YOU IMAGINE THAT?
TOO SPIRITED. TOO FIERCE. TOO CLEVER. "THE GOAT," THEY CALLED HER.
WE FELL IN LOVE THE NIGHT SHE BURNED MY HOME TO THE GROUND.
FIRESTORM IS A GENEROUS AND HONORABLE YOUNG MAN WHO HAS BEFRIENDED DAWN.
THAT MAKES HER HAPPY. IT MAKES ME HAPPY.
THE CEREMONY YOU INTERRUPTED WAS MEANT TO DIVINE THE SECRET NAME OF HIS ATTACKER... NO MORE.
HEH, I FIGURED.
WHEN I ACCEPTED THIS JOB, KYLE SHARED ALL OF HIS THOUGHTS ABOUT THE TEAM WITH ME VIA THE RING.
I KNOW WHAT YOU TWO WENT THROUGH, INTIMATELY. HE TRUSTED YOU WITH HIS SOUL. I'M A CYNIC.
IT WAS RIGHT OF YOU TO ASK. THERE SHOULD BE NO SECRETS BETWEEN WARRIORS.
SHE REALLY BURNED YOUR HOUSE DOWN?
AND SOLD MY HORSES. AND BIT MY DOG, AND--

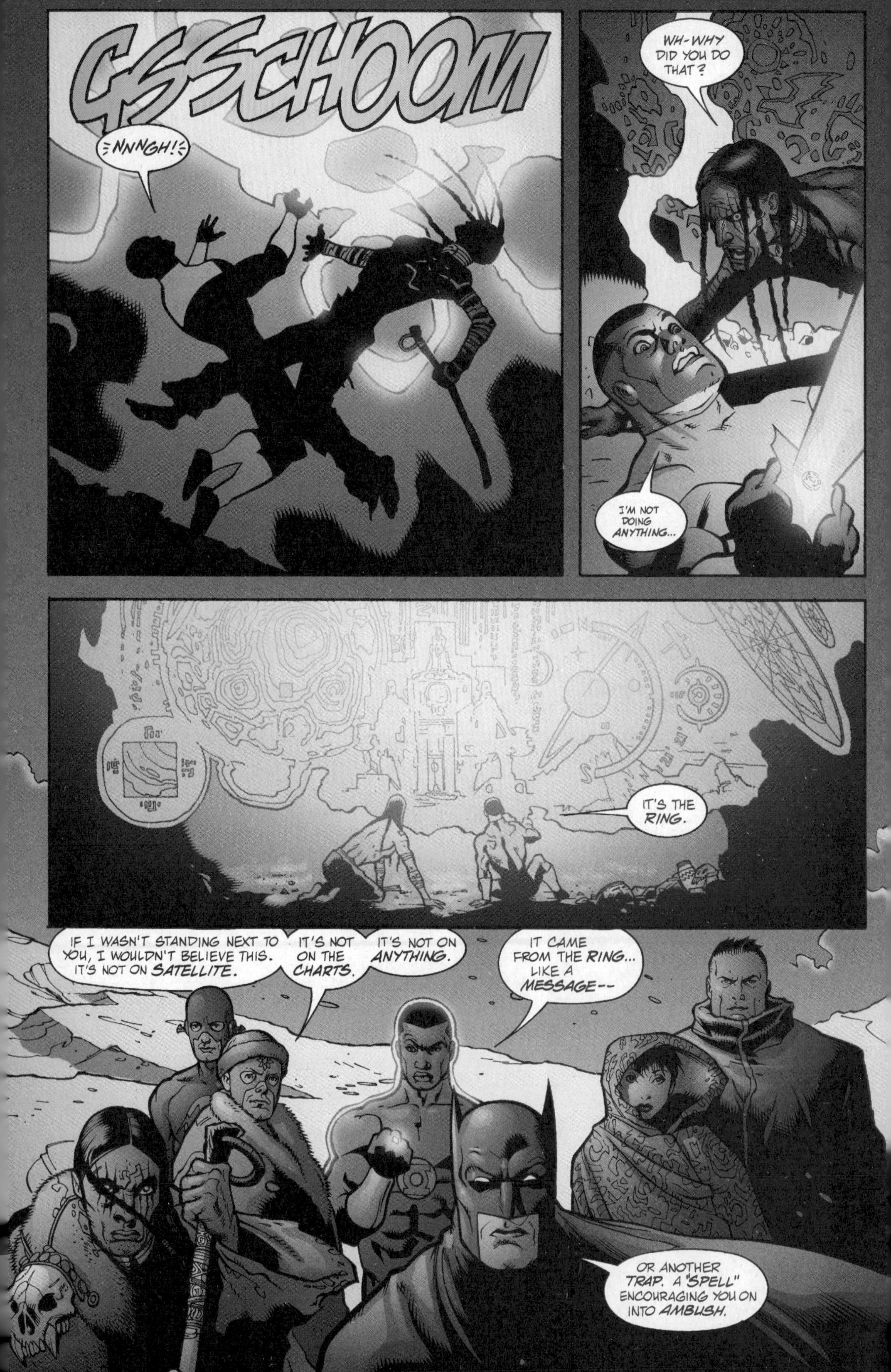
GSSCHOOM
NNNGH!
WH-WHY DID YOU DO THAT?
I'M NOT DOING ANYTHING...
IT'S THE RING.
IF I WASN'T STANDING NEXT TO YOU, I WOULDN'T BELIEVE THIS. IT'S NOT ON SATELLITE.
IT'S NOT ON THE CHARTS.
IT'S NOT ON ANYTHING.
IT CAME FROM THE RING... LIKE A MESSAGE--
OR ANOTHER TRAP. A "SPELL" ENCOURAGING YOU ON INTO AMBUSH.

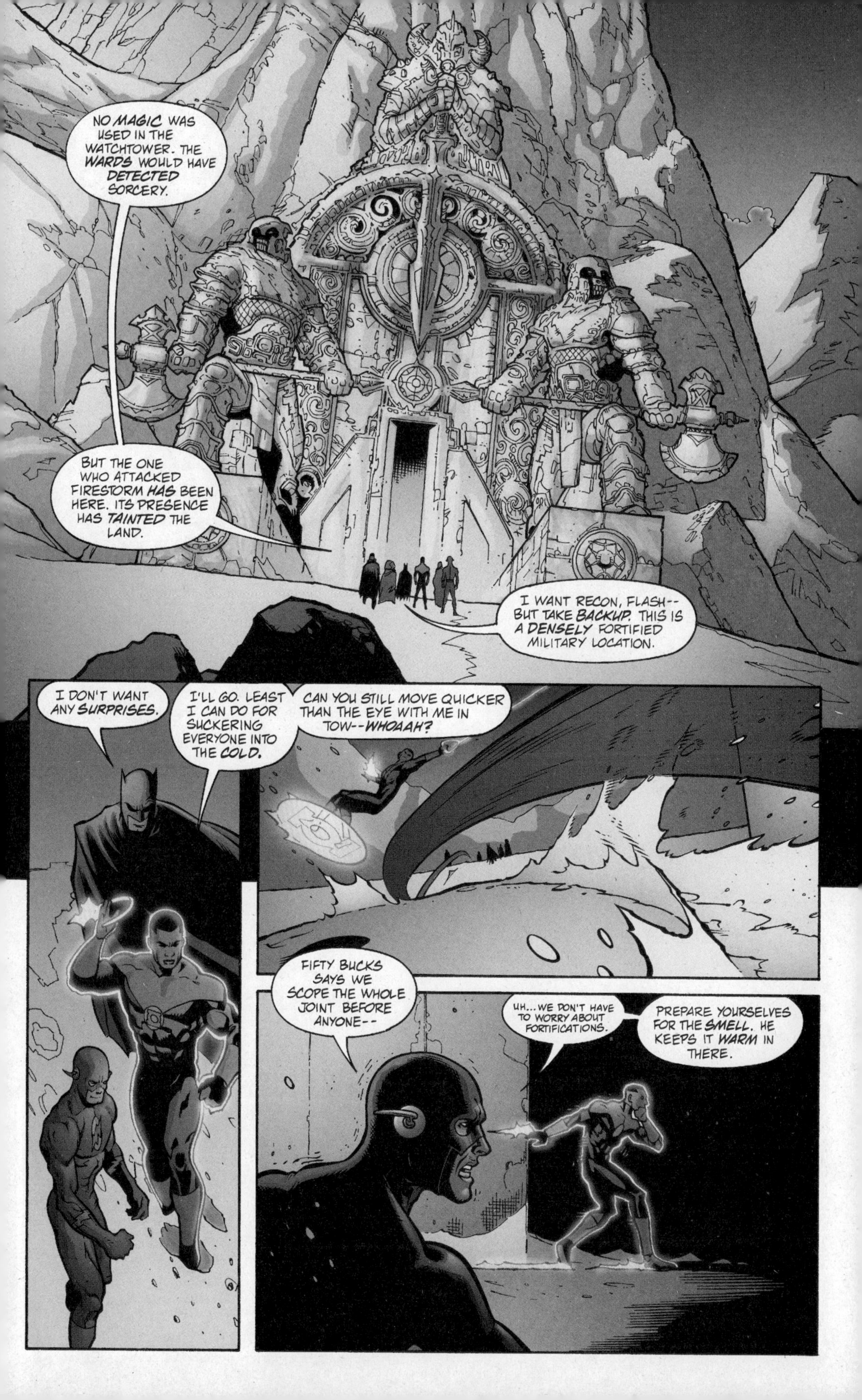
NO MAGIC WAS USED IN THE WATCHTOWER. THE WARDS WOULD HAVE DETECTED SORCERY.
BUT THE ONE WHO ATTACKED FIRESTORM HAS BEEN HERE. ITS PRESENCE HAS TAINTED THE LAND.
I WANT RECON, FLASH-- BUT TAKE BACKUP. THIS IS A DENSELY FORTIFIED MILITARY LOCATION.
I DON'T WANT ANY SURPRISES.
I'LL GO. LEAST I CAN DO FOR SUCKERING EVERYONE INTO THE COLD.
CAN YOU STILL MOVE QUICKER THAN THE EYE WITH ME IN TOW--WHOAAH?
FIFTY BUCKS SAYS WE SCOPE THE WHOLE JOINT BEFORE ANYONE--
UH... WE DON'T HAVE TO WORRY ABOUT FORTIFICATIONS.
PREPARE YOURSELVES FOR THE SMELL. HE KEEPS IT WARM IN THERE.

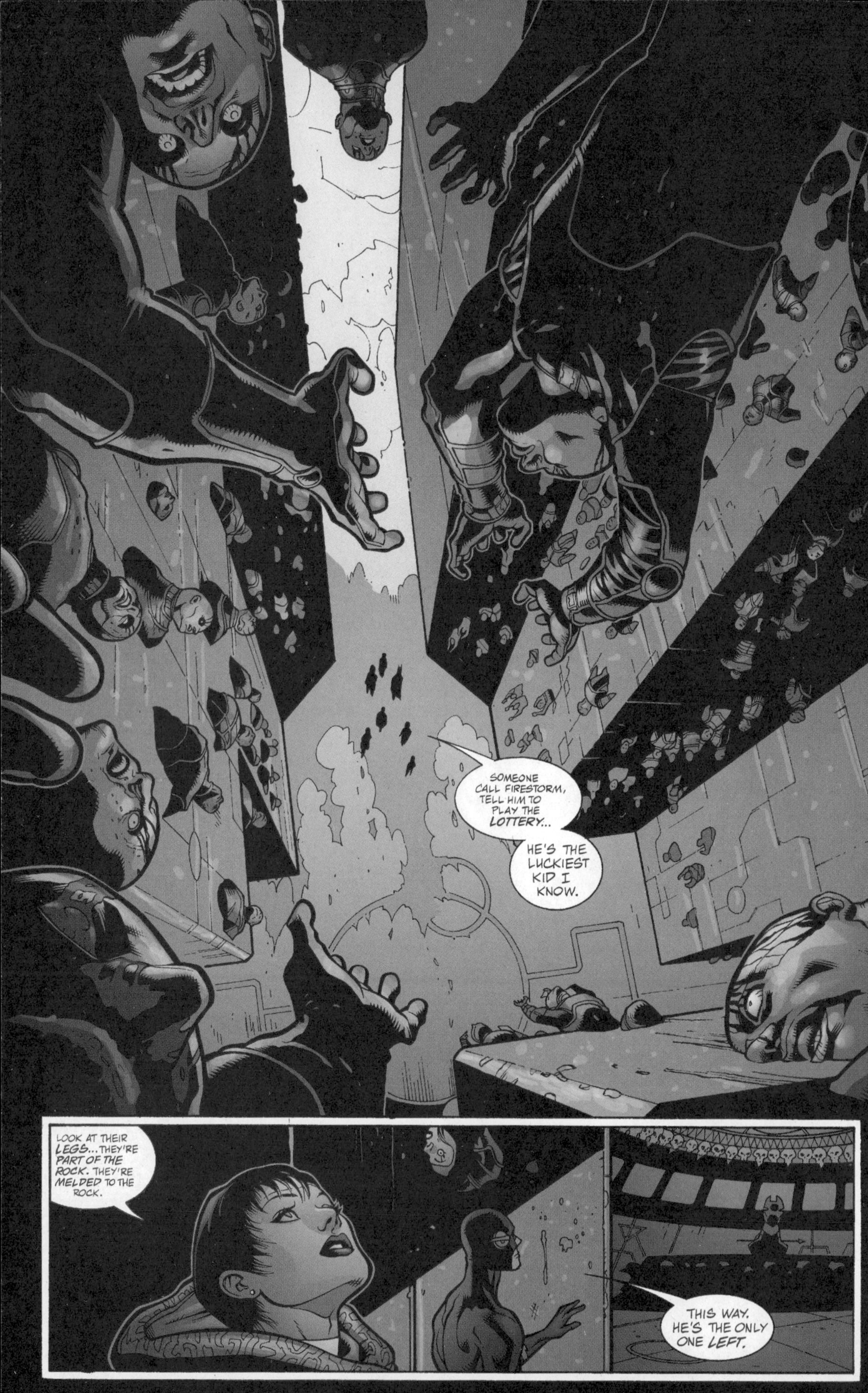
SOMEONE CALL FIRESTORM, TELL HIM TO PLAY THE LOTTERY...
HE'S THE LUCKIEST KID I KNOW.
LOOK AT THEIR LEGS... THEY'RE PART OF THE ROCK. THEY'RE MELDED TO THE ROCK.
THIS WAY. HE'S THE ONLY ONE LEFT.

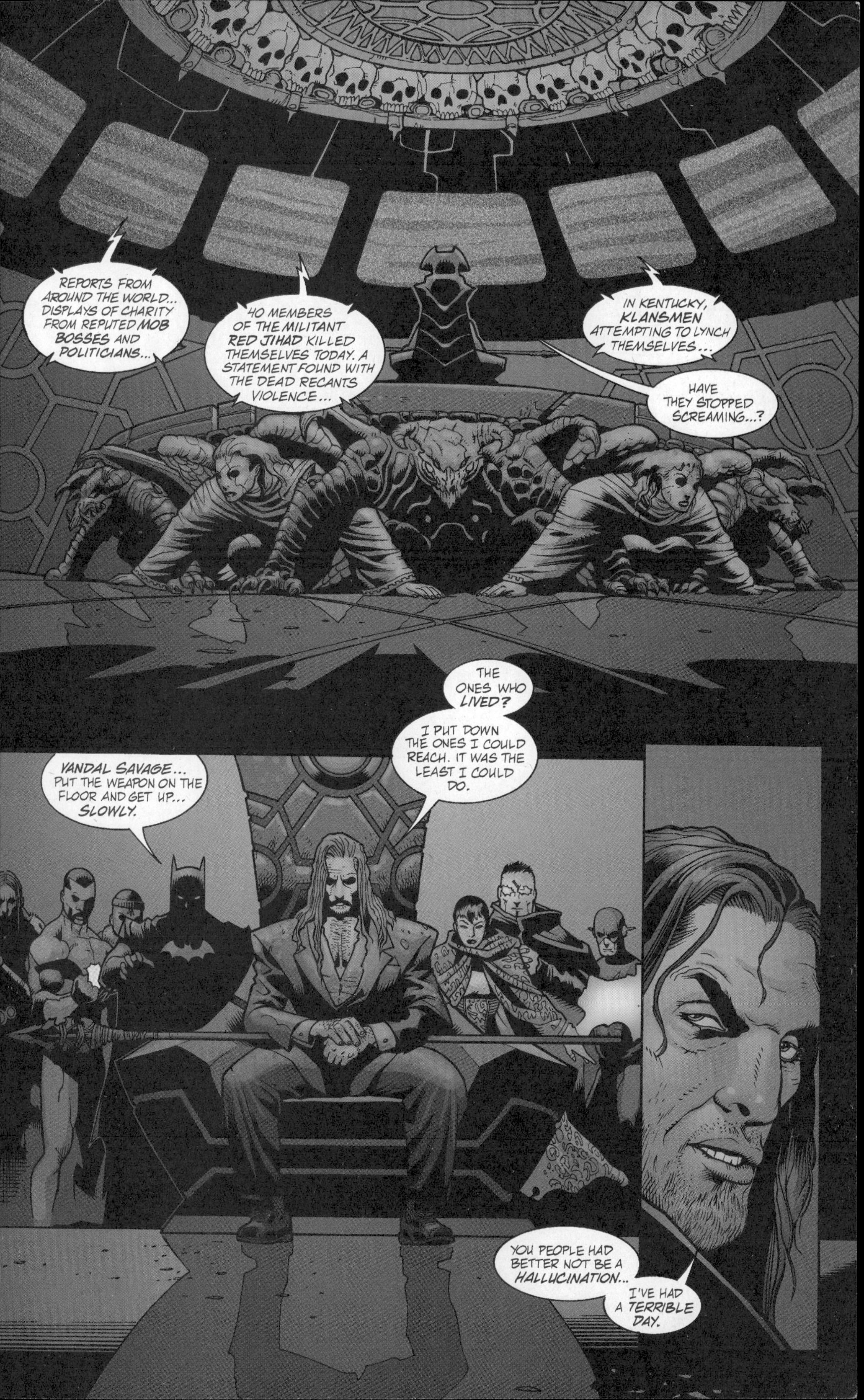
REPORTS FROM AROUND THE WORLD... DISPLAYS OF CHARITY FROM REPUTED MOB BOSSES AND POLITICIANS...
40 MEMBERS OF THE MILITANT RED JIHAD KILLED THEMSELVES TODAY. A STATEMENT FOUND WITH THE DEAD RECANTS VIOLENCE...
IN KENTUCKY, KLANSMEN ATTEMPTING TO LYNCH THEMSELVES...
HAVE THEY STOPPED SCREAMING...?
THE ONES WHO LIVED?
I PUT DOWN THE ONES I COULD REACH. IT WAS THE LEAST I COULD DO.
VANDAL SAVAGE... PUT THE WEAPON ON THE FLOOR AND GET UP... SLOWLY.
YOU PEOPLE HAD BETTER NOT BE A HALLUCINATION...
I'VE HAD A TERRIBLE DAY.

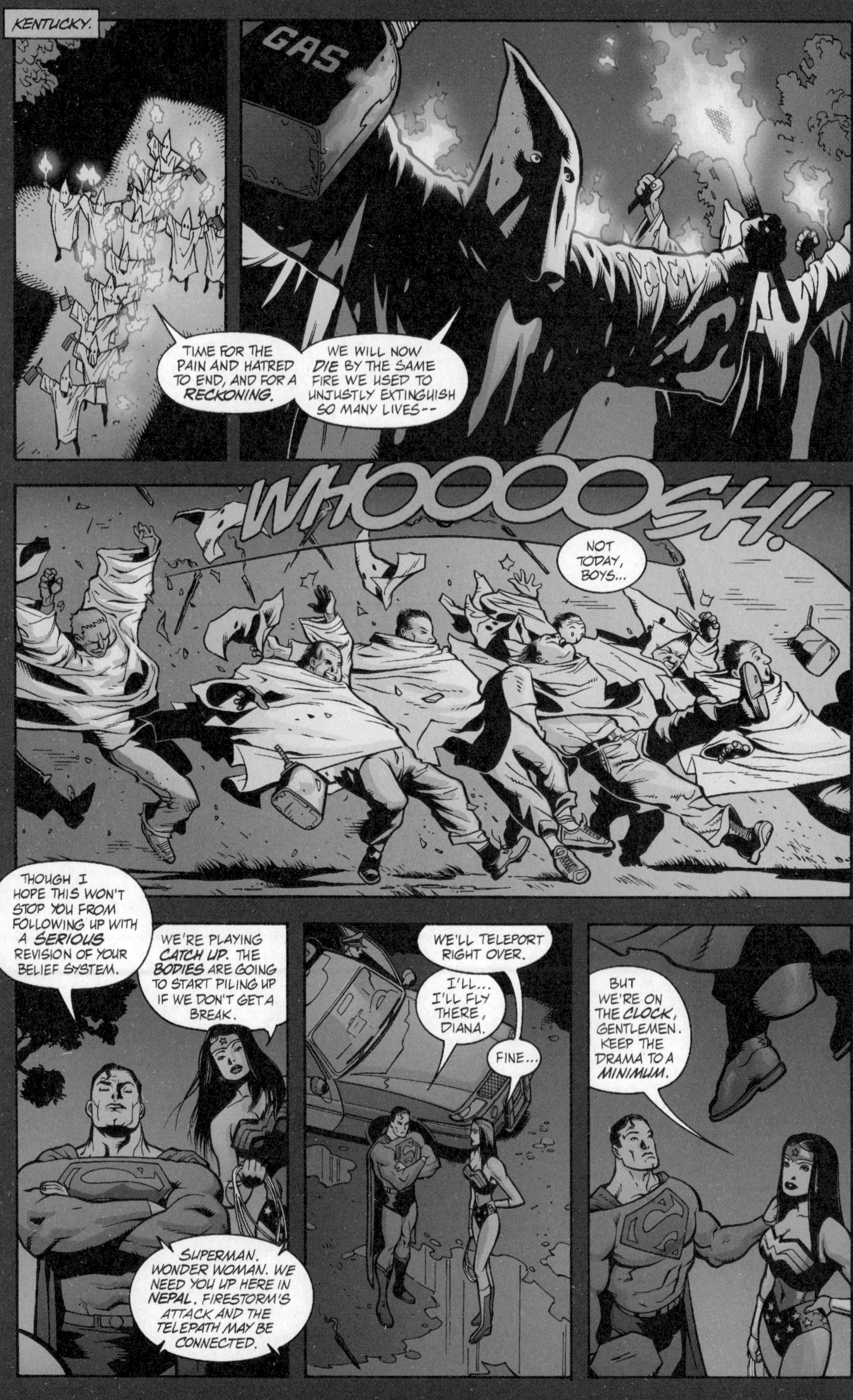
KENTUCKY.
GAS
TIME FOR THE PAIN AND HATRED TO END, AND FOR A RECKONING.
WE WILL NOW DIE BY THE SAME FIRE WE USED TO UNJUSTLY EXTINGUISH SO MANY LIVES--
WHOOOOOSH!
NOT TODAY, BOYS...
THOUGH I HOPE THIS WON'T STOP YOU FROM FOLLOWING UP WITH A SERIOUS REVISION OF YOUR BELIEF SYSTEM.
WE'RE PLAYING CATCH UP. THE BODIES ARE GOING TO START PILING UP IF WE DON'T GET A BREAK.
SUPERMAN. WONDER WOMAN. WE NEED YOU UP HERE IN NEPAL. FIRESTORM'S ATTACK AND THE TELEPATH MAY BE CONNECTED.
WE'LL TELEPORT RIGHT OVER.
I'LL... I'LL FLY THERE, DIANA.
FINE...
BUT WE'RE ON THE CLOCK, GENTLEMEN. KEEP THE DRAMA TO A MINIMUM.

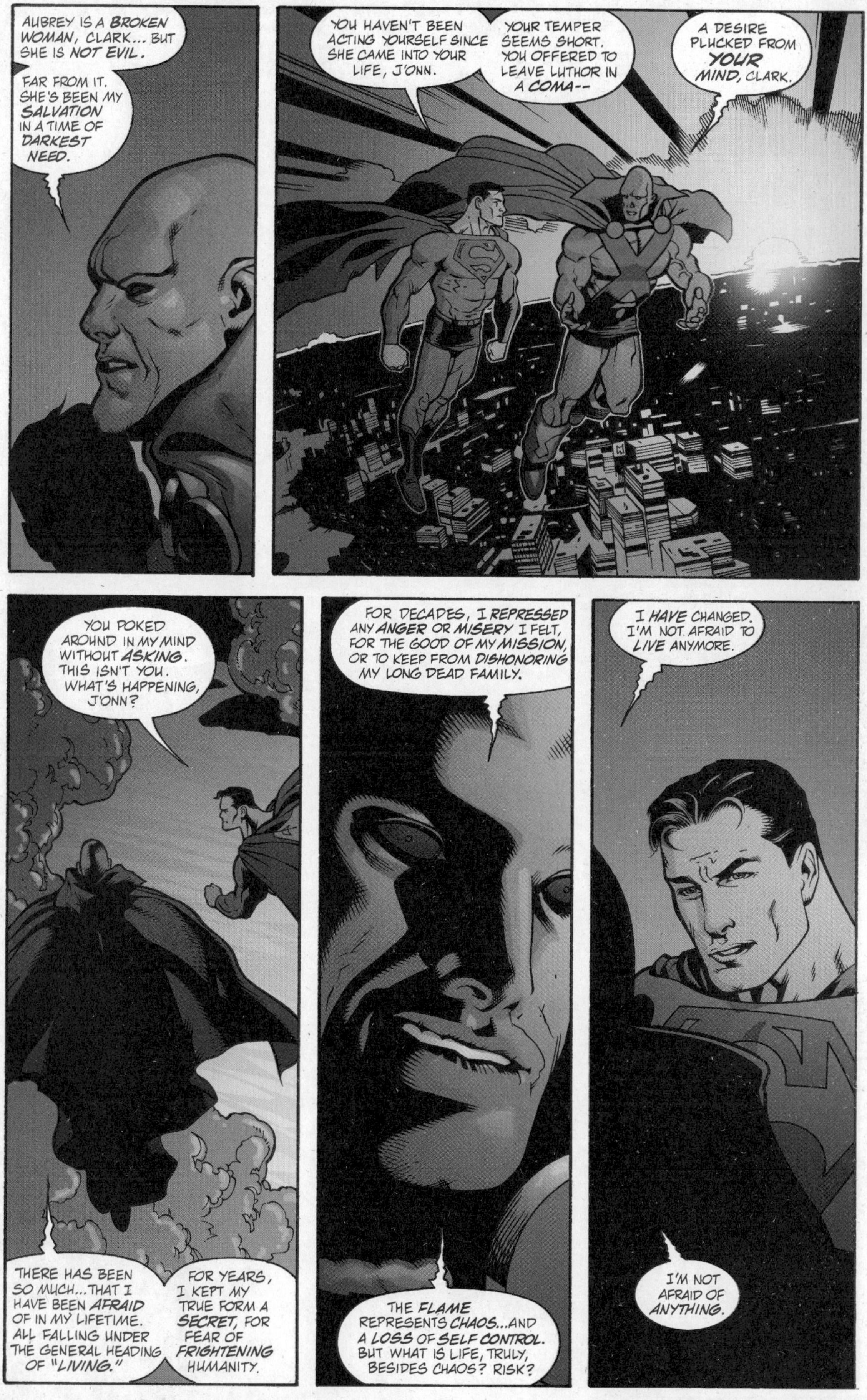
AUBREY IS A BROKEN WOMAN, CLARK... BUT SHE IS NOT EVIL.
FAR FROM IT. SHE'S BEEN MY SALVATION IN A TIME OF DARKEST NEED.
YOU HAVEN'T BEEN ACTING YOURSELF SINCE SHE CAME INTO YOUR LIFE, J'ONN.
YOUR TEMPER SEEMS SHORT. YOU OFFERED TO LEAVE LUTHOR IN A COMA--
A DESIRE PLUCKED FROM YOUR MIND, CLARK.
YOU POKED AROUND IN MY MIND WITHOUT ASKING. THIS ISN'T YOU. WHAT'S HAPPENING, J'ONN?
THERE HAS BEEN SO MUCH... THAT I HAVE BEEN AFRAID OF IN MY LIFETIME. ALL FALLING UNDER THE GENERAL HEADING OF "LIVING."
FOR YEARS, I KEPT MY TRUE FORM A SECRET, FOR FEAR OF FRIGHTENING HUMANITY.
FOR DECADES, I REPRESSED ANY ANGER OR MISERY I FELT, FOR THE GOOD OF MY MISSION, OR TO KEEP FROM DISHONORING MY LONG DEAD FAMILY.
THE FLAME REPRESENTS CHAOS... AND A LOSS OF SELF CONTROL. BUT WHAT IS LIFE, TRULY, BESIDES CHAOS? RISK?
I HAVE CHANGED. I'M NOT AFRAID TO LIVE ANYMORE.
I'M NOT AFRAID OF ANYTHING.

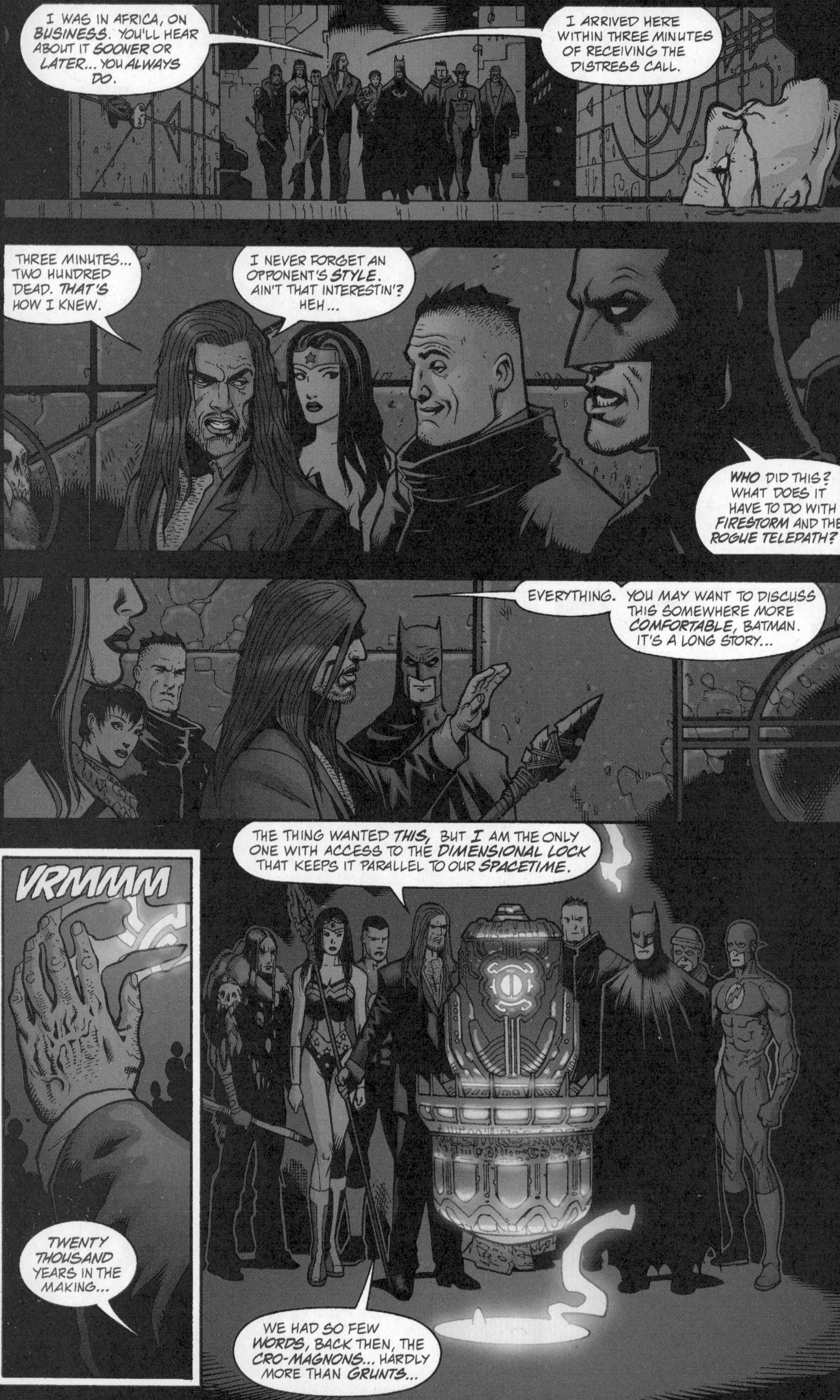

I WAS IN AFRICA, ON BUSINESS. YOU'LL HEAR ABOUT IT SOONER OR LATER... YOU ALWAYS DO.
I ARRIVED HERE WITHIN THREE MINUTES OF RECEIVING THE DISTRESS CALL.
THREE MINUTES... TWO HUNDRED DEAD. THAT'S HOW I KNEW.
I NEVER FORGET AN OPPONENT'S STYLE. AIN'T THAT INTERESTIN'? HEH...
WHO DID THIS? WHAT DOES IT HAVE TO DO WITH FIRESTORM AND THE ROGUE TELEPATH?
EVERYTHING. YOU MAY WANT TO DISCUSS THIS SOMEWHERE MORE COMFORTABLE, BATMAN. IT'S A LONG STORY...
VRMMM
TWENTY THOUSAND YEARS IN THE MAKING...
THE THING WANTED THIS, BUT I AM THE ONLY ONE WITH ACCESS TO THE DIMENSIONAL LOCK THAT KEEPS IT PARALLEL TO OUR SPACETIME.
WE HAD SO FEW WORDS, BACK THEN, THE CRO-MAGNONS... HARDLY MORE THAN GRUNTS...

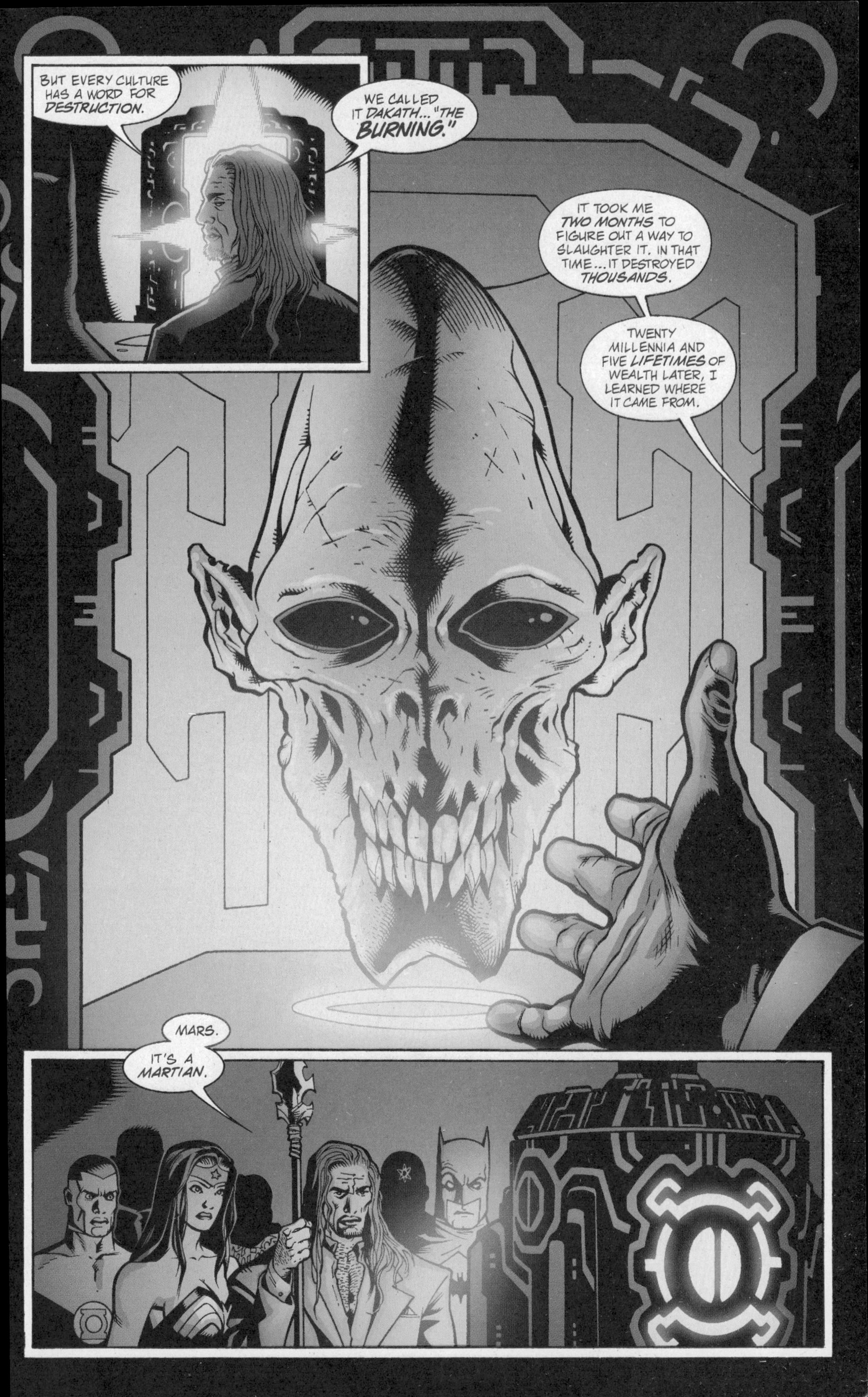
BUT EVERY CULTURE HAS A WORD FOR DESTRUCTION.
WE CALLED IT DAKATH... "THE BURNING."
IT TOOK ME TWO MONTHS TO FIGURE OUT A WAY TO SLAUGHTER IT. IN THAT TIME... IT DESTROYED THOUSANDS.
TWENTY MILLENNIA AND FIVE LIFETIMES OF WEALTH LATER, I LEARNED WHERE IT CAME FROM.
MARS.
IT'S A MARTIAN.

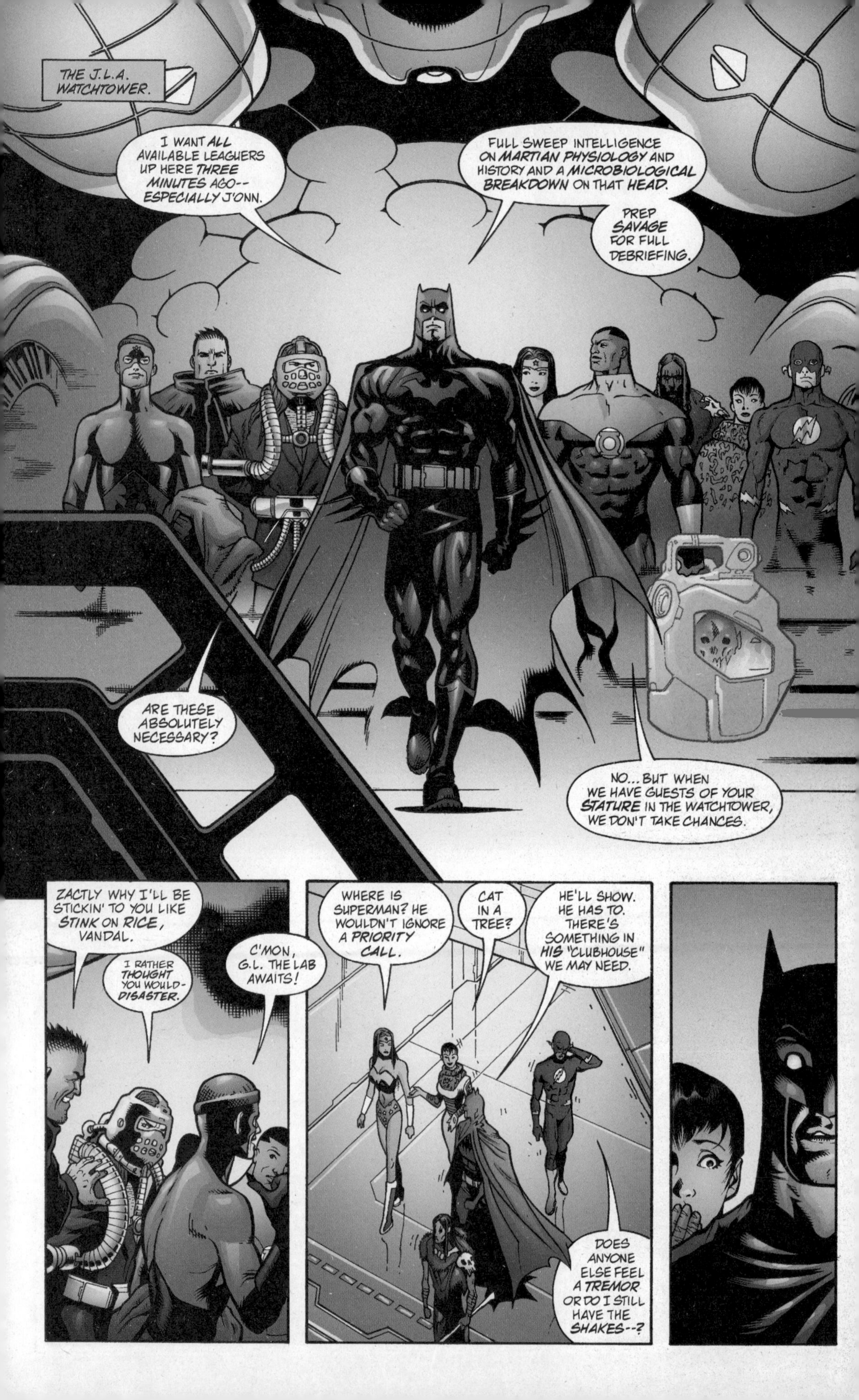
THE J.L.A. WATCHTOWER.
I WANT ALL AVAILABLE LEAGUERS UP HERE THREE MINUTES AGO-- ESPECIALLY J'ONN.
FULL SWEEP INTELLIGENCE ON MARTIAN PHYSIOLOGY AND HISTORY AND A MICROBIOLOGICAL BREAKDOWN ON THAT HEAD.
PREP SAVAGE FOR FULL DEBRIEFING.
ARE THESE ABSOLUTELY NECESSARY?
NO... BUT WHEN WE HAVE GUESTS OF YOUR STATURE IN THE WATCHTOWER, WE DON'T TAKE CHANCES.
ZACTLY WHY I'LL BE STICKIN' TO YOU LIKE STINK ON RICE, VANDAL.
I RATHER THOUGHT YOU WOULD-DISASTER.
C'MON, G.L. THE LAB AWAITS!
WHERE IS SUPERMAN? HE WOULDN'T IGNORE A PRIORITY CALL.
CAT IN A TREE?
HE'LL SHOW. HE HAS TO. THERE'S SOMETHING IN HIS "CLUBHOUSE" WE MAY NEED.
DOES ANYONE ELSE FEEL A TREMOR OR DO I STILL HAVE THE SHAKES--?

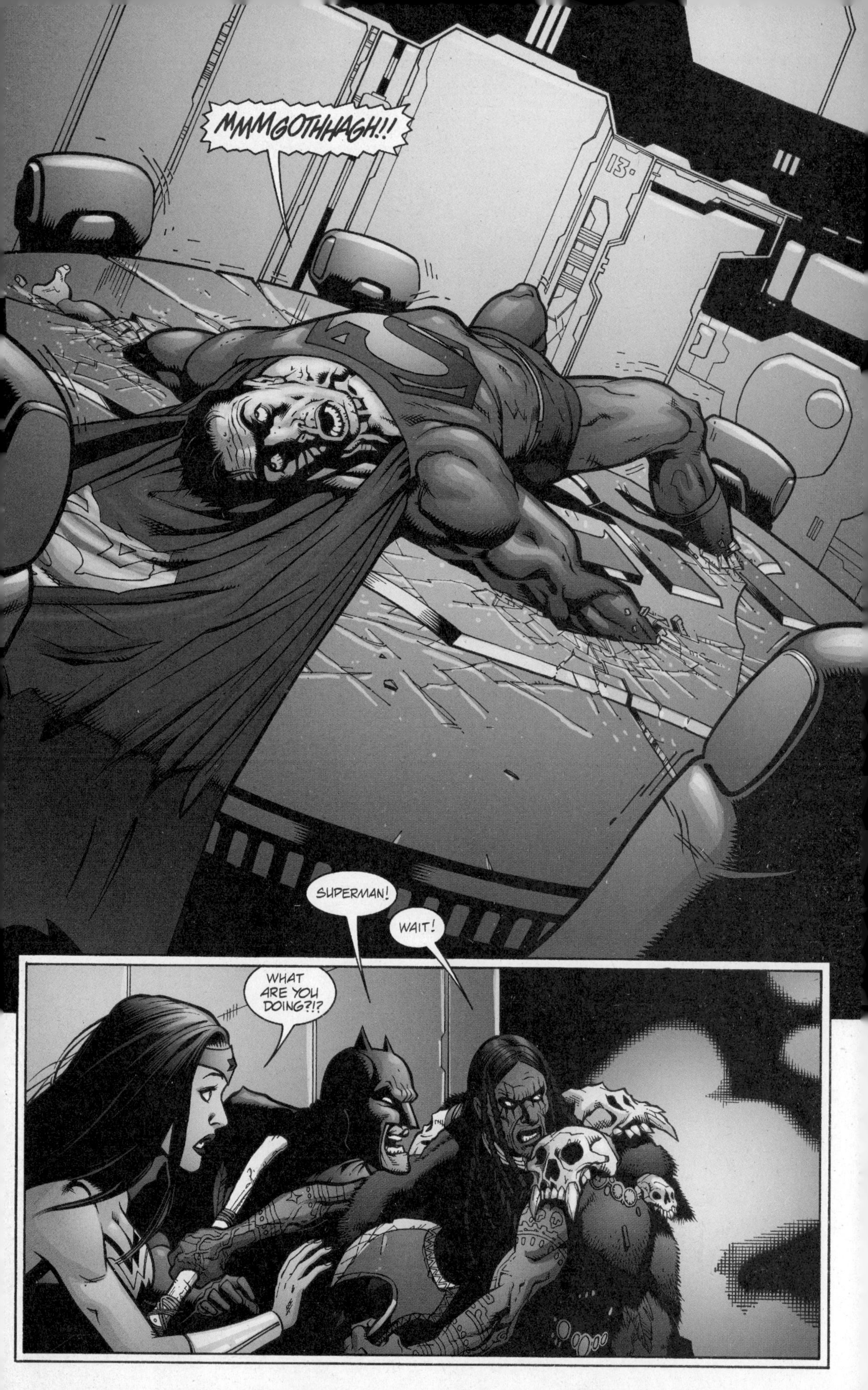
MMMGOTHHAGH!!
SUPERMAN!
WAIT!
WHAT ARE YOU DOING?!?

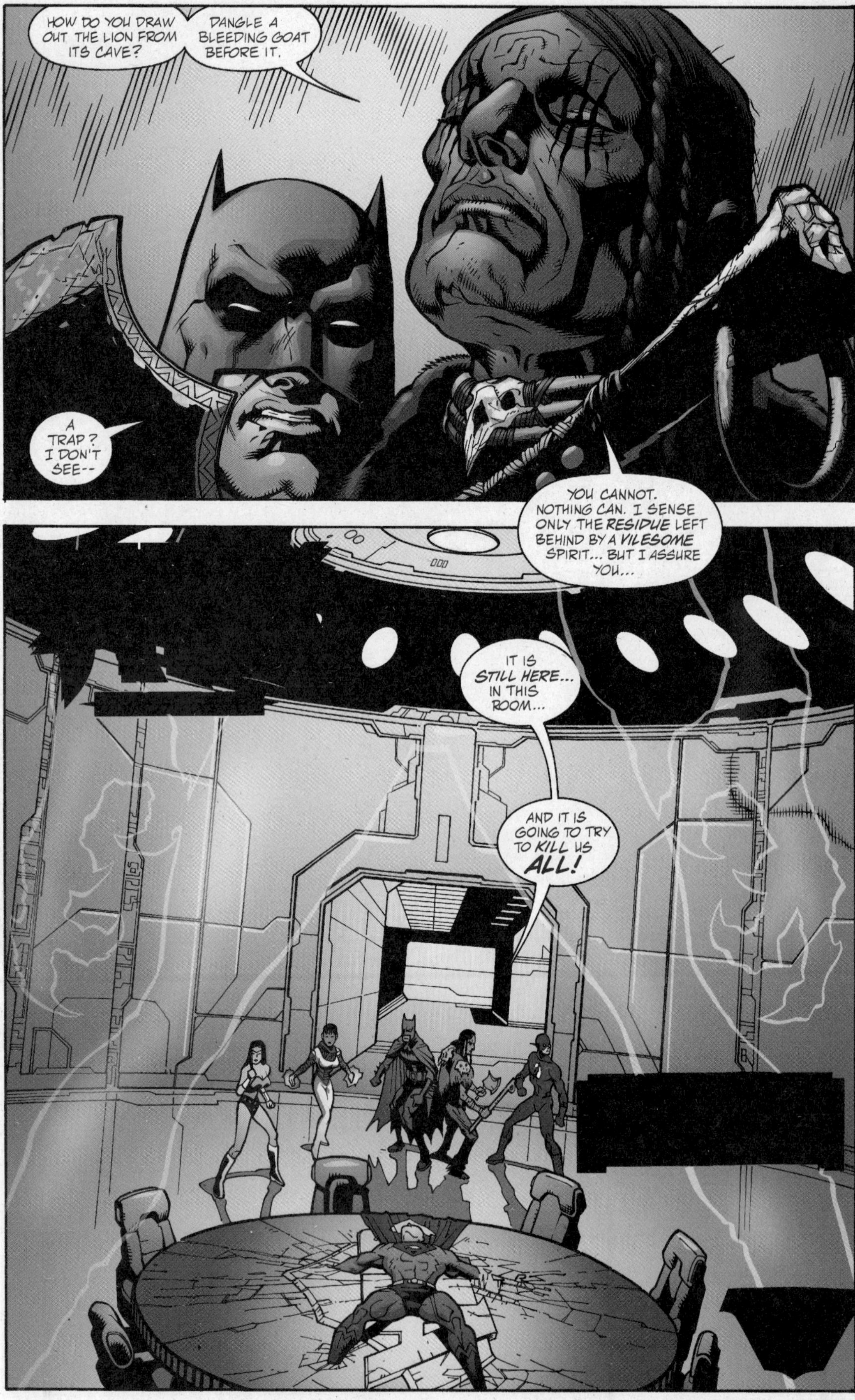
HOW DO YOU DRAW OUT THE LION FROM ITS CAVE?
DANGLE A BLEEDING GOAT BEFORE IT.
A TRAP? I DON'T SEE--
YOU CANNOT. NOTHING CAN. I SENSE ONLY THE *RESIDUE* LEFT BEHIND BY A *VILESOME* SPIRIT... BUT I ASSURE YOU...
IT IS *STILL HERE*... IN THIS ROOM...
AND IT IS GOING TO TRY TO *KILL* US ***ALL!***

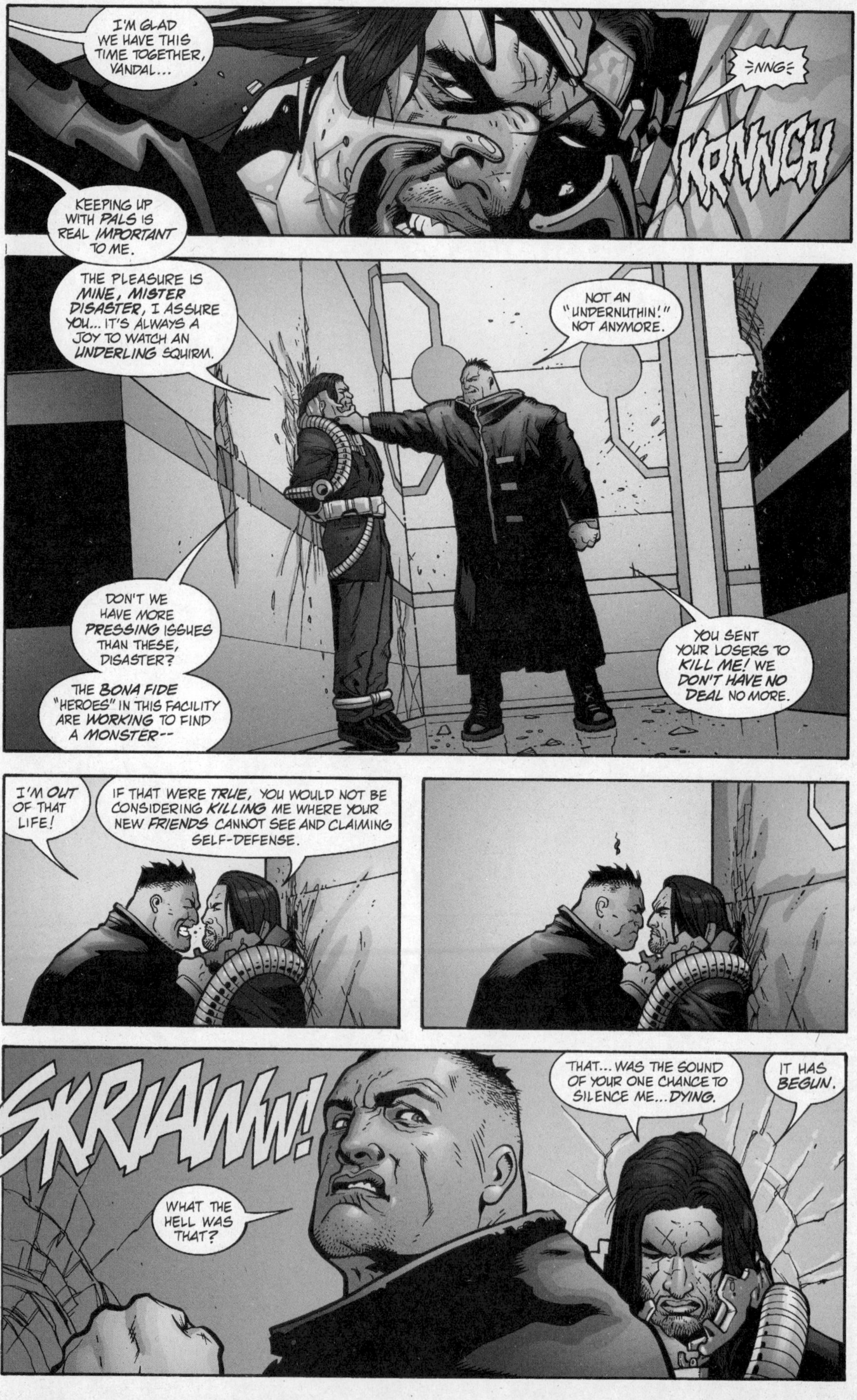
I'M GLAD WE HAVE THIS TIME TOGETHER, VANDAL...
NNG
KRNNCH
KEEPING UP WITH PALS IS REAL IMPORTANT TO ME.
THE PLEASURE IS MINE, MISTER DISASTER, I ASSURE YOU... IT'S ALWAYS A JOY TO WATCH AN UNDERLING SQUIRM.
NOT AN "UNDERNUTHIN'." NOT ANYMORE.
DON'T WE HAVE MORE PRESSING ISSUES THAN THESE, DISASTER?
THE BONA FIDE "HEROES" IN THIS FACILITY ARE WORKING TO FIND A MONSTER--
YOU SENT YOUR LOSERS TO KILL ME! WE DON'T HAVE NO DEAL NO MORE.
I'M OUT OF THAT LIFE!
IF THAT WERE TRUE, YOU WOULD NOT BE CONSIDERING KILLING ME WHERE YOUR NEW FRIENDS CANNOT SEE AND CLAIMING SELF-DEFENSE.
SKRIAWW!
THAT... WAS THE SOUND OF YOUR ONE CHANCE TO SILENCE ME... DYING.
IT HAS BEGUN.
WHAT THE HELL WAS THAT?

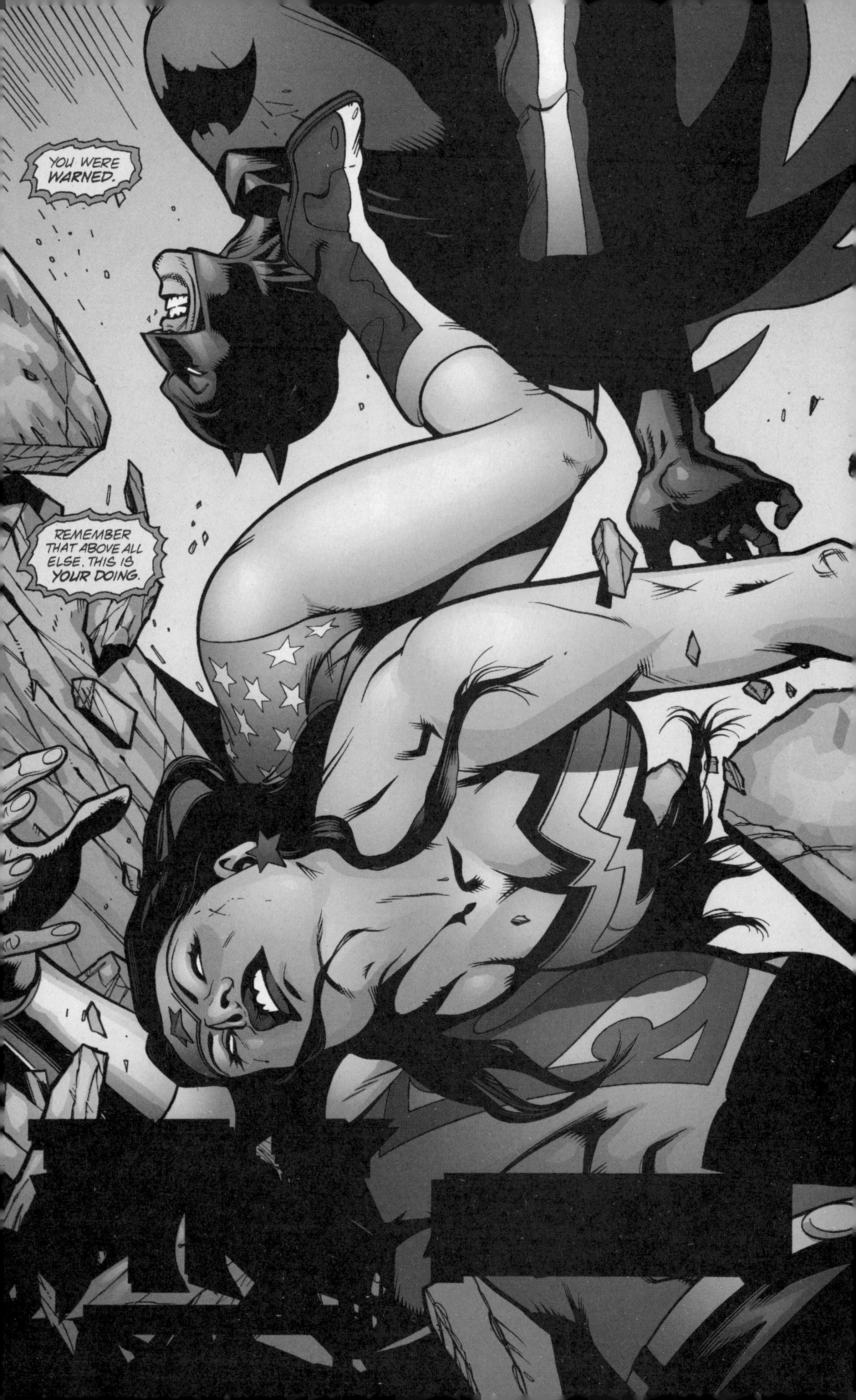
YOU WERE WARNED.
REMEMBER THAT ABOVE ALL ELSE. THIS IS YOUR DOING.

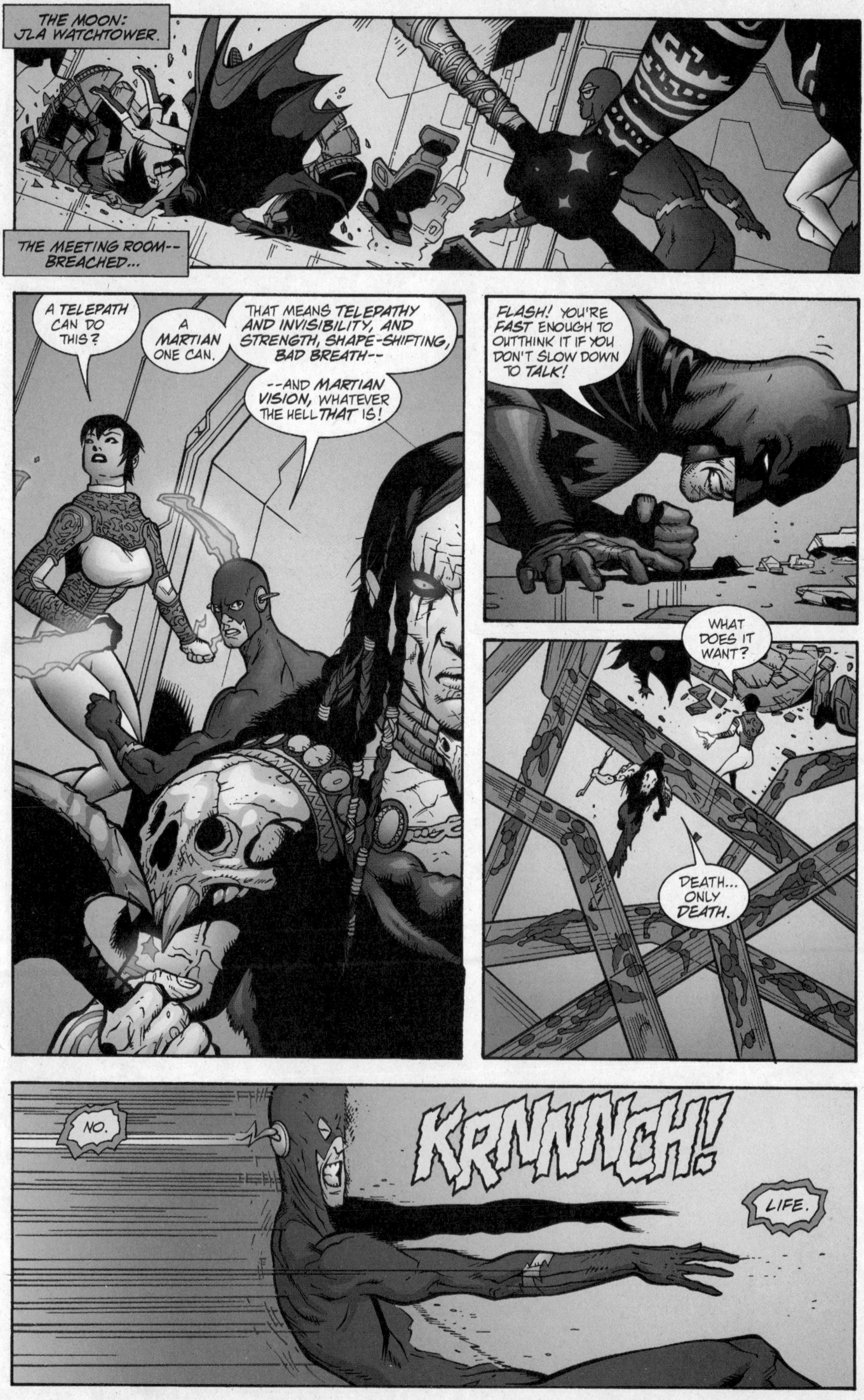
THE MOON: JLA WATCHTOWER.
THE MEETING ROOM-- BREACHED...
A TELEPATH CAN DO THIS?
A MARTIAN ONE CAN.
THAT MEANS TELEPATHY AND INVISIBILITY, AND STRENGTH, SHAPE-SHIFTING, BAD BREATH--
--AND MARTIAN VISION, WHATEVER THE HELL THAT IS!
FLASH! YOU'RE FAST ENOUGH TO OUTTHINK IT IF YOU DON'T SLOW DOWN TO TALK!
WHAT DOES IT WANT?
DEATH... ONLY DEATH.
NO.
KRNNNCH!
LIFE.

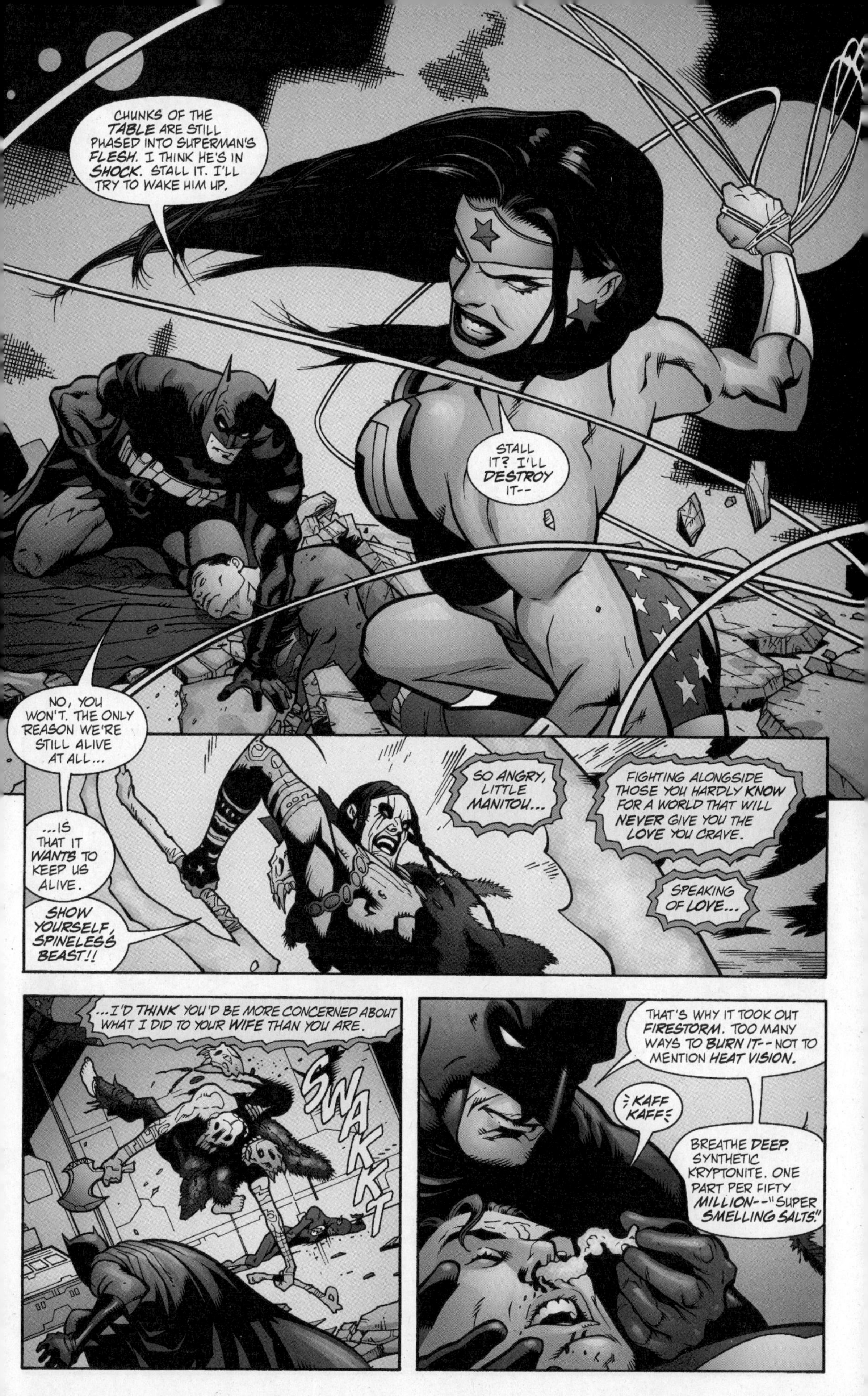
CHUNKS OF THE TABLE ARE STILL PHASED INTO SUPERMAN'S FLESH. I THINK HE'S IN SHOCK. STALL IT. I'LL TRY TO WAKE HIM UP.
STALL IT? I'LL DESTROY IT--
NO, YOU WON'T. THE ONLY REASON WE'RE STILL ALIVE AT ALL...
...IS THAT IT WANTS TO KEEP US ALIVE.
SHOW YOURSELF, SPINELESS BEAST!!
SO ANGRY, LITTLE MANITOU...
FIGHTING ALONGSIDE THOSE YOU HARDLY KNOW FOR A WORLD THAT WILL NEVER GIVE YOU THE LOVE YOU CRAVE.
SPEAKING OF LOVE...
...I'D THINK YOU'D BE MORE CONCERNED ABOUT WHAT I DID TO YOUR WIFE THAN YOU ARE.
SNAKT
THAT'S WHY IT TOOK OUT FIRESTORM. TOO MANY WAYS TO BURN IT-- NOT TO MENTION HEAT VISION.
KAFF KAFF
BREATHE DEEP. SYNTHETIC KRYPTONITE. ONE PART PER FIFTY MILLION--"SUPER SMELLING SALTS."

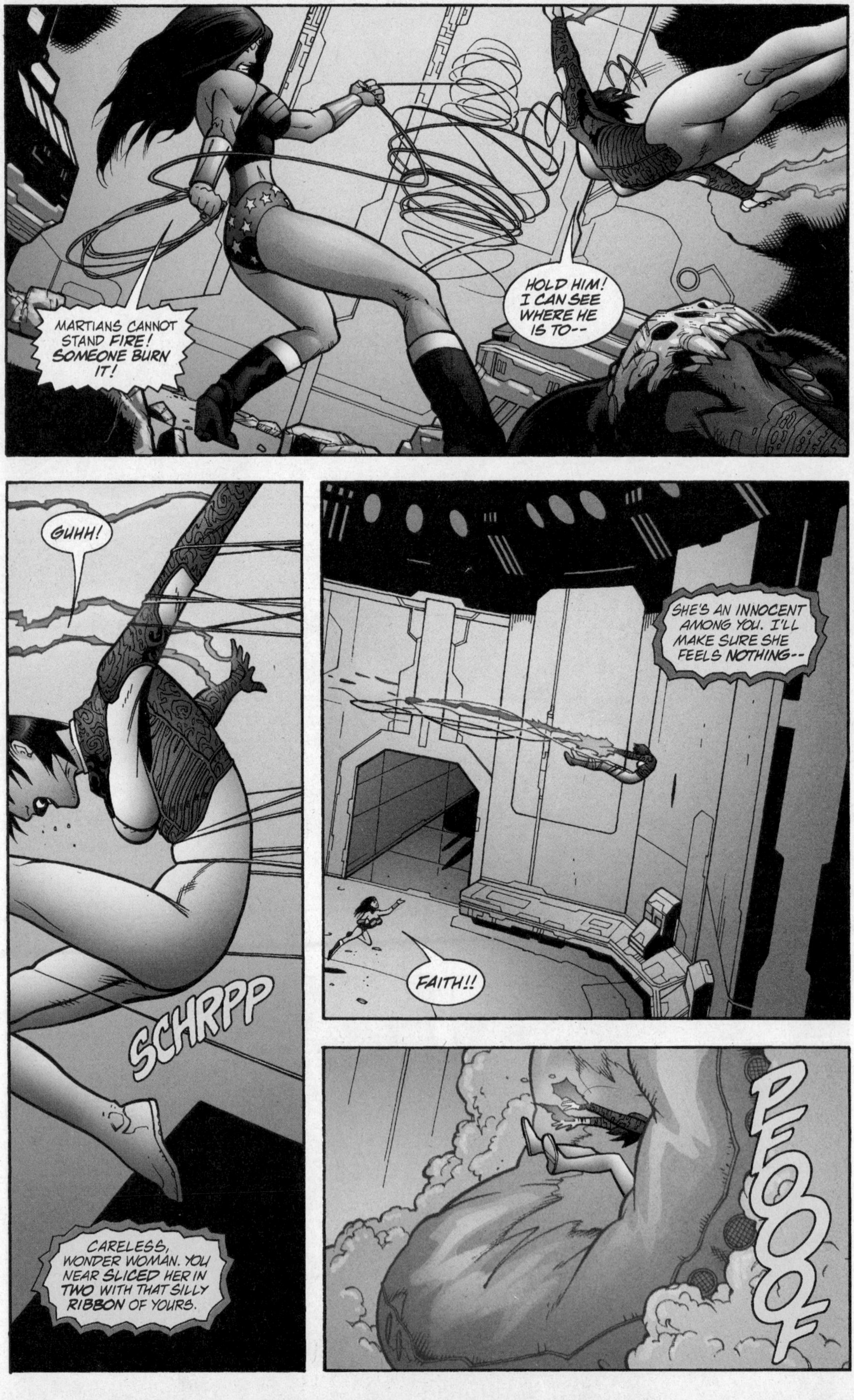
MARTIANS CANNOT STAND **FIRE**! **SOMEONE BURN IT**!
HOLD HIM! I CAN SEE WHERE HE IS TO--
GUHH!
SCHRPP
CARELESS, WONDER WOMAN. YOU NEAR **SLICED** HER IN **TWO** WITH THAT SILLY **RIBBON** OF YOURS.
SHE'S AN INNOCENT AMONG YOU. I'LL MAKE SURE SHE FEELS **NOTHING**--
FAITH!!
PFOOOF

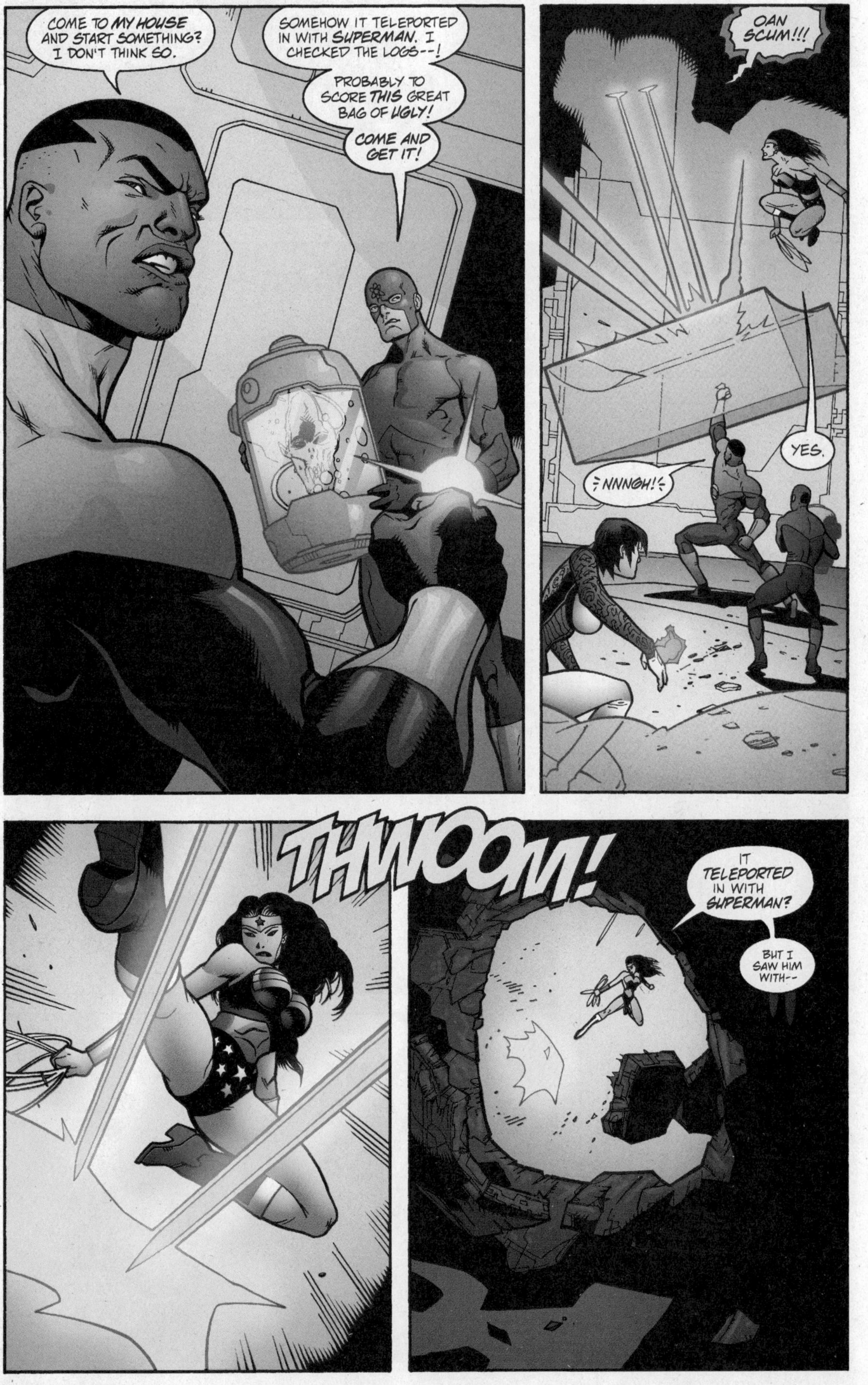

COME TO MY HOUSE AND START SOMETHING? I DON'T THINK SO.
SOMEHOW IT TELEPORTED IN WITH SUPERMAN. I CHECKED THE LOGS--!
PROBABLY TO SCORE THIS GREAT BAG OF UGLY!
COME AND GET IT!
OAN SCUM!!!
YES.
NNNGH!
THWOOM!
IT TELEPORTED IN WITH SUPERMAN?
BUT I SAW HIM WITH--

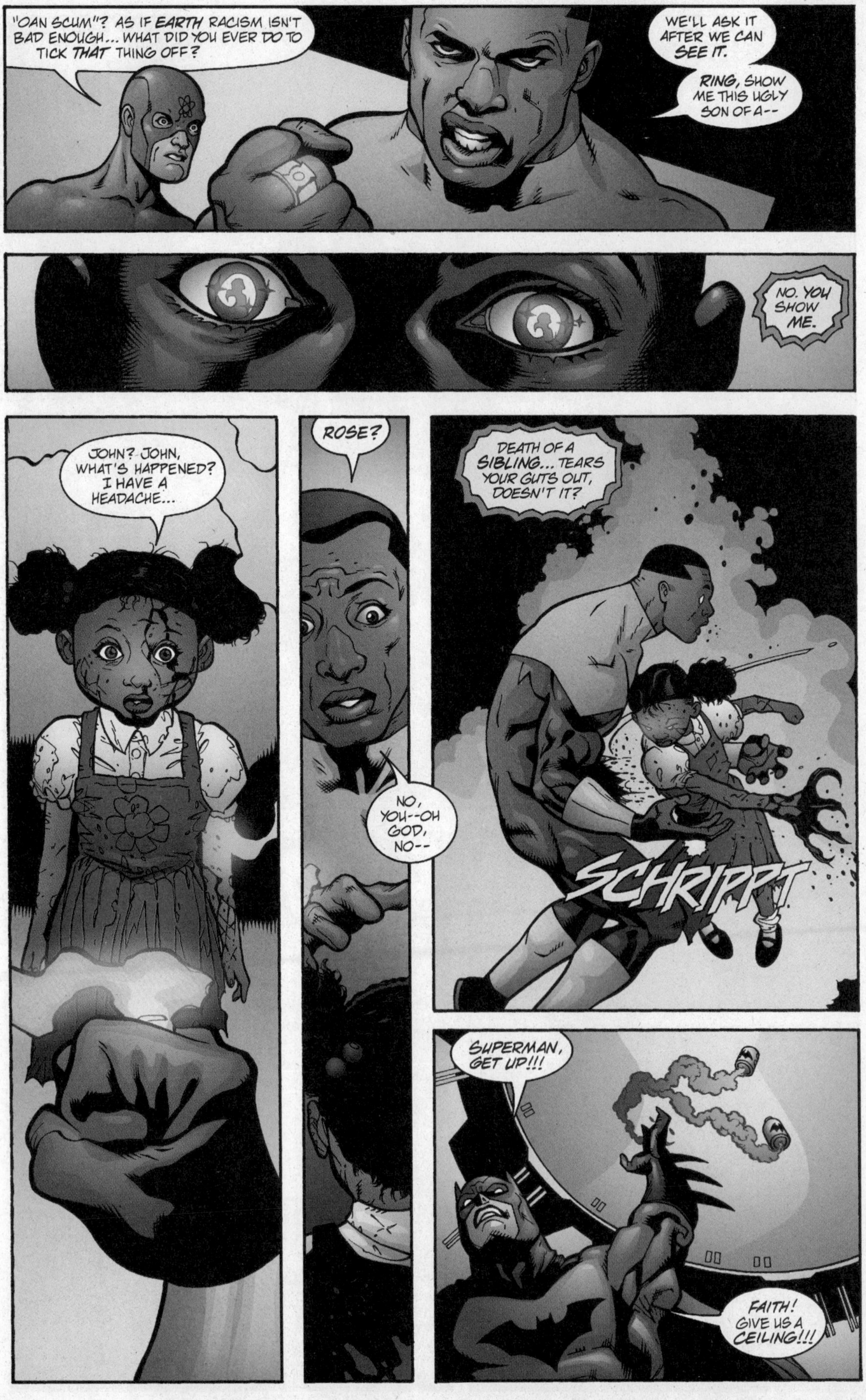
"OAN SCUM"? AS IF EARTH RACISM ISN'T BAD ENOUGH... WHAT DID YOU EVER DO TO TICK THAT THING OFF?
WE'LL ASK IT AFTER WE CAN SEE IT.
RING, SHOW ME THIS UGLY SON OF A--
NO. YOU SHOW ME.
JOHN? JOHN, WHAT'S HAPPENED? I HAVE A HEADACHE...
ROSE?
NO, YOU--OH GOD, NO--
DEATH OF A SIBLING... TEARS YOUR GUTS OUT, DOESN'T IT?
SCHRIPPT
SUPERMAN, GET UP!!!
FAITH! GIVE US A CEILING!!!

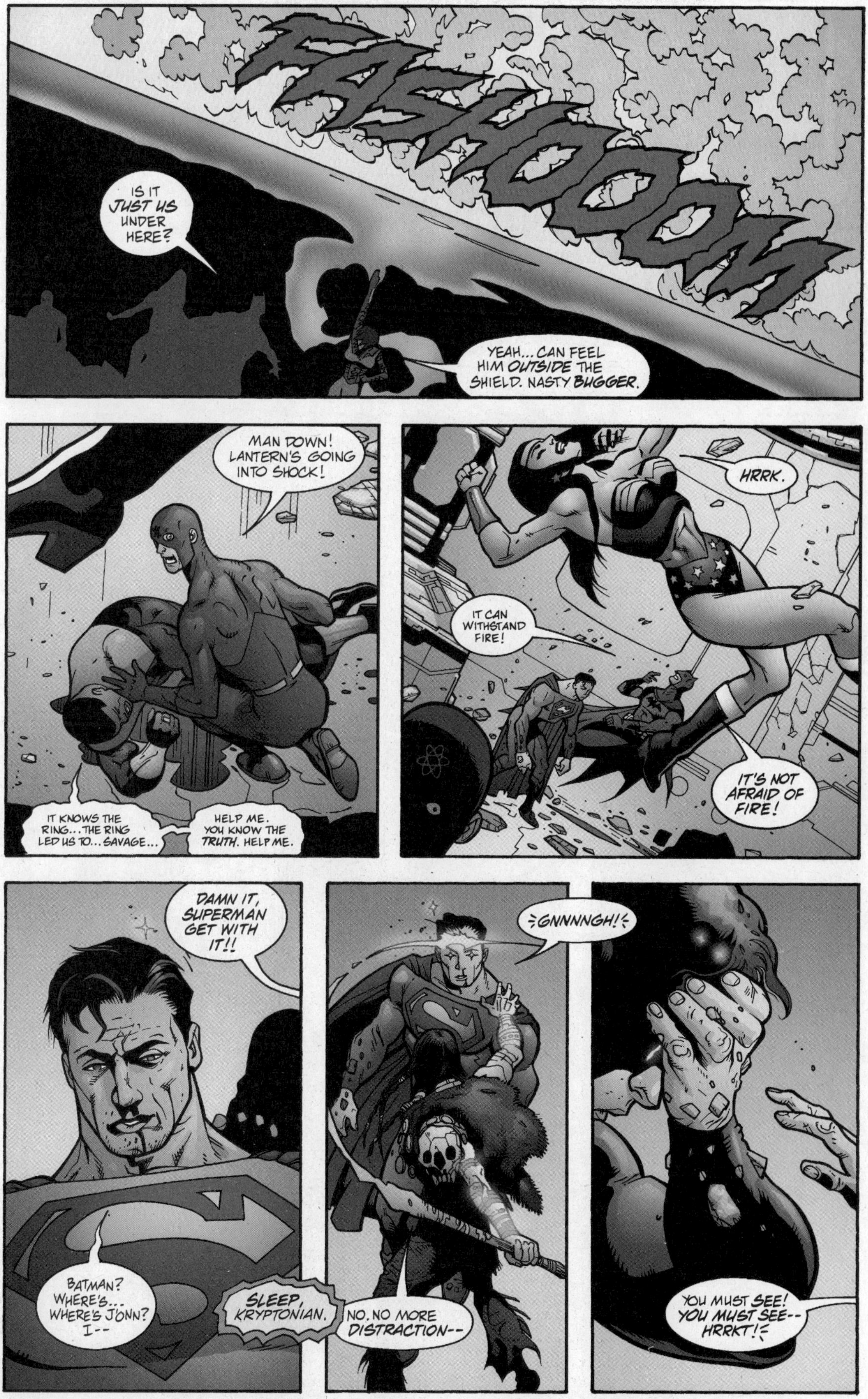
FASHOOOM
IS IT JUST US UNDER HERE?
YEAH... CAN FEEL HIM OUTSIDE THE SHIELD. NASTY BUGGER.
MAN DOWN! LANTERN'S GOING INTO SHOCK!
IT KNOWS THE RING... THE RING LED US TO... SAVAGE...
HELP ME. YOU KNOW THE TRUTH. HELP ME.
HRRK.
IT CAN WITHSTAND FIRE!
IT'S NOT AFRAID OF FIRE!
DAMN IT, SUPERMAN GET WITH IT!!
BATMAN? WHERE'S... WHERE'S J'ONN? I--
SLEEP, KRYPTONIAN.
GNNNNGH!
NO. NO MORE DISTRACTION--
YOU MUST SEE! YOU MUST SEE--HRRKT!

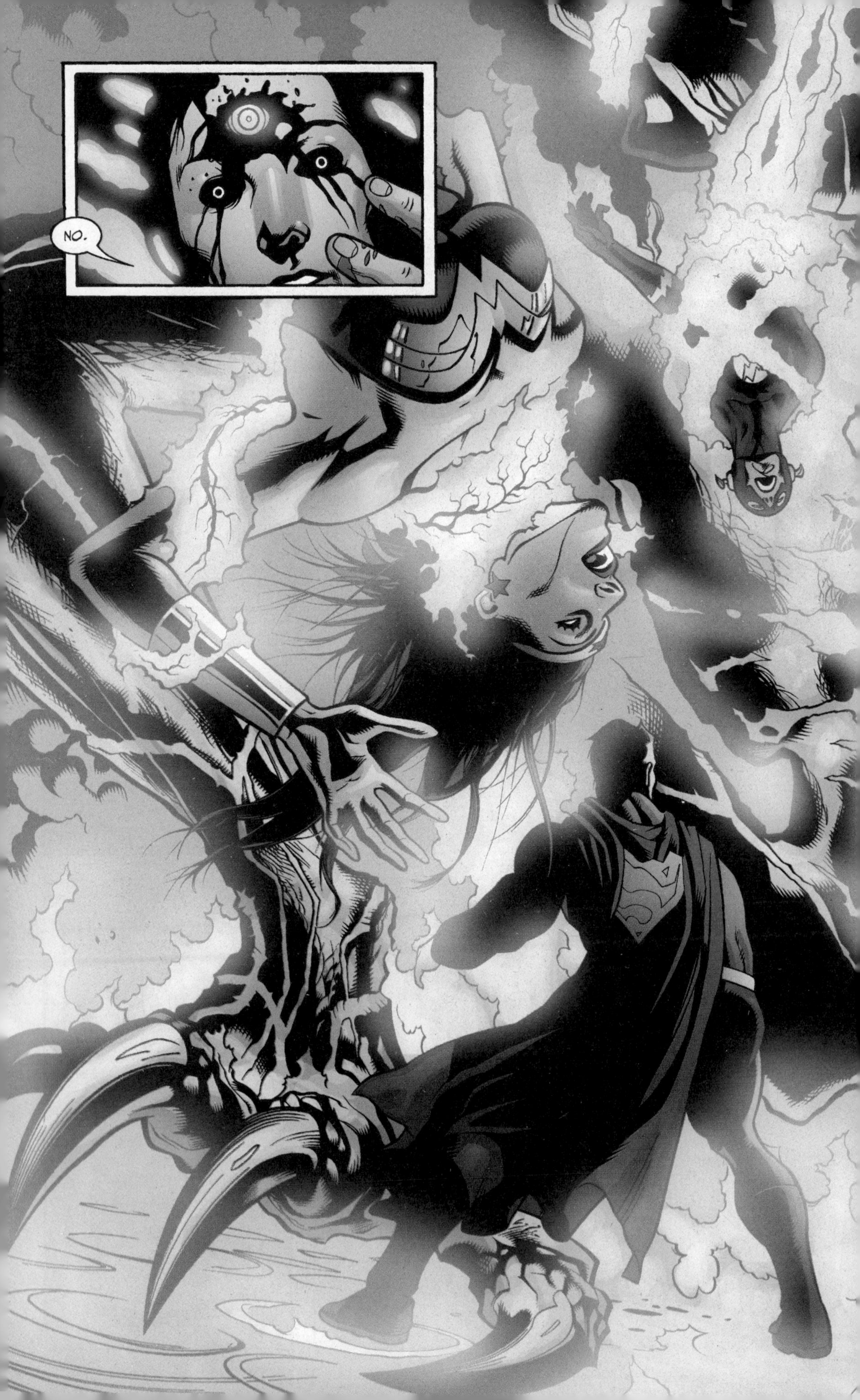
NO.

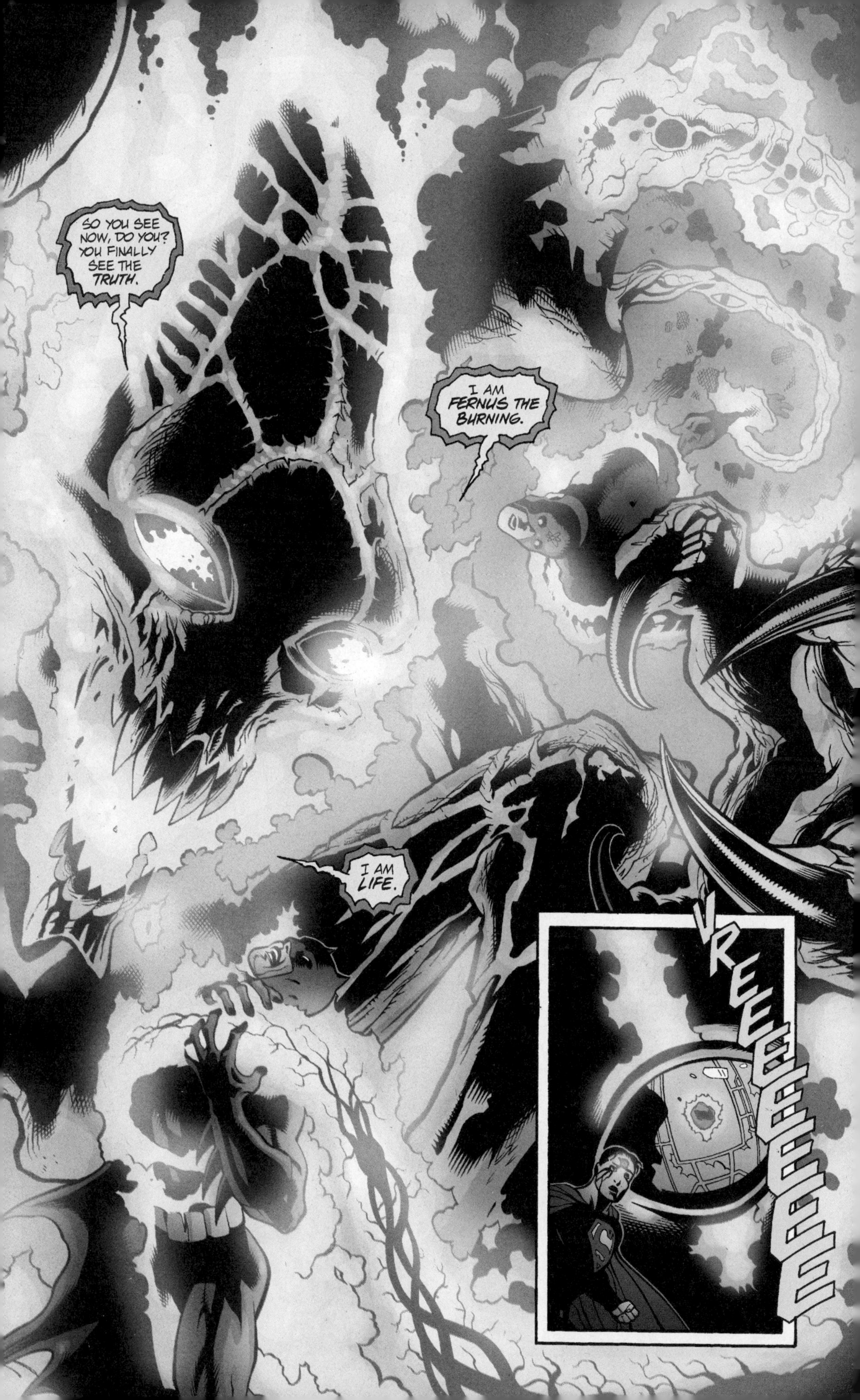
SO YOU SEE NOW, DO YOU? YOU FINALLY SEE THE TRUTH.
I AM FERNUS THE BURNING.
I AM LIFE.
VREEEEEEEEE

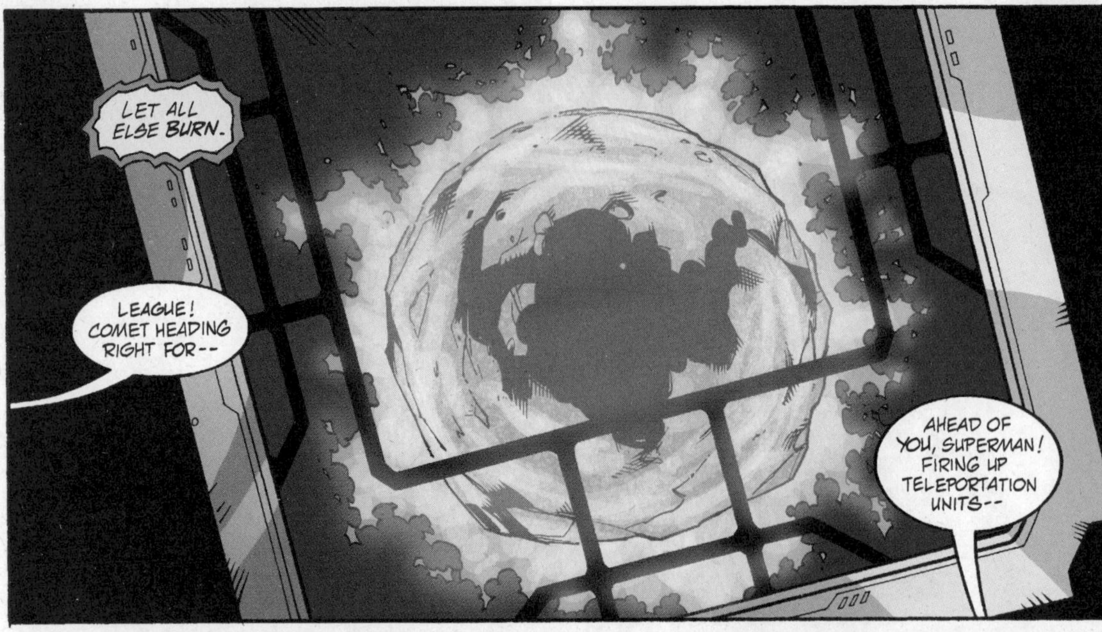
LET ALL ELSE BURN.
LEAGUE! COMET HEADING RIGHT FOR--
AHEAD OF YOU, SUPERMAN! FIRING UP TELEPORTATION UNITS--

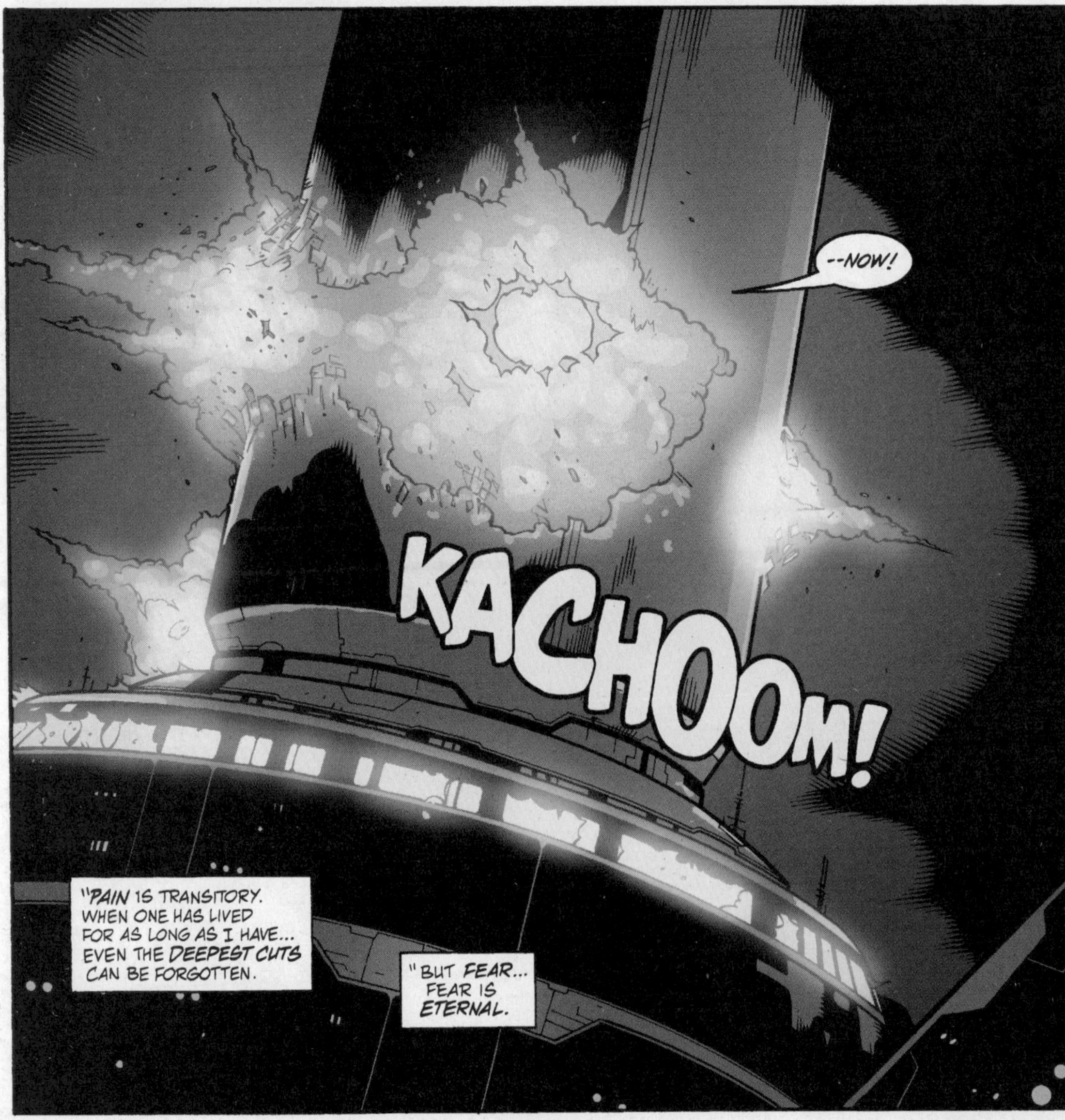
--NOW!
KACHOOM!
"PAIN IS TRANSITORY. WHEN ONE HAS LIVED FOR AS LONG AS I HAVE... EVEN THE DEEPEST CUTS CAN BE FORGOTTEN.
"BUT FEAR... FEAR IS ETERNAL.

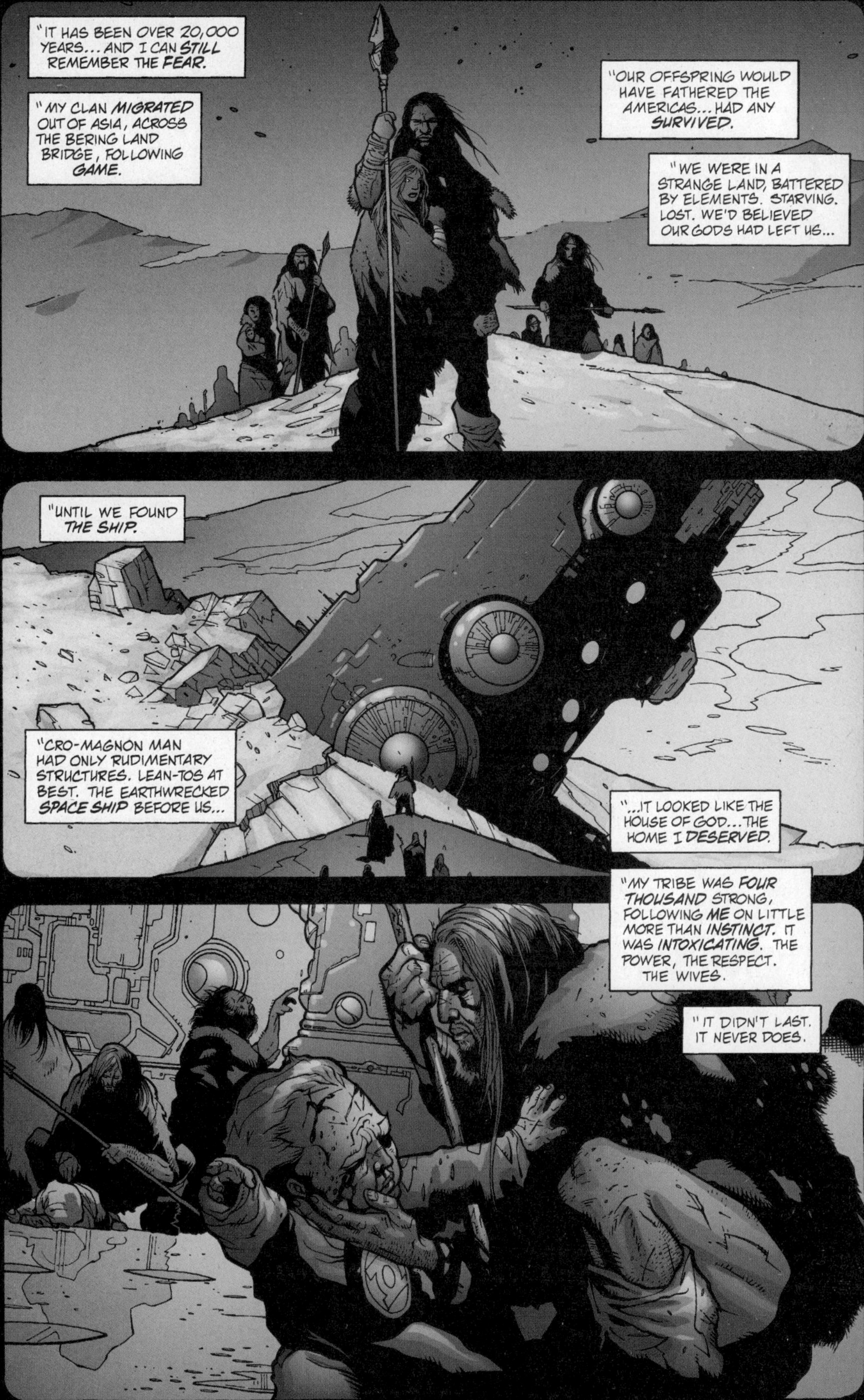
"IT HAS BEEN OVER 20,000 YEARS... AND I CAN STILL REMEMBER THE FEAR.
"MY CLAN MIGRATED OUT OF ASIA, ACROSS THE BERING LAND BRIDGE, FOLLOWING GAME.
"OUR OFFSPRING WOULD HAVE FATHERED THE AMERICAS... HAD ANY SURVIVED.
"WE WERE IN A STRANGE LAND, BATTERED BY ELEMENTS. STARVING. LOST. WE'D BELIEVED OUR GODS HAD LEFT US...
"UNTIL WE FOUND THE SHIP.
"CRO-MAGNON MAN HAD ONLY RUDIMENTARY STRUCTURES. LEAN-TOS AT BEST. THE EARTHWRECKED SPACE SHIP BEFORE US...
"...IT LOOKED LIKE THE HOUSE OF GOD... THE HOME I DESERVED.
"MY TRIBE WAS FOUR THOUSAND STRONG, FOLLOWING ME ON LITTLE MORE THAN INSTINCT. IT WAS INTOXICATING. THE POWER, THE RESPECT. THE WIVES.
"IT DIDN'T LAST. IT NEVER DOES.

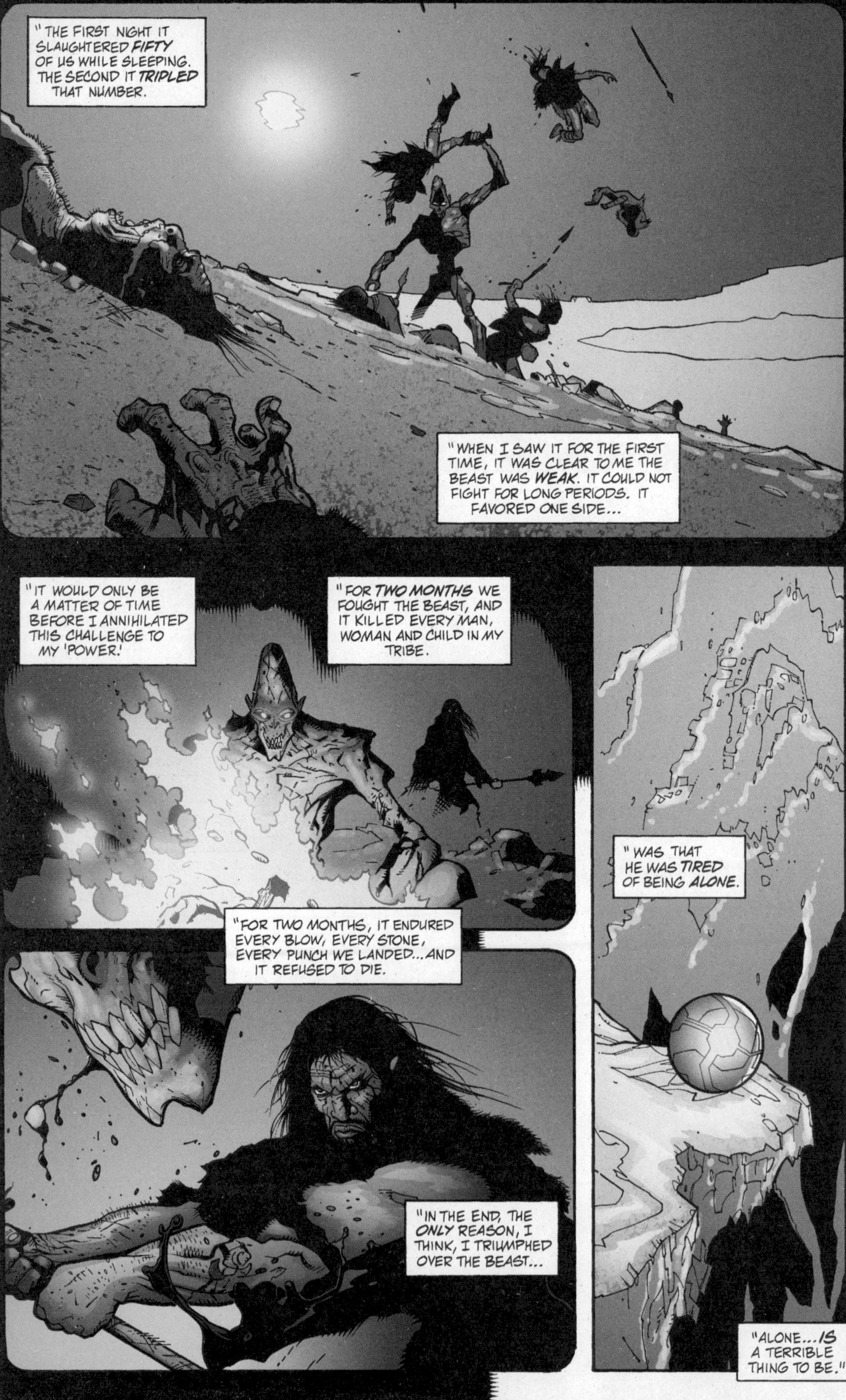
"THE FIRST NIGHT IT SLAUGHTERED *FIFTY* OF US WHILE SLEEPING. THE SECOND IT *TRIPLED* THAT NUMBER.
"WHEN I SAW IT FOR THE FIRST TIME, IT WAS CLEAR TO ME THE BEAST WAS *WEAK*. IT COULD NOT FIGHT FOR LONG PERIODS. IT FAVORED ONE SIDE...
"IT WOULD ONLY BE A MATTER OF TIME BEFORE I ANNIHILATED THIS CHALLENGE TO MY 'POWER.'
"FOR *TWO MONTHS* WE FOUGHT THE BEAST, AND IT KILLED EVERY MAN, WOMAN AND CHILD IN MY TRIBE.
"FOR TWO MONTHS, IT ENDURED EVERY BLOW, EVERY STONE, EVERY PUNCH WE LANDED... AND IT REFUSED TO DIE.
"IN THE END, THE *ONLY* REASON, I THINK, I TRIUMPHED OVER THE BEAST...
"WAS THAT HE WAS *TIRED* OF BEING *ALONE*.
"ALONE... *IS* A TERRIBLE THING TO BE."

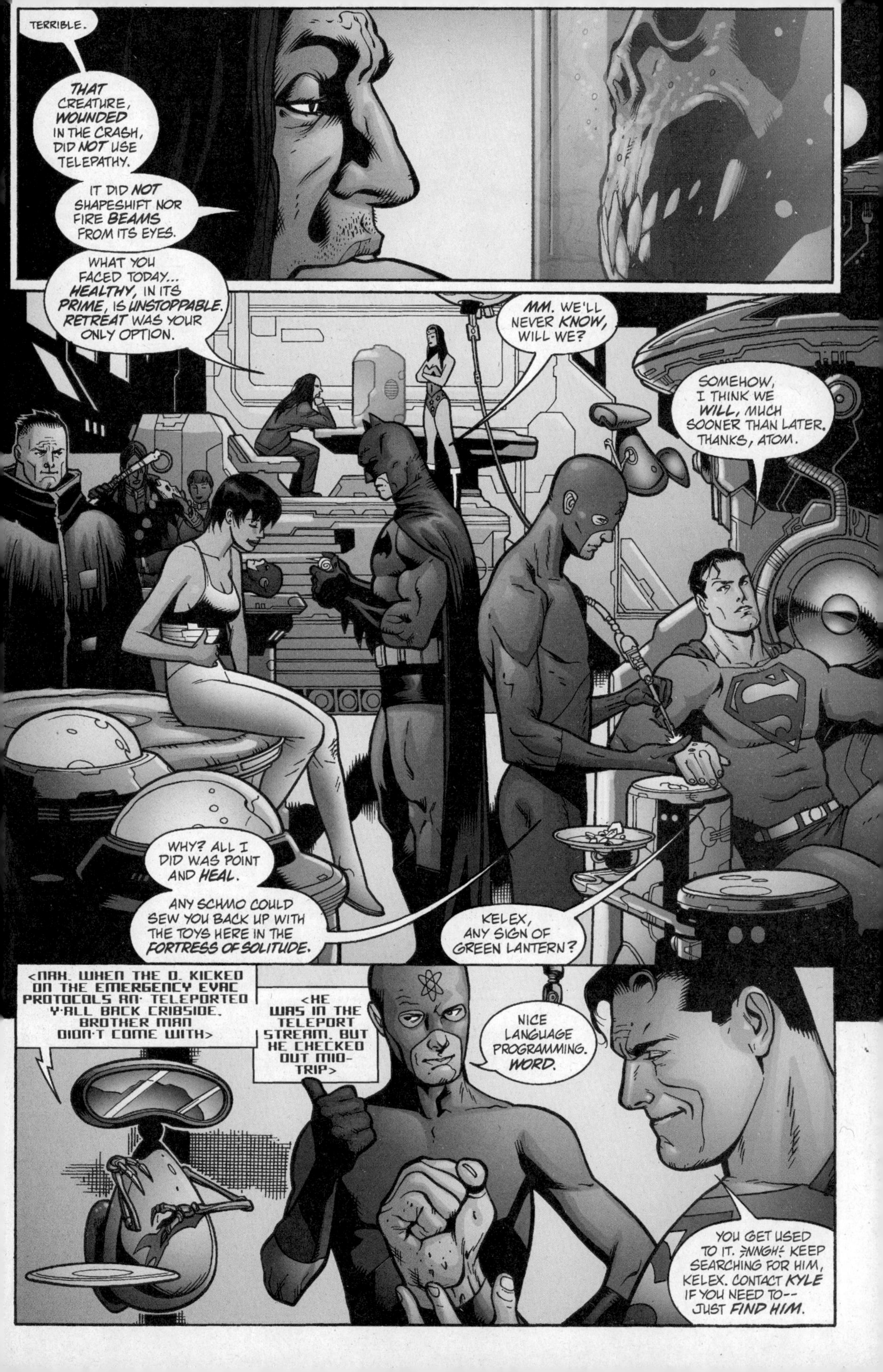

TERRIBLE.
THAT CREATURE, WOUNDED IN THE CRASH, DID NOT USE TELEPATHY.
IT DID NOT SHAPESHIFT NOR FIRE BEAMS FROM ITS EYES.
WHAT YOU FACED TODAY... HEALTHY, IN ITS PRIME, IS UNSTOPPABLE. RETREAT WAS YOUR ONLY OPTION.
MM. WE'LL NEVER KNOW, WILL WE?
SOMEHOW, I THINK WE WILL, MUCH SOONER THAN LATER. THANKS, ATOM.
WHY? ALL I DID WAS POINT AND HEAL.
ANY SCHMO COULD SEW YOU BACK UP WITH THE TOYS HERE IN THE FORTRESS OF SOLITUDE.
KELEX, ANY SIGN OF GREEN LANTERN?
<NAH. WHEN THE O. KICKED ON THE EMERGENCY EVAC PROTOCOLS AN' TELEPORTED Y'ALL BACK CRIBSIDE, BROTHER MAN DIDN'T COME WITH>
<HE WAS IN THE TELEPORT STREAM, BUT HE CHECKED OUT MID-TRIP>
NICE LANGUAGE PROGRAMMING. WORD.
YOU GET USED TO IT. <NNGH> KEEP SEARCHING FOR HIM, KELEX. CONTACT KYLE IF YOU NEED TO-- JUST FIND HIM.

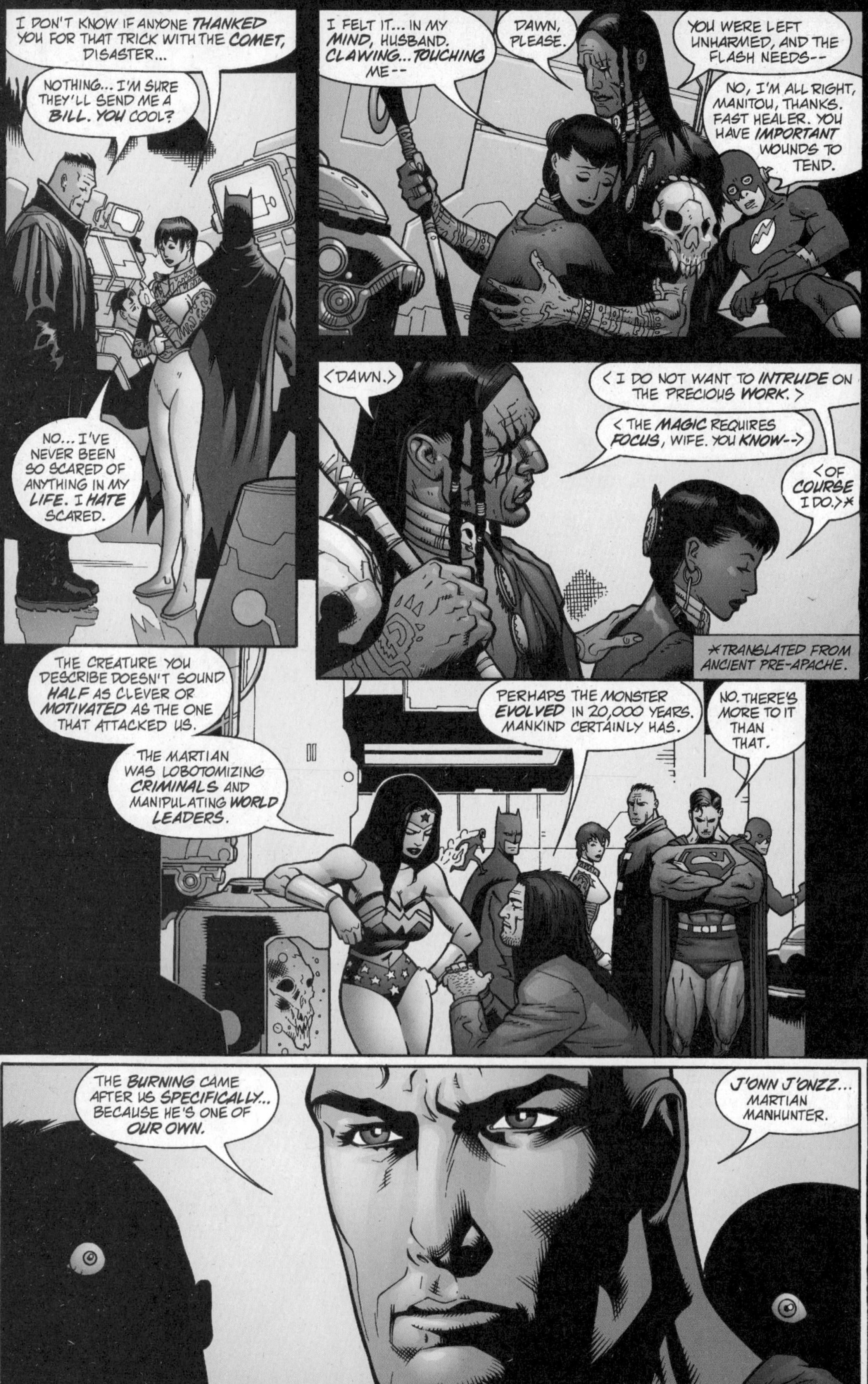
I DON'T KNOW IF ANYONE THANKED YOU FOR THAT TRICK WITH THE COMET, DISASTER...
NOTHING... I'M SURE THEY'LL SEND ME A BILL. YOU COOL?
NO... I'VE NEVER BEEN SO SCARED OF ANYTHING IN MY LIFE. I HATE SCARED.
I FELT IT... IN MY MIND, HUSBAND. CLAWING... TOUCHING ME--
DAWN, PLEASE.
YOU WERE LEFT UNHARMED, AND THE FLASH NEEDS--
NO, I'M ALL RIGHT, MANITOU, THANKS. FAST HEALER. YOU HAVE IMPORTANT WOUNDS TO TEND.
<DAWN.>
< I DO NOT WANT TO INTRUDE ON THE PRECIOUS WORK. >
< THE MAGIC REQUIRES FOCUS, WIFE. YOU KNOW-->
<OF COURSE I DO.>*
*TRANSLATED FROM ANCIENT PRE-APACHE.
THE CREATURE YOU DESCRIBE DOESN'T SOUND HALF AS CLEVER OR MOTIVATED AS THE ONE THAT ATTACKED US.
THE MARTIAN WAS LOBOTOMIZING CRIMINALS AND MANIPULATING WORLD LEADERS.
PERHAPS THE MONSTER EVOLVED IN 20,000 YEARS. MANKIND CERTAINLY HAS.
NO. THERE'S MORE TO IT THAN THAT.
THE BURNING CAME AFTER US SPECIFICALLY... BECAUSE HE'S ONE OF OUR OWN.
J'ONN J'ONZZ... MARTIAN MANHUNTER.

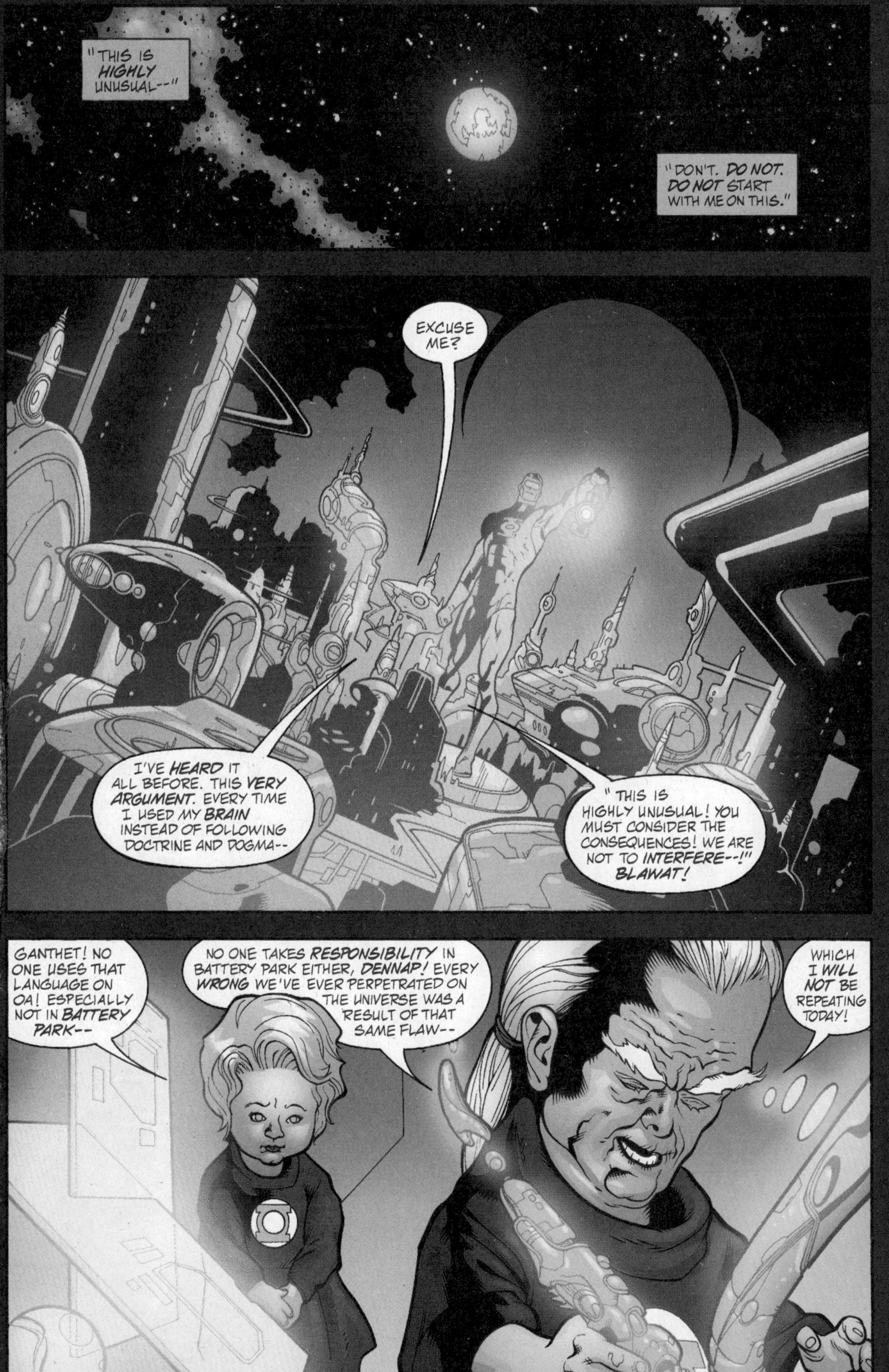
"THIS IS HIGHLY UNUSUAL--"
"DON'T. DO NOT. DO NOT START WITH ME ON THIS."
EXCUSE ME?
I'VE HEARD IT ALL BEFORE. THIS VERY ARGUMENT. EVERY TIME I USED MY BRAIN INSTEAD OF FOLLOWING DOCTRINE AND DOGMA--
"THIS IS HIGHLY UNUSUAL! YOU MUST CONSIDER THE CONSEQUENCES! WE ARE NOT TO INTERFERE--!" BLAWAT!
GANTHET! NO ONE USES THAT LANGUAGE ON OA! ESPECIALLY NOT IN BATTERY PARK--
NO ONE TAKES RESPONSIBILITY IN BATTERY PARK EITHER, DENNAP! EVERY WRONG WE'VE EVER PERPETRATED ON THE UNIVERSE WAS A RESULT OF THAT SAME FLAW--
WHICH I WILL NOT BE REPEATING TODAY!

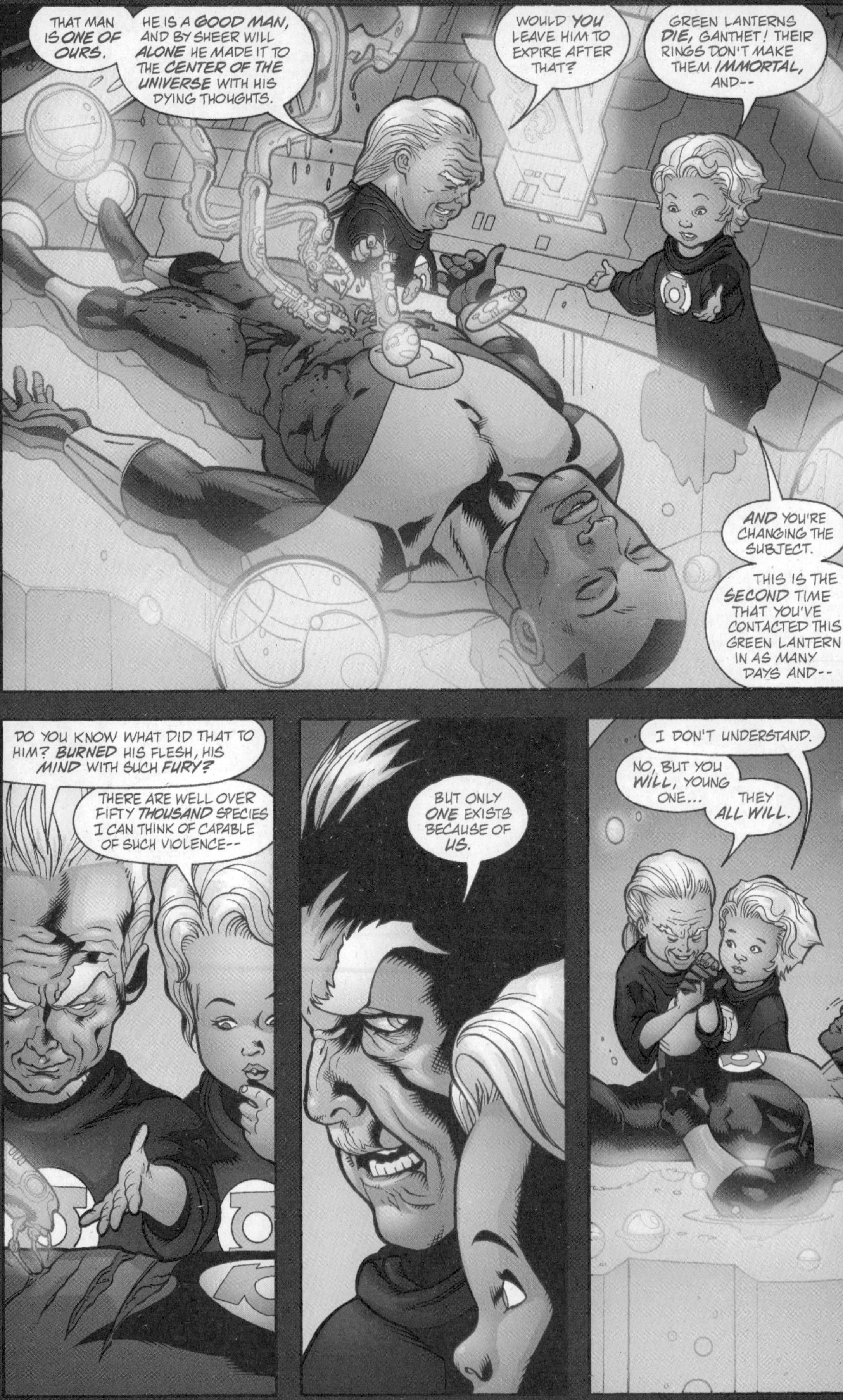

THAT MAN IS ONE OF OURS.
HE IS A GOOD MAN, AND BY SHEER WILL ALONE HE MADE IT TO THE CENTER OF THE UNIVERSE WITH HIS DYING THOUGHTS.
WOULD YOU LEAVE HIM TO EXPIRE AFTER THAT?
GREEN LANTERNS DIE, GANTHET! THEIR RINGS DON'T MAKE THEM IMMORTAL, AND--
AND YOU'RE CHANGING THE SUBJECT.
THIS IS THE SECOND TIME THAT YOU'VE CONTACTED THIS GREEN LANTERN IN AS MANY DAYS AND--
DO YOU KNOW WHAT DID THAT TO HIM? BURNED HIS FLESH, HIS MIND WITH SUCH FURY?
THERE ARE WELL OVER FIFTY THOUSAND SPECIES I CAN THINK OF CAPABLE OF SUCH VIOLENCE--
BUT ONLY ONE EXISTS BECAUSE OF US.
I DON'T UNDERSTAND.
NO, BUT YOU WILL, YOUNG ONE... THEY ALL WILL.

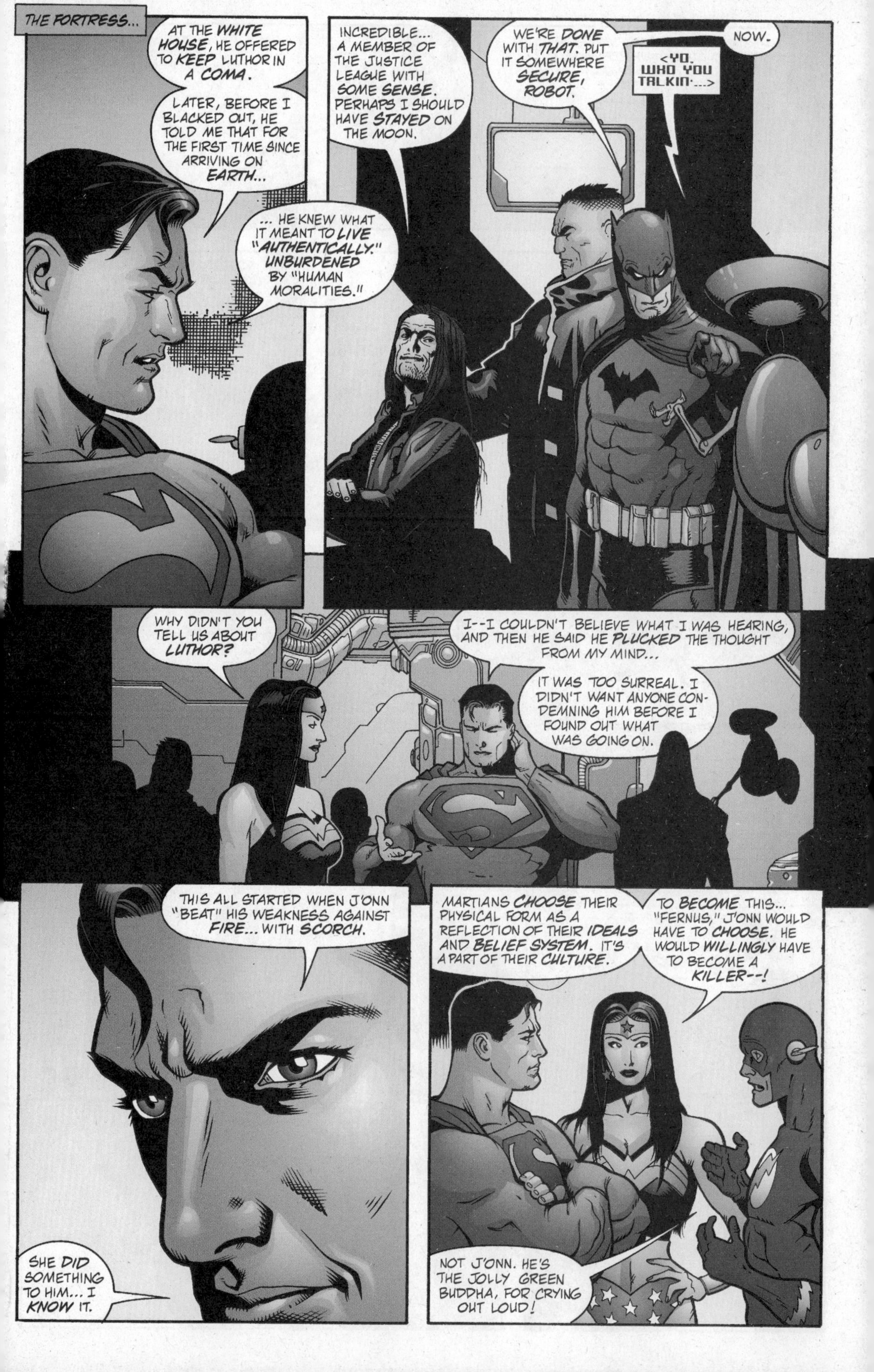

THE FORTRESS...
AT THE WHITE HOUSE, HE OFFERED TO KEEP LUTHOR IN A COMA.
LATER, BEFORE I BLACKED OUT, HE TOLD ME THAT FOR THE FIRST TIME SINCE ARRIVING ON EARTH...
... HE KNEW WHAT IT MEANT TO LIVE "AUTHENTICALLY." UNBURDENED BY "HUMAN MORALITIES."
INCREDIBLE... A MEMBER OF THE JUSTICE LEAGUE WITH SOME SENSE. PERHAPS I SHOULD HAVE STAYED ON THE MOON.
WE'RE DONE WITH THAT. PUT IT SOMEWHERE SECURE, ROBOT.
NOW.
<YO. WHO YOU TALKIN'...>
WHY DIDN'T YOU TELL US ABOUT LUTHOR?
I--I COULDN'T BELIEVE WHAT I WAS HEARING, AND THEN HE SAID HE PLUCKED THE THOUGHT FROM MY MIND...
IT WAS TOO SURREAL. I DIDN'T WANT ANYONE CONDEMNING HIM BEFORE I FOUND OUT WHAT WAS GOING ON.
THIS ALL STARTED WHEN J'ONN "BEAT" HIS WEAKNESS AGAINST FIRE... WITH SCORCH.
SHE DID SOMETHING TO HIM... I KNOW IT.
MARTIANS CHOOSE THEIR PHYSICAL FORM AS A REFLECTION OF THEIR IDEALS AND BELIEF SYSTEM. IT'S A PART OF THEIR CULTURE.
TO BECOME THIS... "FERNUS," J'ONN WOULD HAVE TO CHOOSE. HE WOULD WILLINGLY HAVE TO BECOME A KILLER--!
NOT J'ONN. HE'S THE JOLLY GREEN BUDDHA, FOR CRYING OUT LOUD!

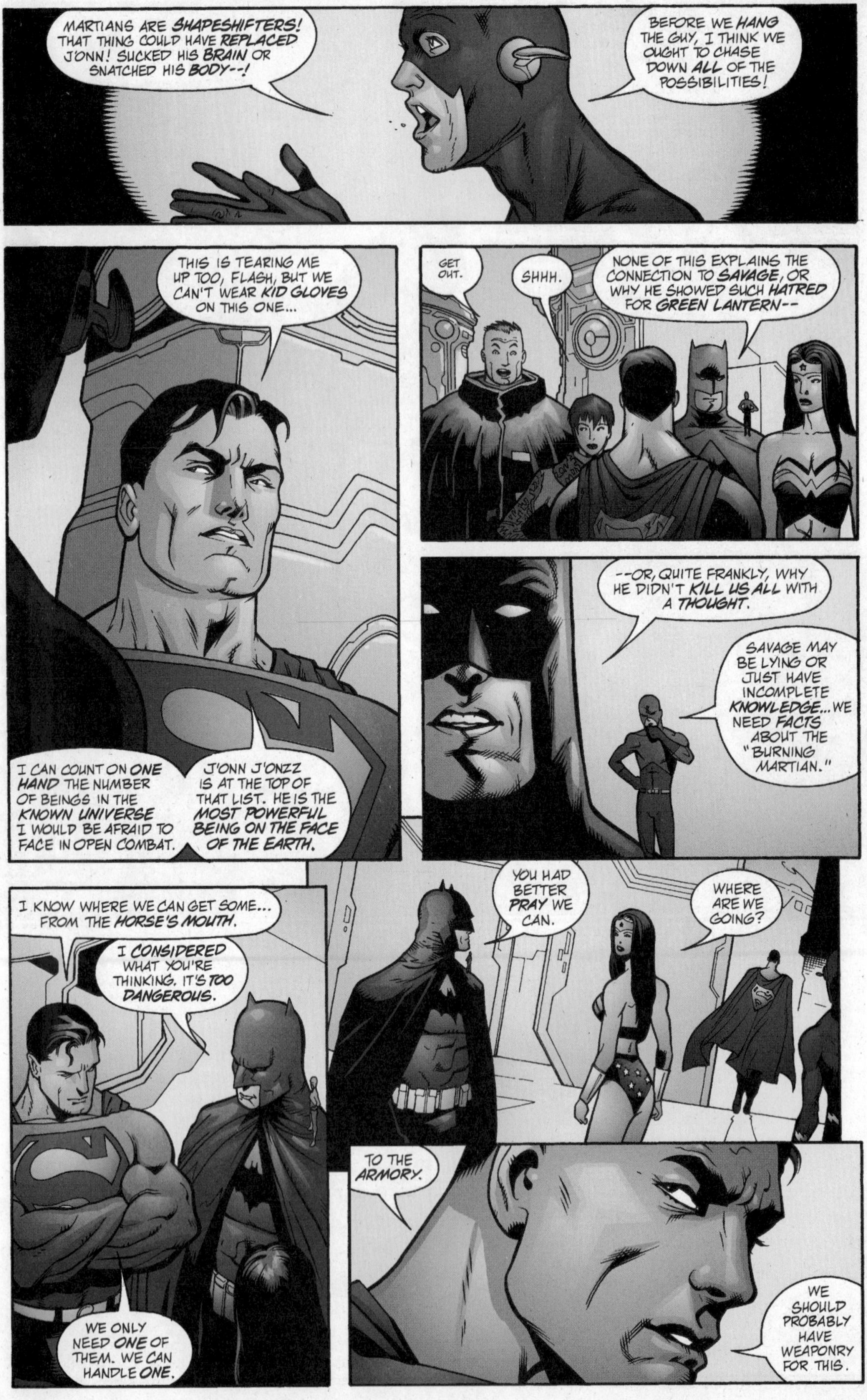
MARTIANS ARE SHAPESHIFTERS! THAT THING COULD HAVE REPLACED J'ONN! SUCKED HIS BRAIN OR SNATCHED HIS BODY--!
BEFORE WE HANG THE GUY, I THINK WE OUGHT TO CHASE DOWN ALL OF THE POSSIBILITIES!
THIS IS TEARING ME UP TOO, FLASH, BUT WE CAN'T WEAR KID GLOVES ON THIS ONE...
I CAN COUNT ON ONE HAND THE NUMBER OF BEINGS IN THE KNOWN UNIVERSE I WOULD BE AFRAID TO FACE IN OPEN COMBAT.
J'ONN J'ONZZ IS AT THE TOP OF THAT LIST. HE IS THE MOST POWERFUL BEING ON THE FACE OF THE EARTH.
GET OUT.
SHHH.
NONE OF THIS EXPLAINS THE CONNECTION TO SAVAGE, OR WHY HE SHOWED SUCH HATRED FOR GREEN LANTERN--
--OR, QUITE FRANKLY, WHY HE DIDN'T KILL US ALL WITH A THOUGHT.
SAVAGE MAY BE LYING OR JUST HAVE INCOMPLETE KNOWLEDGE... WE NEED FACTS ABOUT THE "BURNING MARTIAN."
I KNOW WHERE WE CAN GET SOME... FROM THE HORSE'S MOUTH.
I CONSIDERED WHAT YOU'RE THINKING. IT'S TOO DANGEROUS.
WE ONLY NEED ONE OF THEM. WE CAN HANDLE ONE.
YOU HAD BETTER PRAY WE CAN.
WHERE ARE WE GOING?
TO THE ARMORY.
WE SHOULD PROBABLY HAVE WEAPONRY FOR THIS.

PISBOE, VIRGINIA...

♫ GOIN' OUT ♫ WITH MY BABY TONIGHT... GOIN' OUT FOR A ♫ HOT TIME--

♪ CAUSE HE WANTS TO ASK TO MARRY ME--♫

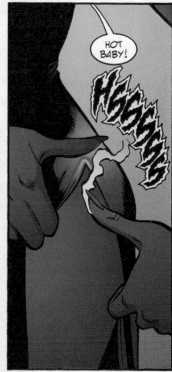

HOT BABY!

HSSSSS

YOU LOOK EXQUISITE, AUBREY.

WHA--? J'ONN?

YES... AND NO. A TELEPATHIC PROJECTION IN LIEU OF THE REAL THING.

OH. I THOUGHT WE WERE--IS SOMETHIN' WRONG? Y'SOUND WEIRD.

BUSINESS, DEAR, UP NORTH. BUT I WANTED TO TALK TO YOU ABOUT SOMETHING, AUBREY...SOMETHING THAT CANNOT WAIT.

SURE--

WHAT ARE YOUR THOUGHTS ON CHILDREN?

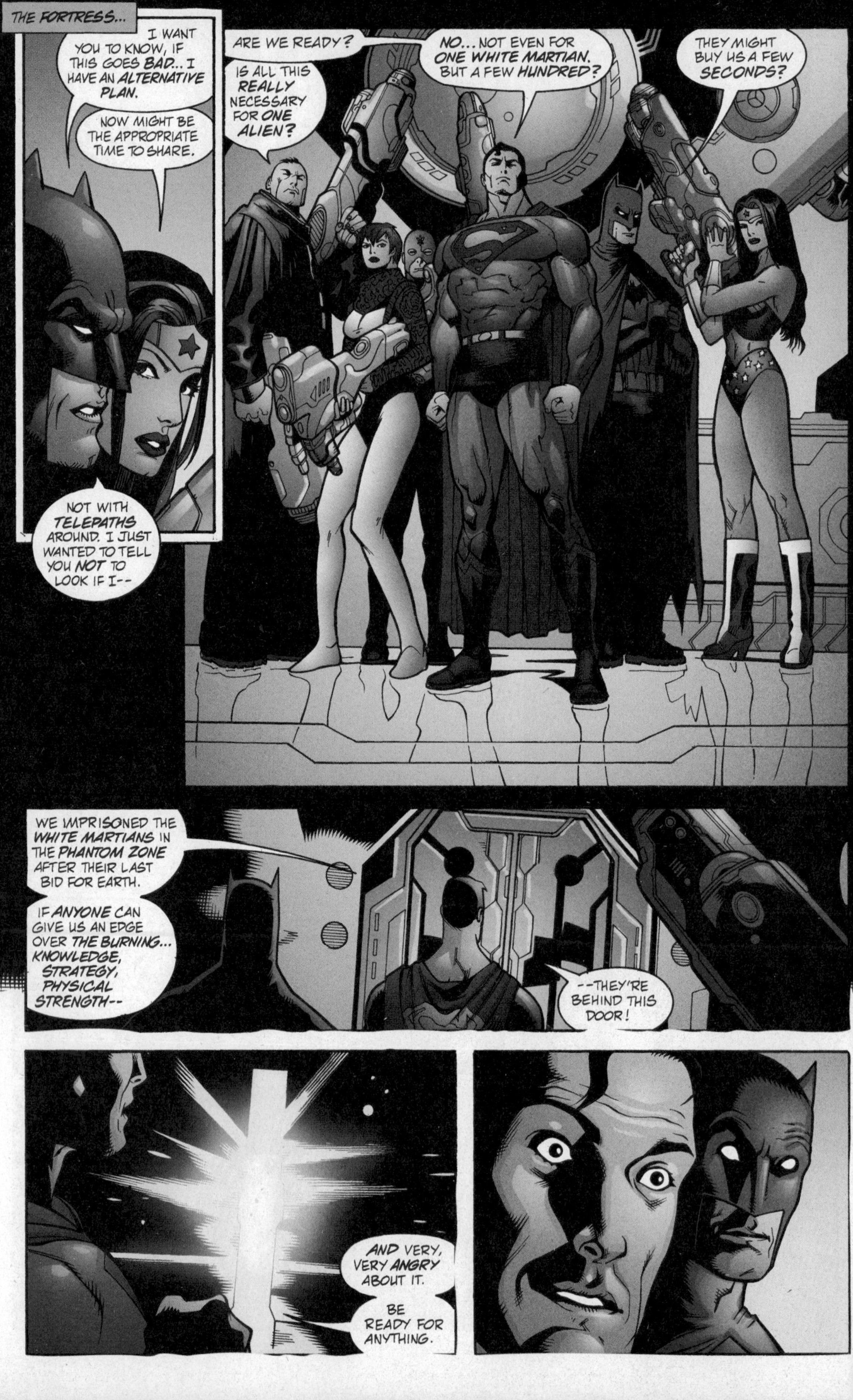
THE FORTRESS...
I WANT YOU TO KNOW, IF THIS GOES BAD... I HAVE AN ALTERNATIVE PLAN.
NOW MIGHT BE THE APPROPRIATE TIME TO SHARE.
NOT WITH TELEPATHS AROUND. I JUST WANTED TO TELL YOU NOT TO LOOK IF I--
ARE WE READY?
IS ALL THIS REALLY NECESSARY FOR ONE ALIEN?
NO... NOT EVEN FOR ONE WHITE MARTIAN. BUT A FEW HUNDRED?
THEY MIGHT BUY US A FEW SECONDS?
WE IMPRISONED THE WHITE MARTIANS IN THE PHANTOM ZONE AFTER THEIR LAST BID FOR EARTH.
IF ANYONE CAN GIVE US AN EDGE OVER THE BURNING... KNOWLEDGE, STRATEGY, PHYSICAL STRENGTH--
--THEY'RE BEHIND THIS DOOR!
AND VERY, VERY ANGRY ABOUT IT.
BE READY FOR ANYTHING.

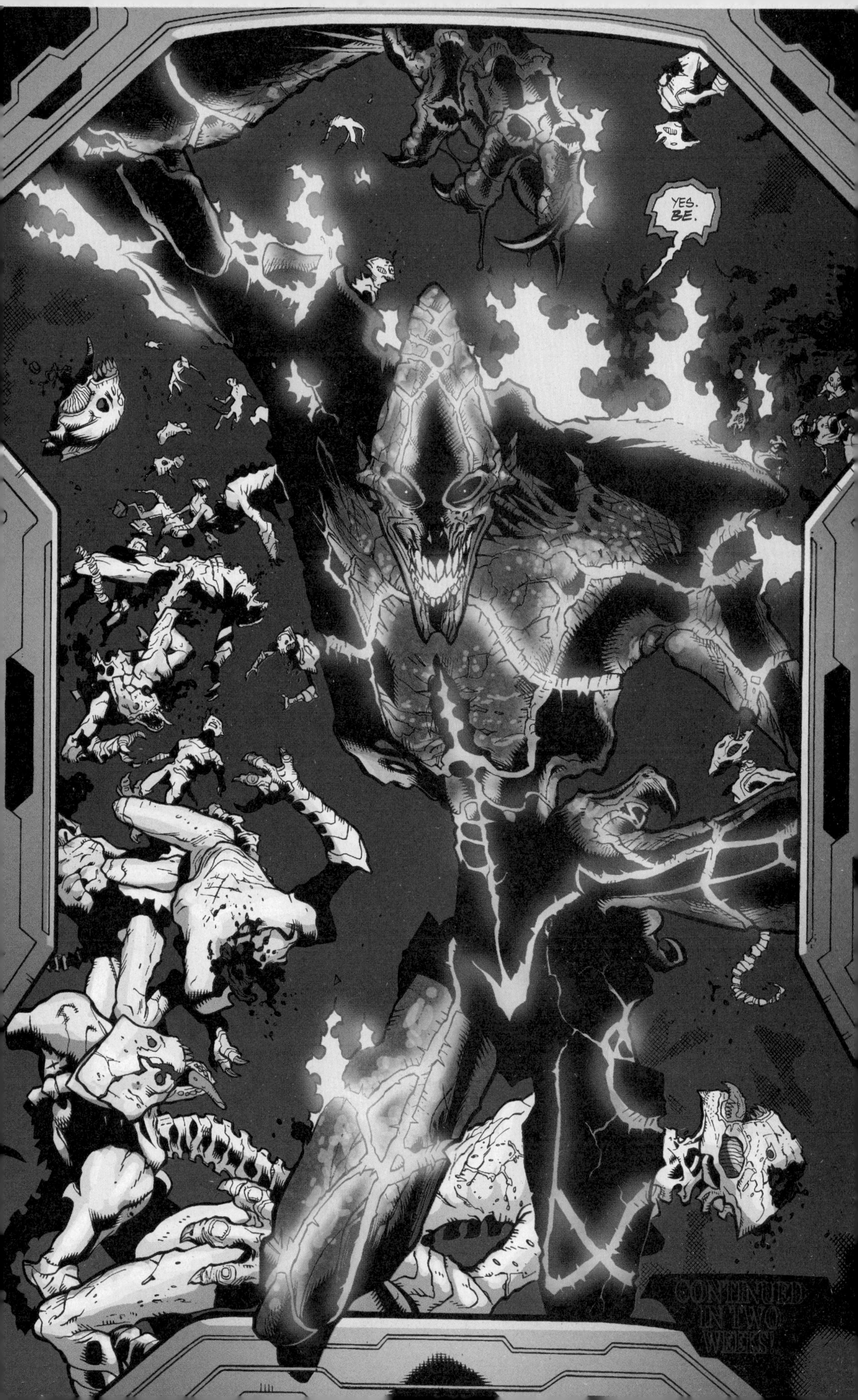
YES. BE.
CONTINUED IN TWO WEEKS!

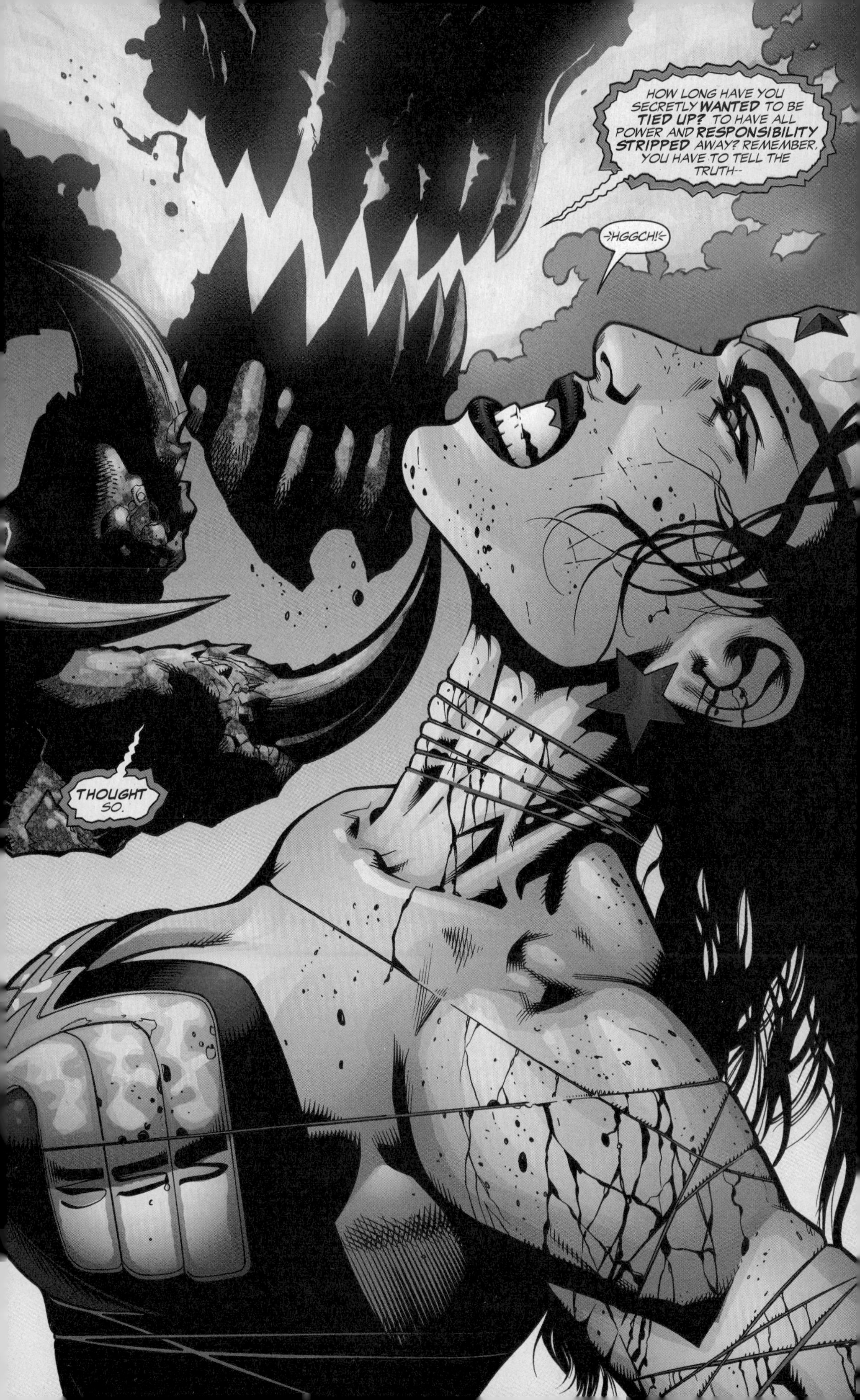
HOW LONG HAVE YOU SECRETLY **WANTED** TO BE **TIED UP?** TO HAVE ALL POWER AND **RESPONSIBILITY STRIPPED** AWAY? REMEMBER, YOU HAVE TO TELL THE TRUTH--
HGGCH!
THOUGHT SO.

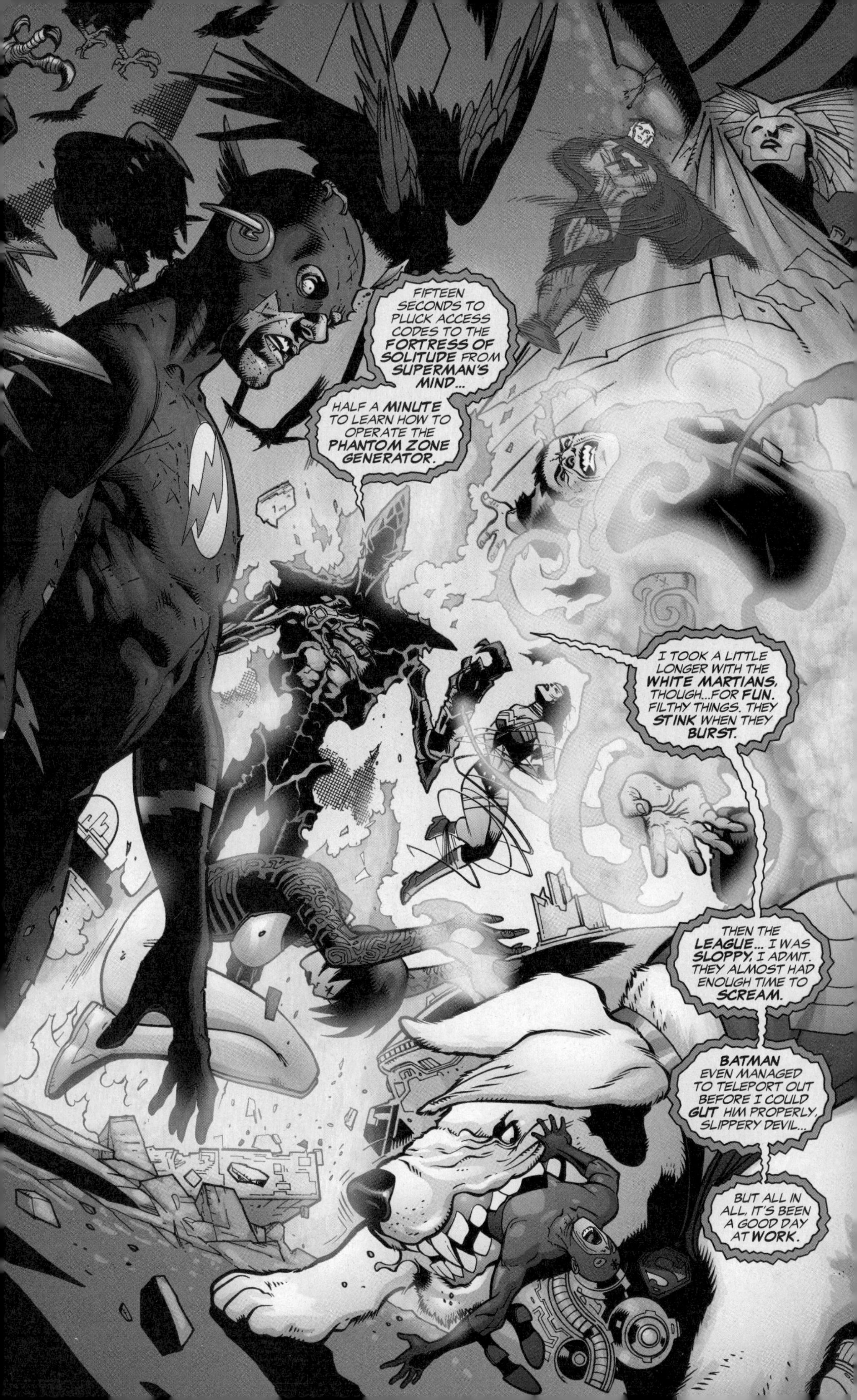
FIFTEEN SECONDS TO PLUCK ACCESS CODES TO THE FORTRESS OF SOLITUDE FROM SUPERMAN'S MIND...
HALF A MINUTE TO LEARN HOW TO OPERATE THE PHANTOM ZONE GENERATOR.
I TOOK A LITTLE LONGER WITH THE WHITE MARTIANS, THOUGH...FOR FUN. FILTHY THINGS. THEY STINK WHEN THEY BURST.
THEN THE LEAGUE... I WAS SLOPPY, I ADMIT. THEY ALMOST HAD ENOUGH TIME TO SCREAM.
BATMAN EVEN MANAGED TO TELEPORT OUT BEFORE I COULD GUT HIM PROPERLY, SLIPPERY DEVIL...
BUT ALL IN ALL, IT'S BEEN A GOOD DAY AT WORK.

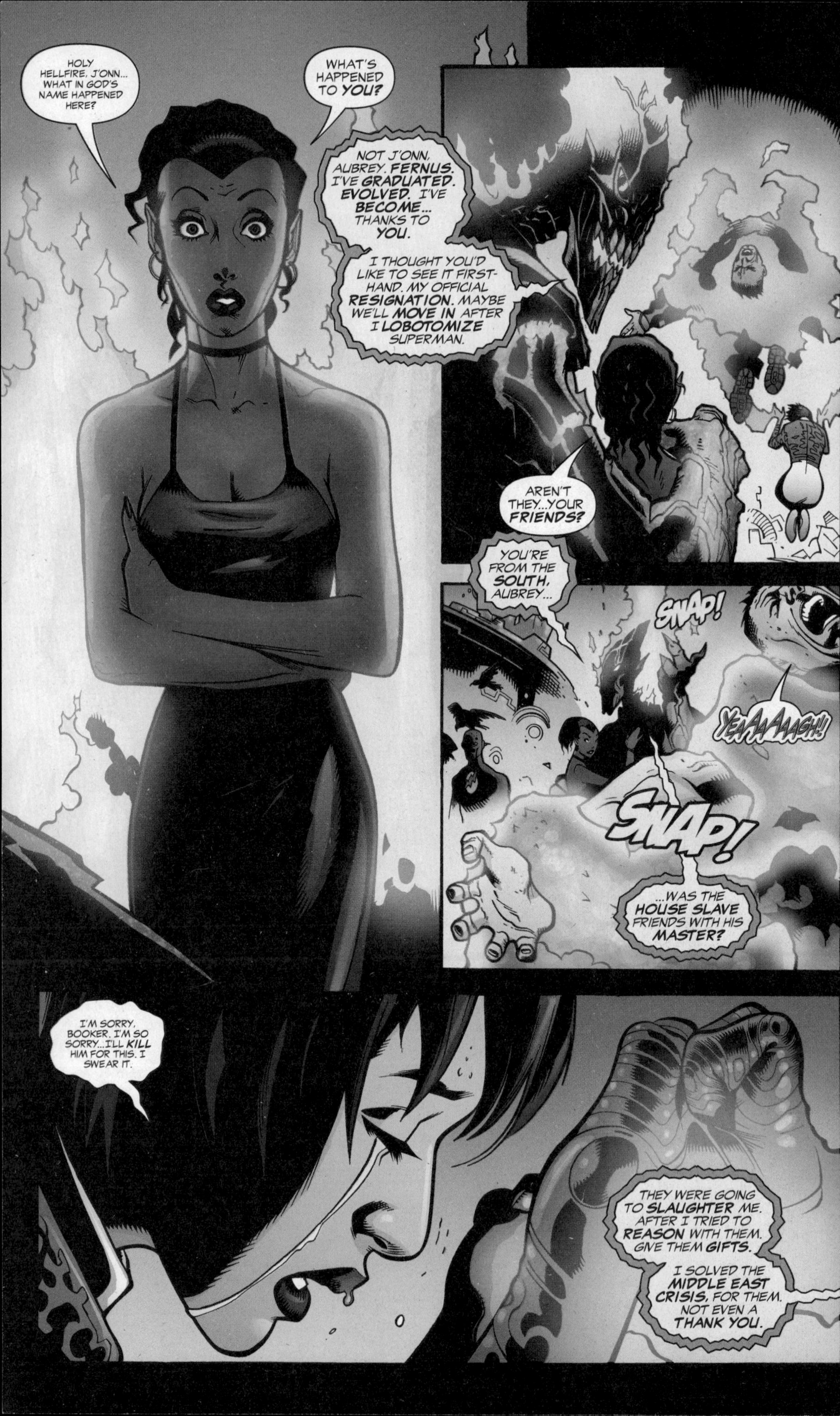
HOLY HELLFIRE, J'ONN... WHAT IN GOD'S NAME HAPPENED HERE?
WHAT'S HAPPENED TO YOU?
NOT J'ONN, AUBREY. FERNUS. I'VE GRADUATED. EVOLVED. I'VE BECOME... THANKS TO YOU.
I THOUGHT YOU'D LIKE TO SEE IT FIRST-HAND. MY OFFICIAL RESIGNATION. MAYBE WE'LL MOVE IN AFTER I LOBOTOMIZE SUPERMAN.
AREN'T THEY...YOUR FRIENDS?
YOU'RE FROM THE SOUTH, AUBREY...
SNAP!
YEAAAAAAGH!!
SNAP!
...WAS THE HOUSE SLAVE FRIENDS WITH HIS MASTER?
I'M SORRY, BOOKER. I'M SO SORRY...I'LL KILL HIM FOR THIS. I SWEAR IT.
THEY WERE GOING TO SLAUGHTER ME. AFTER I TRIED TO REASON WITH THEM. GIVE THEM GIFTS.
I SOLVED THE MIDDLE EAST CRISIS, FOR THEM. NOT EVEN A THANK YOU.

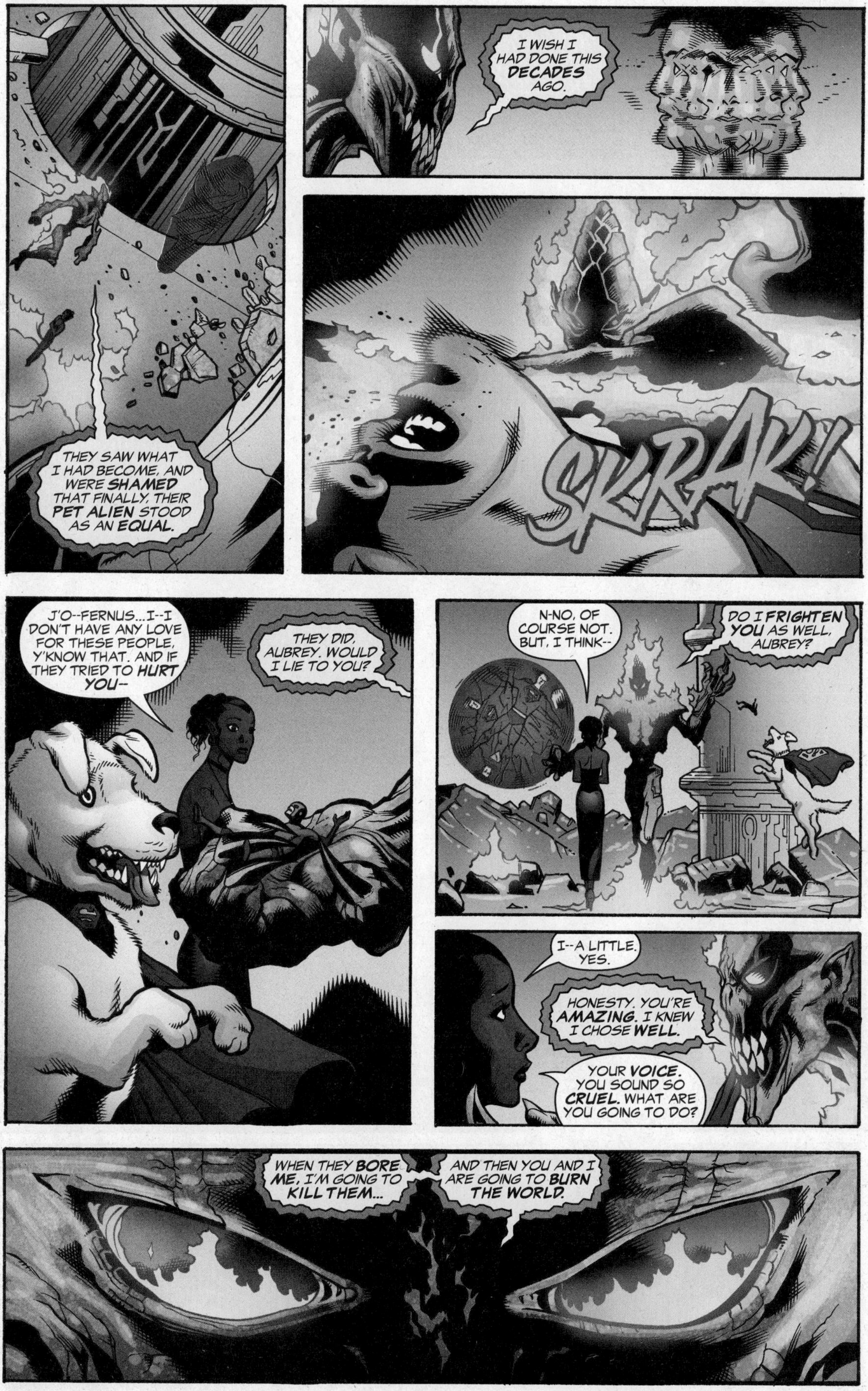

THEY SAW WHAT I HAD BECOME, AND WERE SHAMED THAT FINALLY, THEIR PET ALIEN STOOD AS AN EQUAL.
I WISH I HAD DONE THIS DECADES AGO.
SKRAK!!
J'O--FERNUS... I--I DON'T HAVE ANY LOVE FOR THESE PEOPLE, Y'KNOW THAT. AND IF THEY TRIED TO HURT YOU--
THEY DID, AUBREY. WOULD I LIE TO YOU?
DO I FRIGHTEN YOU AS WELL, AUBREY?
N-NO, OF COURSE NOT. BUT, I THINK--
I--A LITTLE. YES.
HONESTY. YOU'RE AMAZING. I KNEW I CHOSE WELL.
YOUR VOICE. YOU SOUND SO CRUEL. WHAT ARE YOU GOING TO DO?
WHEN THEY BORE ME, I'M GOING TO KILL THEM...
AND THEN YOU AND I ARE GOING TO BURN THE WORLD.

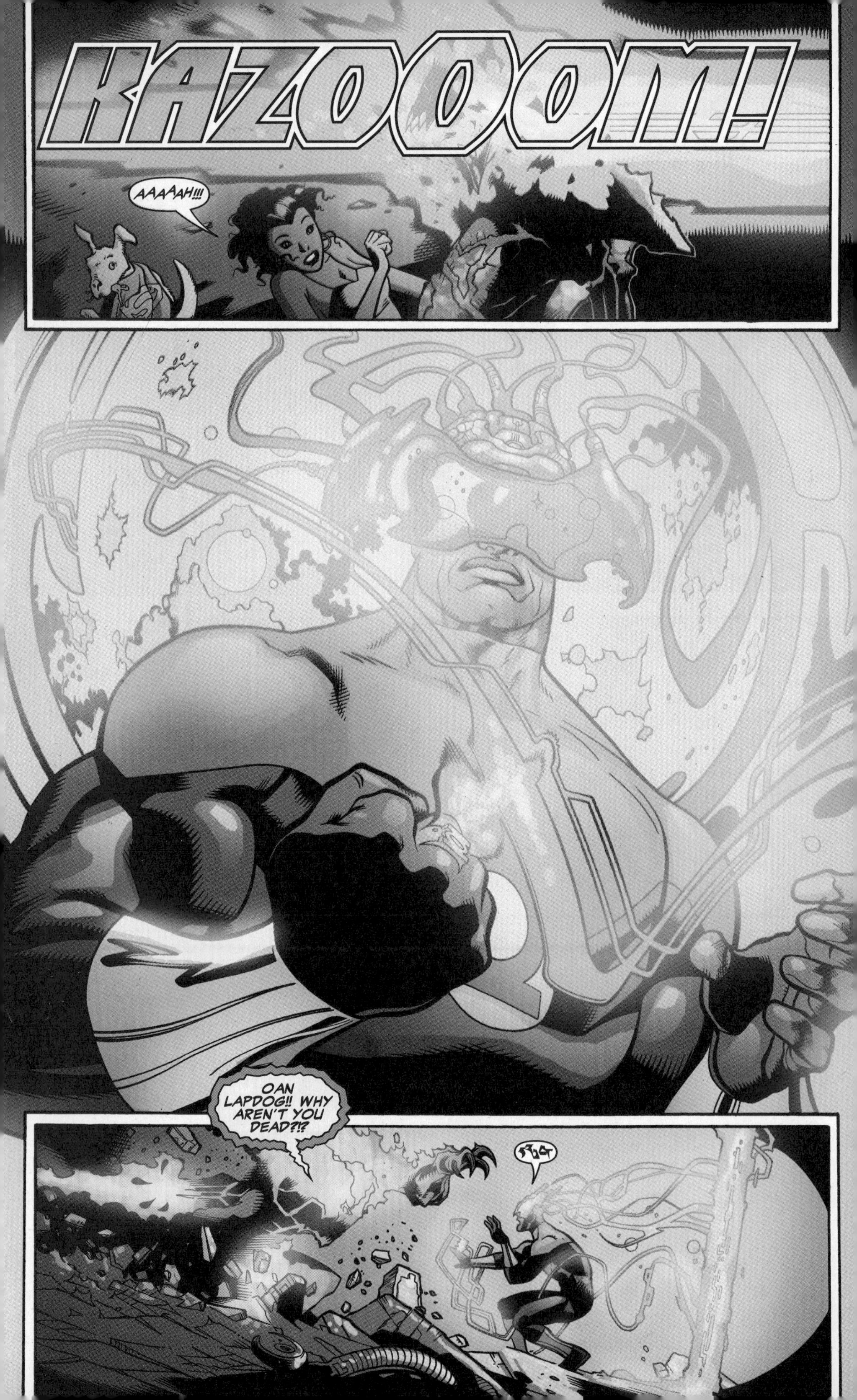
KAZOOOM!
AAAAAH!!!
OAN LAPDOG!! WHY AREN'T YOU DEAD?!?

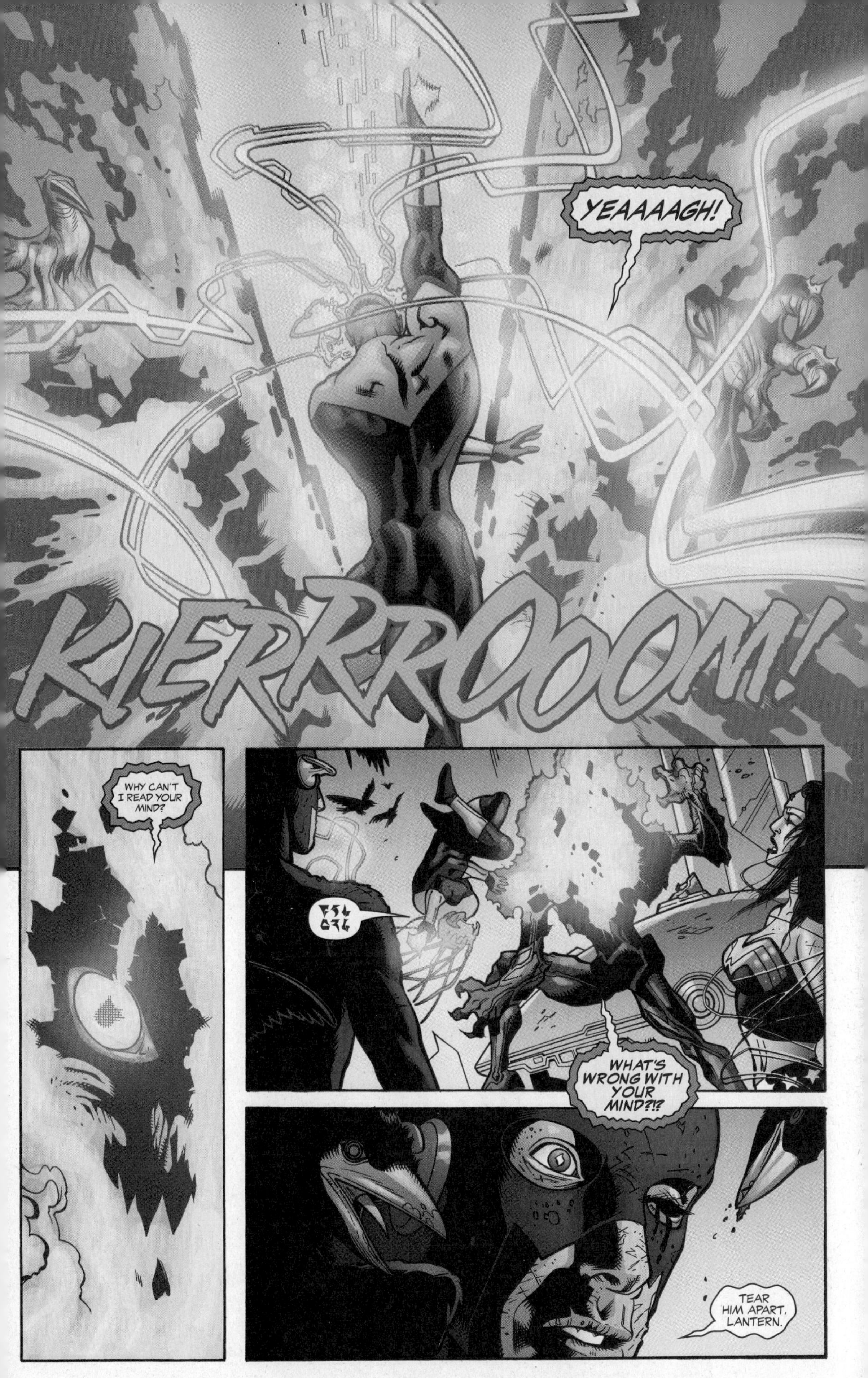
YEAAAAGH!
KIERRROOOM!
WHY CAN'T I READ YOUR MIND?
WHAT'S WRONG WITH YOUR MIND?!?
TEAR HIM APART, LANTERN.

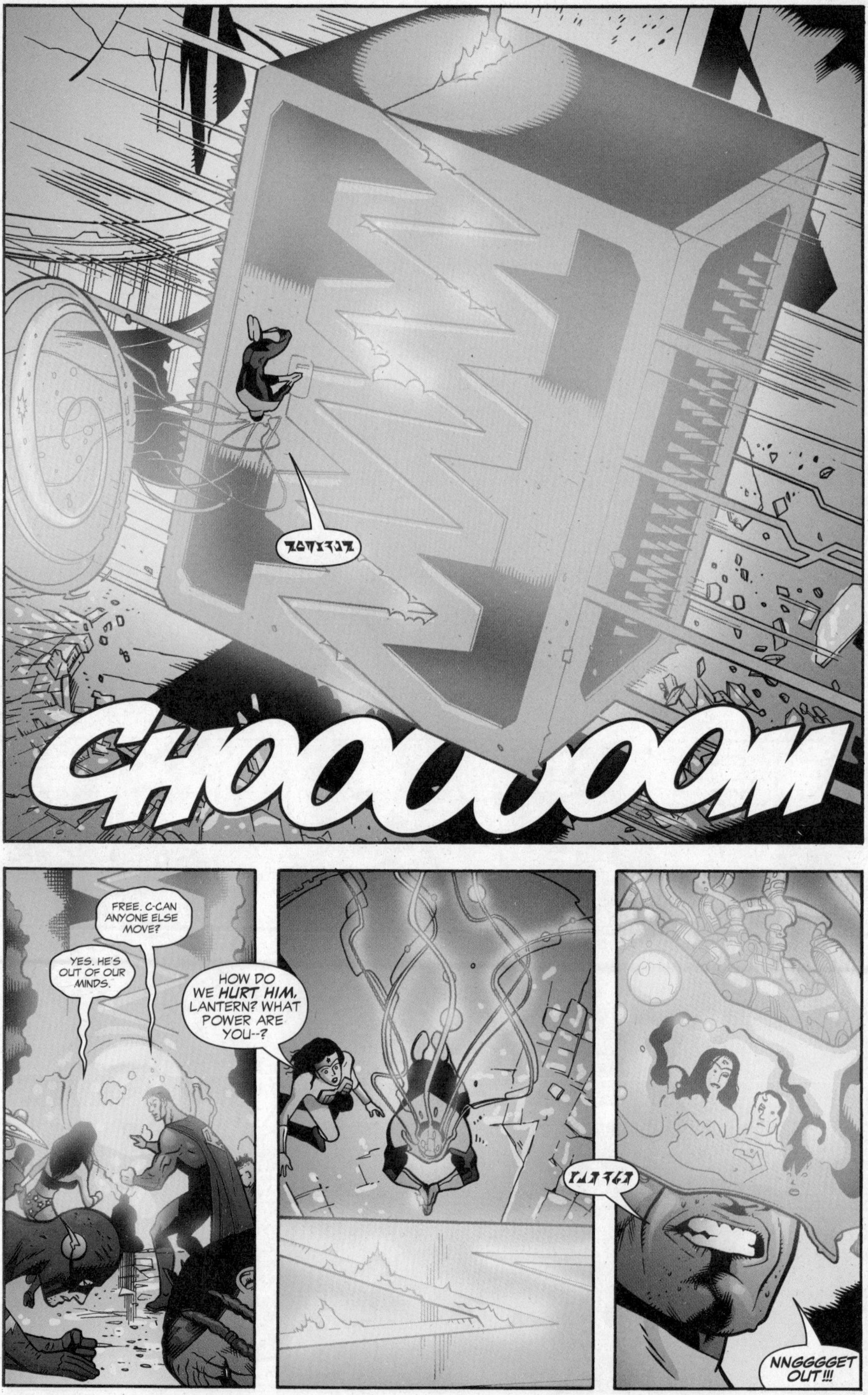
CHOOOOOM
FREE. C-CAN ANYONE ELSE MOVE?
YES. HE'S OUT OF OUR MINDS.
HOW DO WE HURT HIM, LANTERN? WHAT POWER ARE YOU--?
NNGGGGET OUT!!!

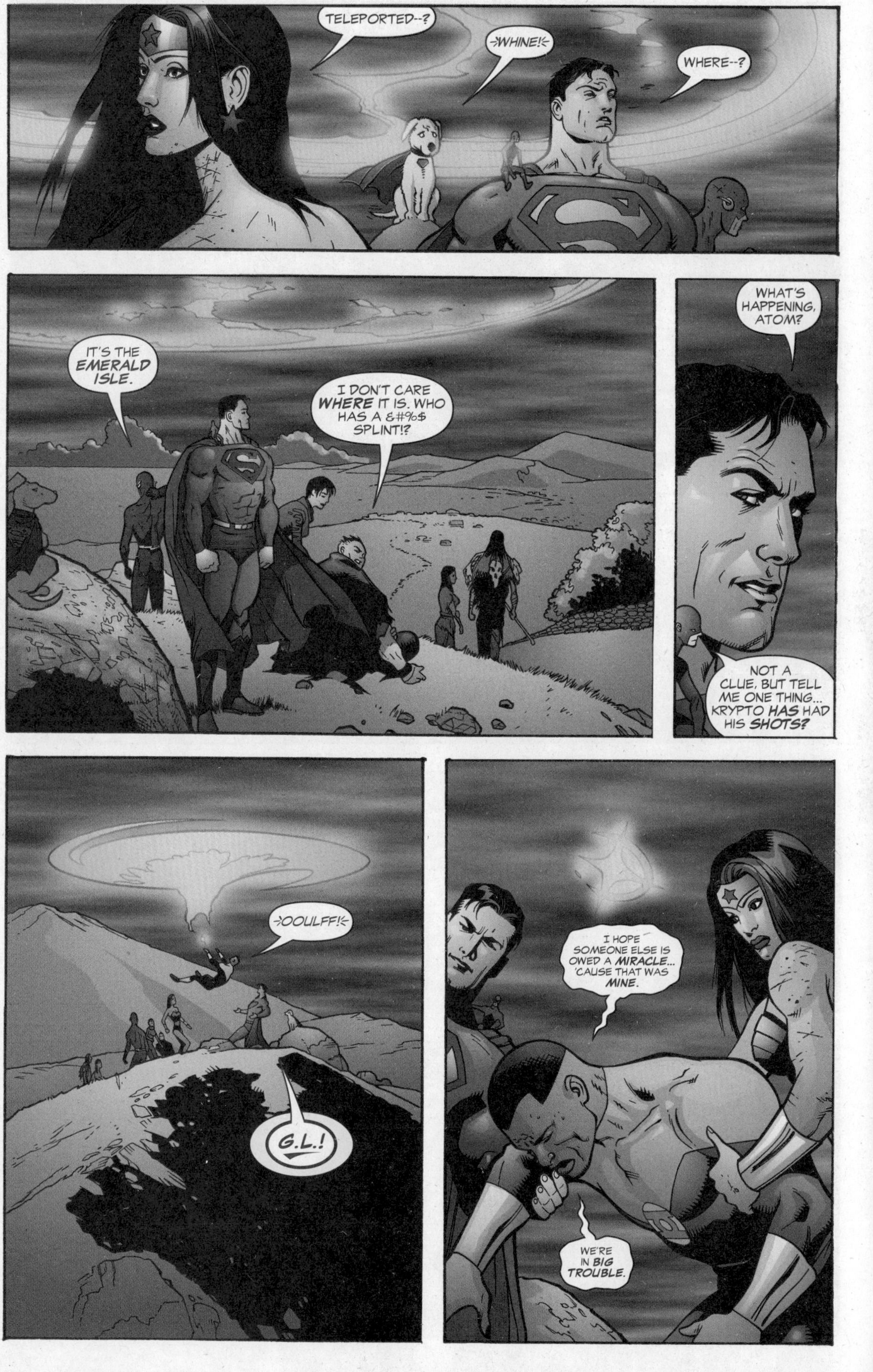
TELEPORTED--?
WHINE!
WHERE--?
IT'S THE EMERALD ISLE.
I DON'T CARE WHERE IT IS. WHO HAS A &#%$ SPLINT!?
WHAT'S HAPPENING, ATOM?
NOT A CLUE, BUT TELL ME ONE THING... KRYPTO HAS HAD HIS SHOTS?
OOULFF!
G.L.!
I HOPE SOMEONE ELSE IS OWED A MIRACLE... 'CAUSE THAT WAS MINE.
WE'RE IN BIG TROUBLE.

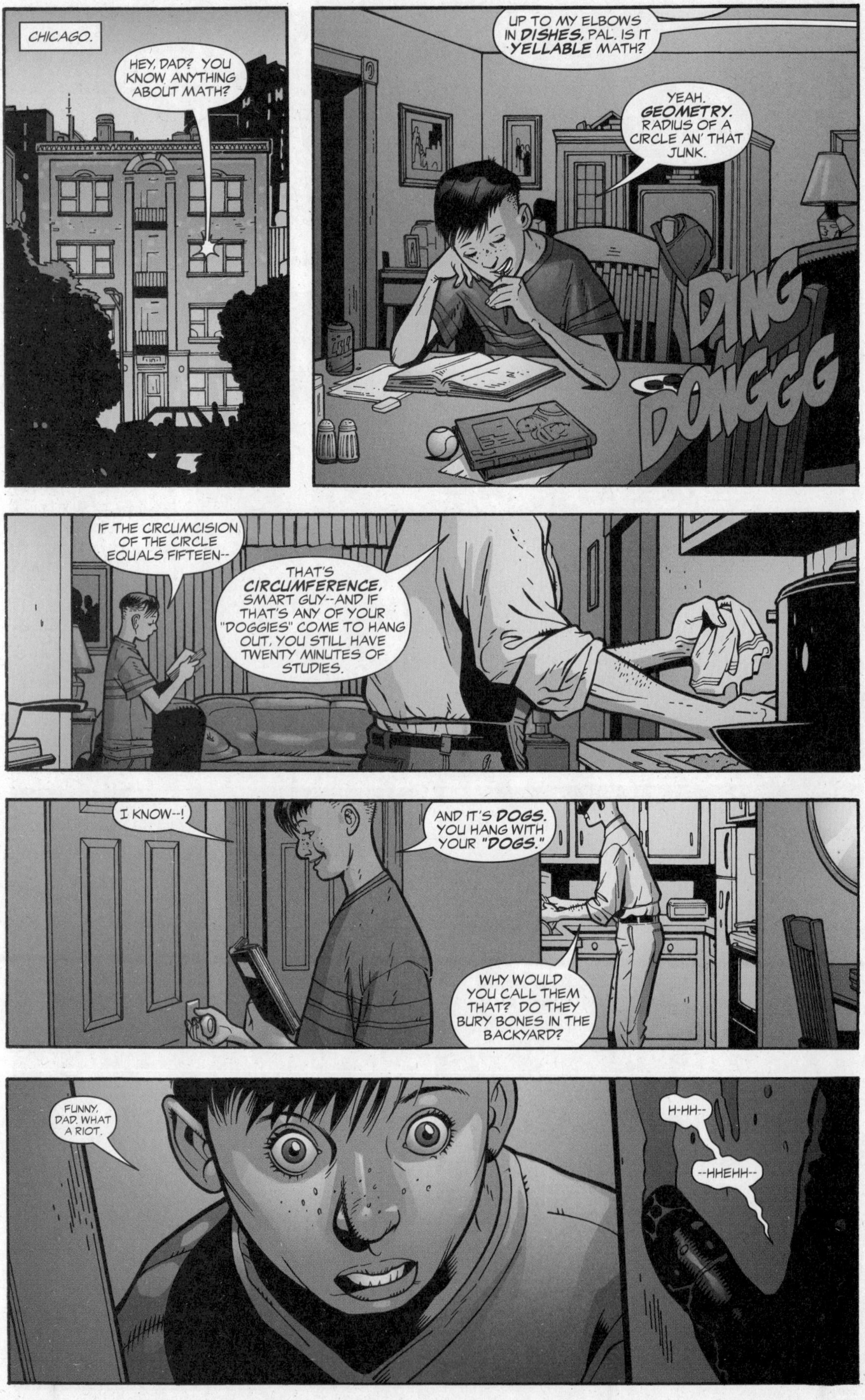
CHICAGO.
HEY, DAD? YOU KNOW ANYTHING ABOUT MATH?
UP TO MY ELBOWS IN DISHES, PAL. IS IT YELLABLE MATH?
YEAH. GEOMETRY. RADIUS OF A CIRCLE AN' THAT JUNK.
DING DONGGG
IF THE CIRCUMCISION OF THE CIRCLE EQUALS FIFTEEN--
THAT'S CIRCUMFERENCE, SMART GUY--AND IF THAT'S ANY OF YOUR "DOGGIES" COME TO HANG OUT, YOU STILL HAVE TWENTY MINUTES OF STUDIES.
I KNOW--!
AND IT'S DOGS. YOU HANG WITH YOUR "DOGS."
WHY WOULD YOU CALL THEM THAT? DO THEY BURY BONES IN THE BACKYARD?
FUNNY, DAD. WHAT A RIOT.
H-HH--
--HHEHH--

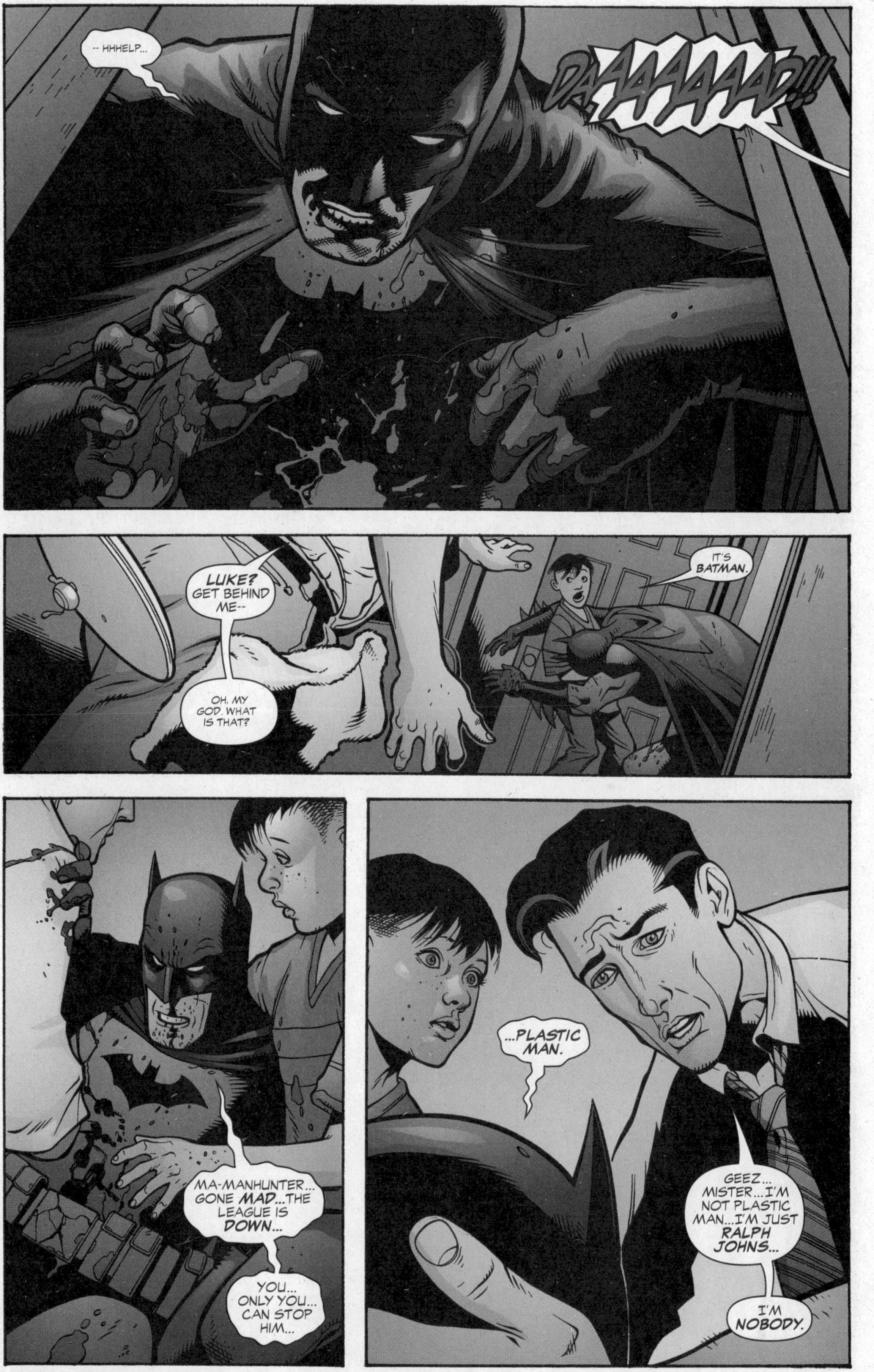
-- HHHELP...
DAAAAAAAD!!!
LUKE? GET BEHIND ME--
OH, MY GOD. WHAT IS THAT?
IT'S BATMAN.
MA-MANHUNTER... GONE MAD...THE LEAGUE IS DOWN...
YOU... ONLY YOU... CAN STOP HIM...
...PLASTIC MAN.
GEEZ... MISTER...I'M NOT PLASTIC MAN...I'M JUST RALPH JOHNS...
I'M NOBODY.

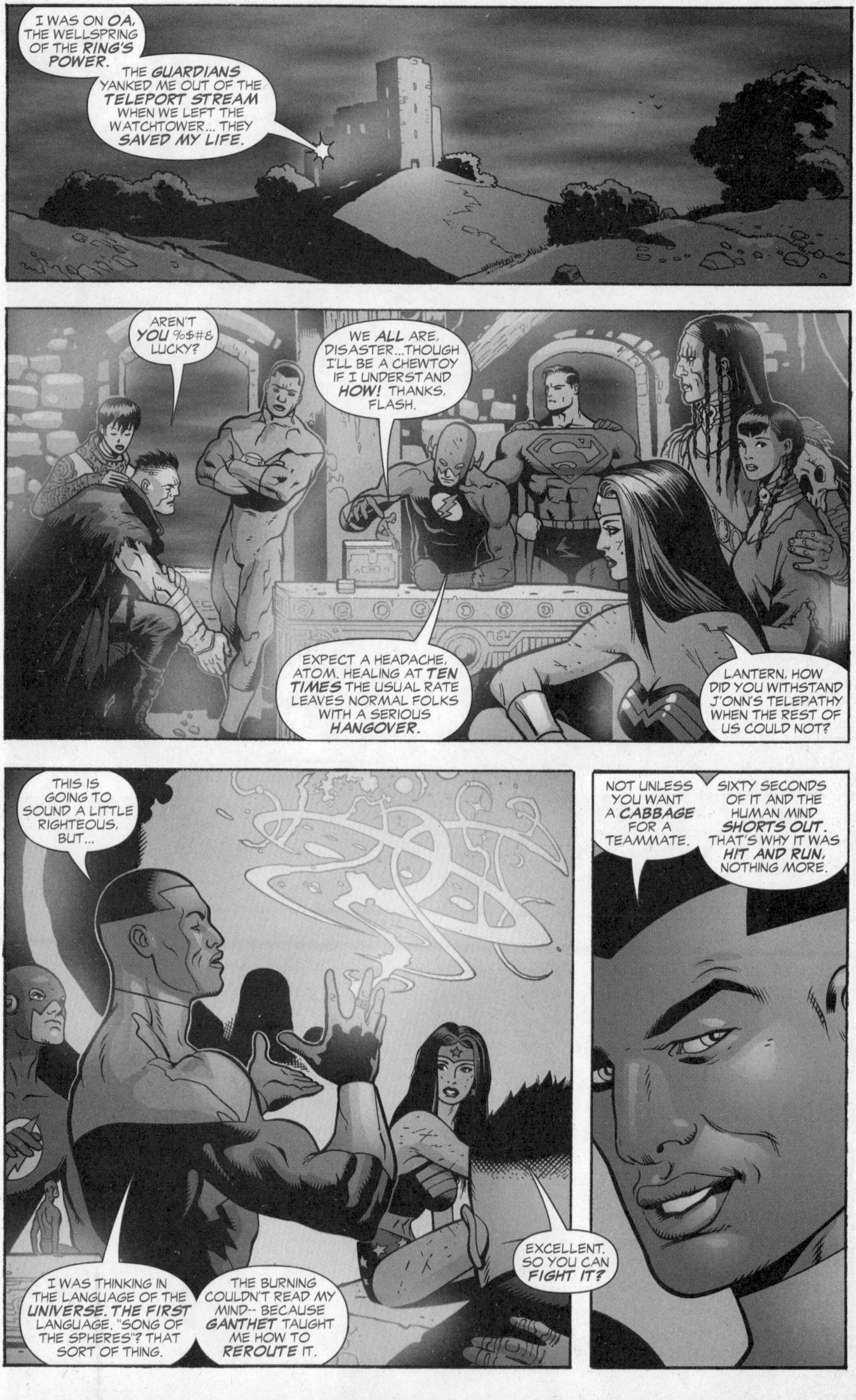
I WAS ON OA, THE WELLSPRING OF THE RING'S POWER.
THE GUARDIANS YANKED ME OUT OF THE TELEPORT STREAM WHEN WE LEFT THE WATCHTOWER... THEY SAVED MY LIFE.
AREN'T YOU %$#& LUCKY?
WE ALL ARE, DISASTER... THOUGH I'LL BE A CHEWTOY IF I UNDERSTAND HOW! THANKS, FLASH.
EXPECT A HEADACHE, ATOM. HEALING AT TEN TIMES THE USUAL RATE LEAVES NORMAL FOLKS WITH A SERIOUS HANGOVER.
LANTERN, HOW DID YOU WITHSTAND J'ONN'S TELEPATHY WHEN THE REST OF US COULD NOT?
THIS IS GOING TO SOUND A LITTLE RIGHTEOUS, BUT...
I WAS THINKING IN THE LANGUAGE OF THE UNIVERSE. THE FIRST LANGUAGE. "SONG OF THE SPHERES"? THAT SORT OF THING.
THE BURNING COULDN'T READ MY MIND-- BECAUSE GANTHET TAUGHT ME HOW TO REROUTE IT.
EXCELLENT. SO YOU CAN FIGHT IT?
NOT UNLESS YOU WANT A CABBAGE FOR A TEAMMATE.
SIXTY SECONDS OF IT AND THE HUMAN MIND SHORTS OUT. THAT'S WHY IT WAS HIT AND RUN, NOTHING MORE.

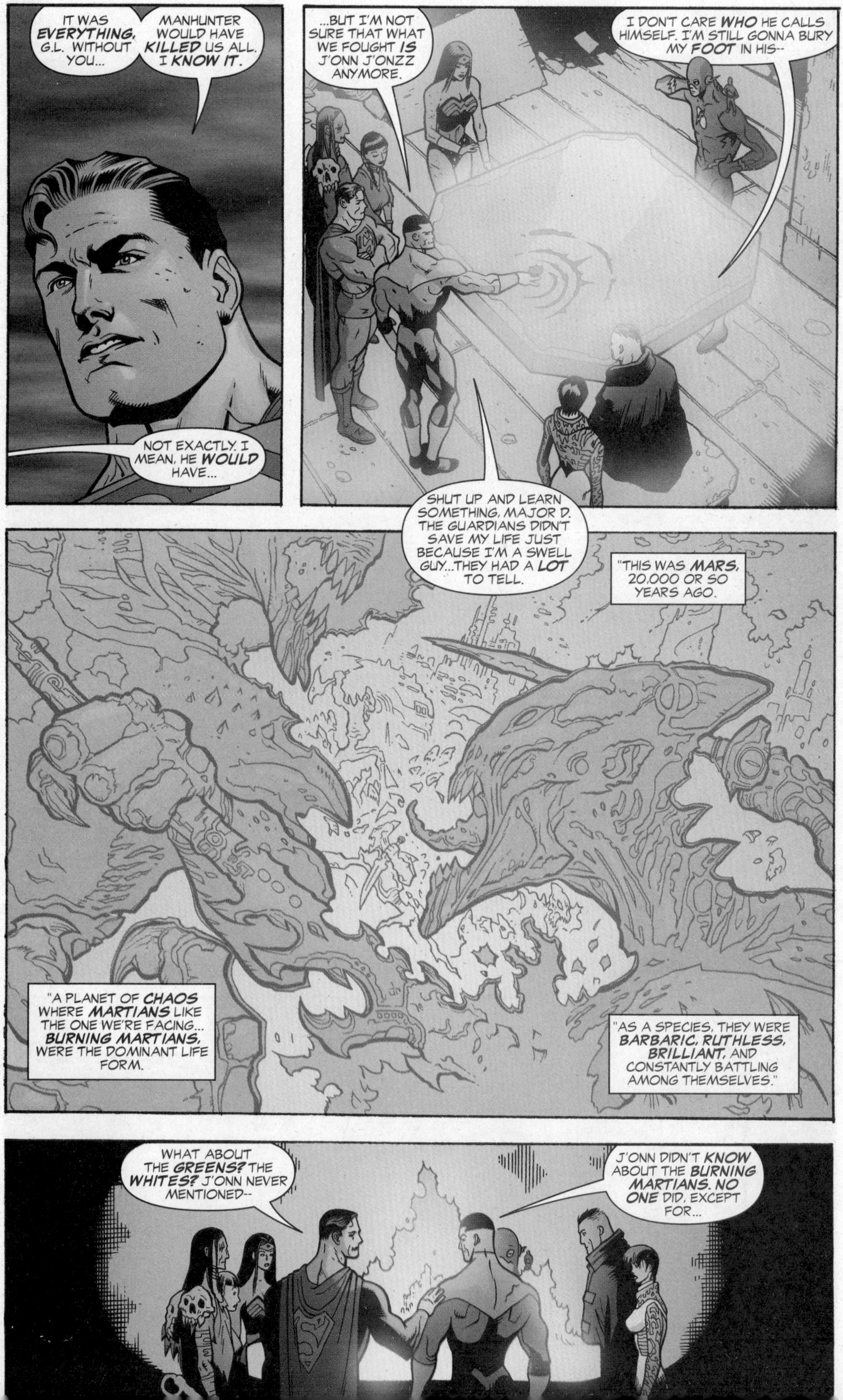
IT WAS EVERYTHING, G.L. WITHOUT YOU...
MANHUNTER WOULD HAVE KILLED US ALL. I KNOW IT.
NOT EXACTLY. I MEAN, HE WOULD HAVE...
...BUT I'M NOT SURE THAT WHAT WE FOUGHT IS J'ONN J'ONZZ ANYMORE.
I DON'T CARE WHO HE CALLS HIMSELF. I'M STILL GONNA BURY MY FOOT IN HIS--
SHUT UP AND LEARN SOMETHING, MAJOR D. THE GUARDIANS DIDN'T SAVE MY LIFE JUST BECAUSE I'M A SWELL GUY...THEY HAD A LOT TO TELL.
"THIS WAS MARS, 20,000 OR SO YEARS AGO.
"A PLANET OF CHAOS WHERE MARTIANS LIKE THE ONE WE'RE FACING... BURNING MARTIANS, WERE THE DOMINANT LIFE FORM.
"AS A SPECIES, THEY WERE BARBARIC, RUTHLESS, BRILLIANT, AND CONSTANTLY BATTLING AMONG THEMSELVES."
WHAT ABOUT THE GREENS? THE WHITES? J'ONN NEVER MENTIONED--
J'ONN DIDN'T KNOW ABOUT THE BURNING MARTIANS. NO ONE DID, EXCEPT FOR...

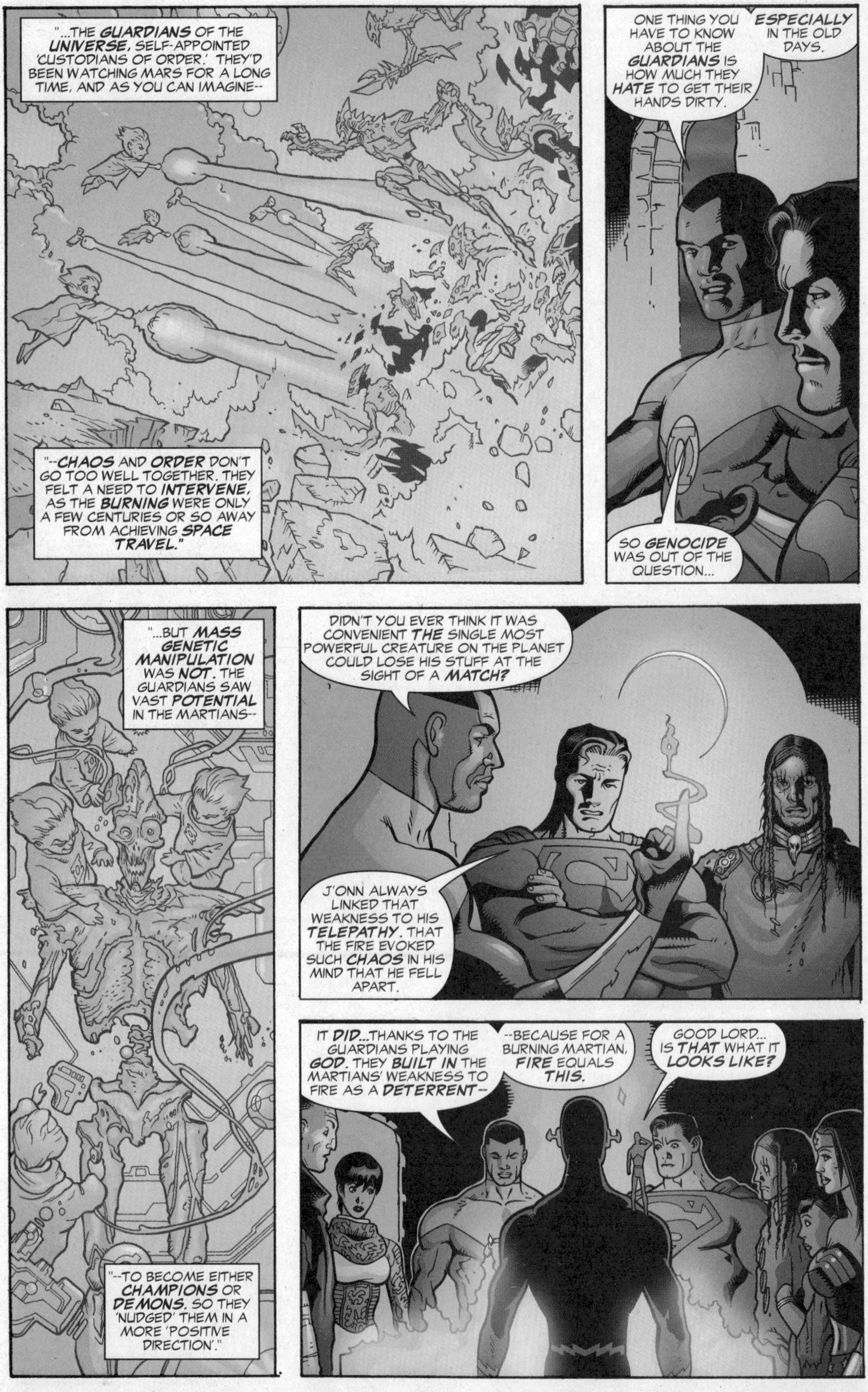
"...THE GUARDIANS OF THE UNIVERSE, SELF-APPOINTED 'CUSTODIANS OF ORDER.' THEY'D BEEN WATCHING MARS FOR A LONG TIME, AND AS YOU CAN IMAGINE--
"--CHAOS AND ORDER DON'T GO TOO WELL TOGETHER. THEY FELT A NEED TO INTERVENE, AS THE BURNING WERE ONLY A FEW CENTURIES OR SO AWAY FROM ACHIEVING SPACE TRAVEL."
ONE THING YOU HAVE TO KNOW ABOUT THE GUARDIANS IS HOW MUCH THEY HATE TO GET THEIR HANDS DIRTY.
ESPECIALLY IN THE OLD DAYS.
SO GENOCIDE WAS OUT OF THE QUESTION...
"...BUT MASS GENETIC MANIPULATION WAS NOT. THE GUARDIANS SAW VAST POTENTIAL IN THE MARTIANS--
"--TO BECOME EITHER CHAMPIONS OR DEMONS. SO THEY 'NUDGED' THEM IN A MORE 'POSITIVE DIRECTION'."
DIDN'T YOU EVER THINK IT WAS CONVENIENT THE SINGLE MOST POWERFUL CREATURE ON THE PLANET COULD LOSE HIS STUFF AT THE SIGHT OF A MATCH?
J'ONN ALWAYS LINKED THAT WEAKNESS TO HIS TELEPATHY. THAT THE FIRE EVOKED SUCH CHAOS IN HIS MIND THAT HE FELL APART.
IT DID...THANKS TO THE GUARDIANS PLAYING GOD. THEY BUILT IN THE MARTIANS' WEAKNESS TO FIRE AS A DETERRENT--
--BECAUSE FOR A BURNING MARTIAN, FIRE EQUALS THIS.
GOOD LORD... IS THAT WHAT IT LOOKS LIKE?

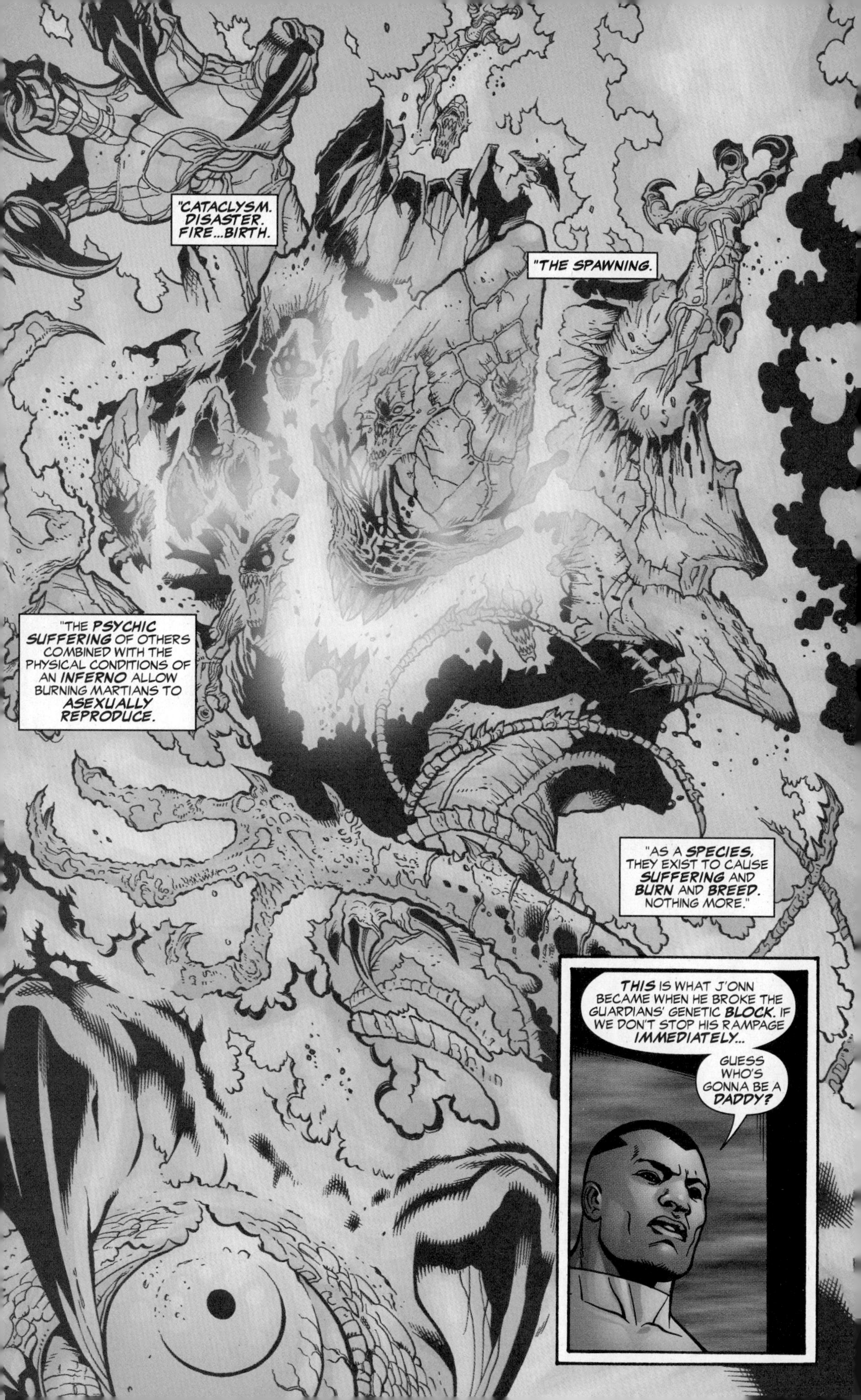
"CATACLYSM. DISASTER. FIRE...BIRTH.
"THE SPAWNING.
"THE PSYCHIC SUFFERING OF OTHERS COMBINED WITH THE PHYSICAL CONDITIONS OF AN INFERNO ALLOW BURNING MARTIANS TO ASEXUALLY REPRODUCE.
"AS A SPECIES, THEY EXIST TO CAUSE SUFFERING AND BURN AND BREED. NOTHING MORE."
THIS IS WHAT J'ONN BECAME WHEN HE BROKE THE GUARDIANS' GENETIC BLOCK. IF WE DON'T STOP HIS RAMPAGE IMMEDIATELY...
GUESS WHO'S GONNA BE A DADDY?

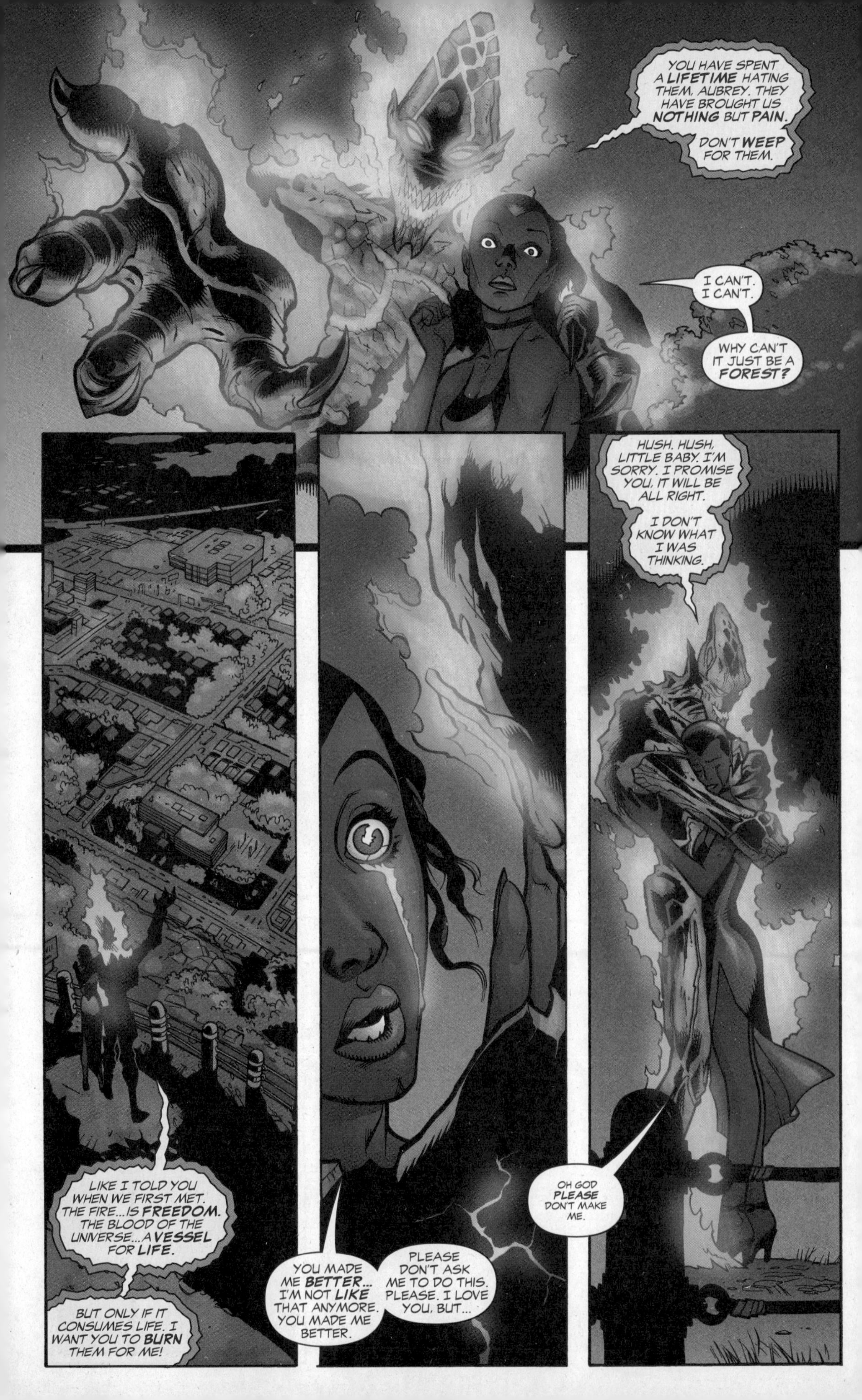

YOU HAVE SPENT A LIFETIME HATING THEM, AUBREY. THEY HAVE BROUGHT US NOTHING BUT PAIN.
DON'T WEEP FOR THEM.
I CAN'T. I CAN'T.
WHY CAN'T IT JUST BE A FOREST?
LIKE I TOLD YOU WHEN WE FIRST MET. THE FIRE...IS FREEDOM. THE BLOOD OF THE UNIVERSE...A VESSEL FOR LIFE.
BUT ONLY IF IT CONSUMES LIFE. I WANT YOU TO BURN THEM FOR ME!
YOU MADE ME BETTER... I'M NOT LIKE THAT ANYMORE. YOU MADE ME BETTER.
PLEASE DON'T ASK ME TO DO THIS. PLEASE. I LOVE YOU, BUT...
HUSH. HUSH, LITTLE BABY. I'M SORRY. I PROMISE YOU, IT WILL BE ALL RIGHT.
I DON'T KNOW WHAT I WAS THINKING.
OH GOD PLEASE DON'T MAKE ME.

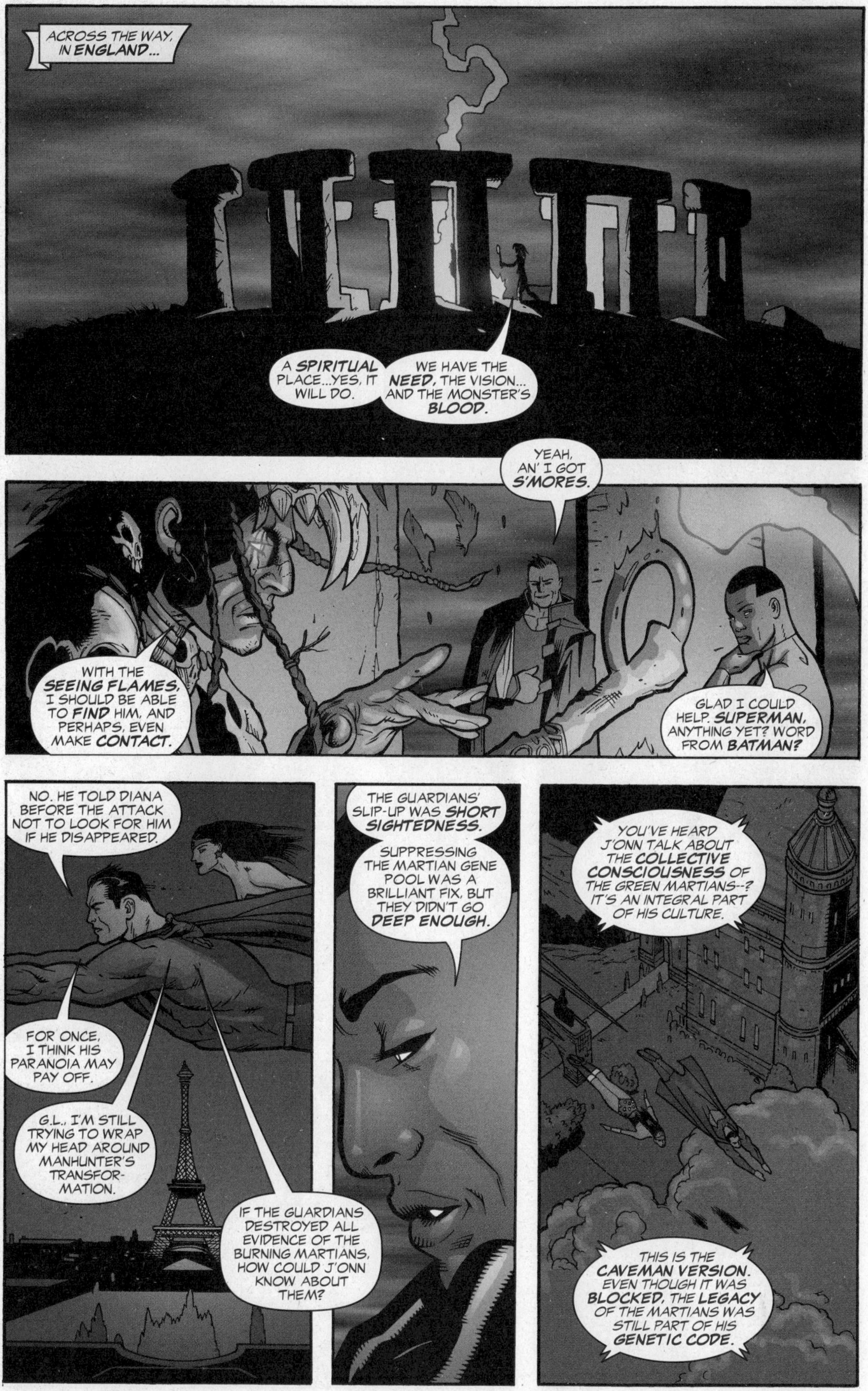
ACROSS THE WAY, IN ENGLAND...
A SPIRITUAL PLACE...YES, IT WILL DO.
WE HAVE THE NEED, THE VISION... AND THE MONSTER'S BLOOD.
YEAH, AN' I GOT S'MORES.
WITH THE SEEING FLAMES, I SHOULD BE ABLE TO FIND HIM, AND PERHAPS, EVEN MAKE CONTACT.
GLAD I COULD HELP. SUPERMAN, ANYTHING YET? WORD FROM BATMAN?
NO. HE TOLD DIANA BEFORE THE ATTACK NOT TO LOOK FOR HIM IF HE DISAPPEARED.
FOR ONCE, I THINK HIS PARANOIA MAY PAY OFF.
G.L., I'M STILL TRYING TO WRAP MY HEAD AROUND MANHUNTER'S TRANSFOR-MATION.
IF THE GUARDIANS DESTROYED ALL EVIDENCE OF THE BURNING MARTIANS, HOW COULD J'ONN KNOW ABOUT THEM?
THE GUARDIANS' SLIP-UP WAS SHORT SIGHTEDNESS.
SUPPRESSING THE MARTIAN GENE POOL WAS A BRILLIANT FIX, BUT THEY DIDN'T GO DEEP ENOUGH.
YOU'VE HEARD J'ONN TALK ABOUT THE COLLECTIVE CONSCIOUSNESS OF THE GREEN MARTIANS--? IT'S AN INTEGRAL PART OF HIS CULTURE.
THIS IS THE CAVEMAN VERSION. EVEN THOUGH IT WAS BLOCKED, THE LEGACY OF THE MARTIANS WAS STILL PART OF HIS GENETIC CODE.

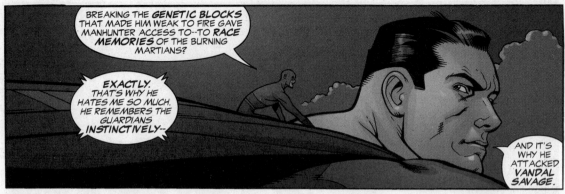

BREAKING THE **GENETIC BLOCKS** THAT MADE HIM WEAK TO FIRE GAVE MANHUNTER ACCESS TO--TO **RACE MEMORIES** OF THE BURNING MARTIANS?

EXACTLY. THAT'S WHY HE HATES ME SO MUCH. HE REMEMBERS THE GUARDIANS **INSTINCTIVELY--**

AND IT'S WHY HE ATTACKED **VANDAL SAVAGE.**

RIGHT. THAT LITTLE NUMBER WAS AN **OAN** TRANSPORT SHIP THAT WENT DOWN EN ROUTE TO **OA**--WITH A HALF-DEAD **BURNING** IN THE HOLD.

GEE, I HOPE THE POOR GUY'S **ALL RIGHT** LOCKED UP IN THE **FORTRESS--**

BOOKER? HOW'S THAT ARM?

PERFECT.

SO HAS MARTIAN MANHUNTER **BECOME** THE BURNING? OR DID IT **CONSUME** HIM?

I DON'T KNOW. I WISH I DID, BUT I DON'T KNOW.

MARTIANS CAN RECONFIGURE THEIR **PHYSIOLOGY** TO REFLECT THEIR **PHILOSOPHY.** HENCE THE WHITES AND THE GREENS...

IT'S POSSIBLE, THAT THIS IS J'ONN THAT WE'RE DEALING WITH, "RECLAIMING HIS PAST."

OR THE BURNING MARTIAN **INSTINCTS** HAVE **CONSUMED** J'ONN. DESPITE IT ALL, I'M NOT READY TO HANG HIM YET.

SUPERMAN... IF J'ONN HAS **TURNED,** WILLINGLY OR **OTHERWISE,** WE MIGHT--

DON'T. DON'T YOU GIVE UP ON HIM. NOT **YOU.**

NOT YET.

FRIENDS, I...I **FELT** HIM, SOMEWHERE. FELT HIS **LINGERING AURA,** AS I HAVE IN THE PAST...

WHAT'S IN **METROPOLIS?**

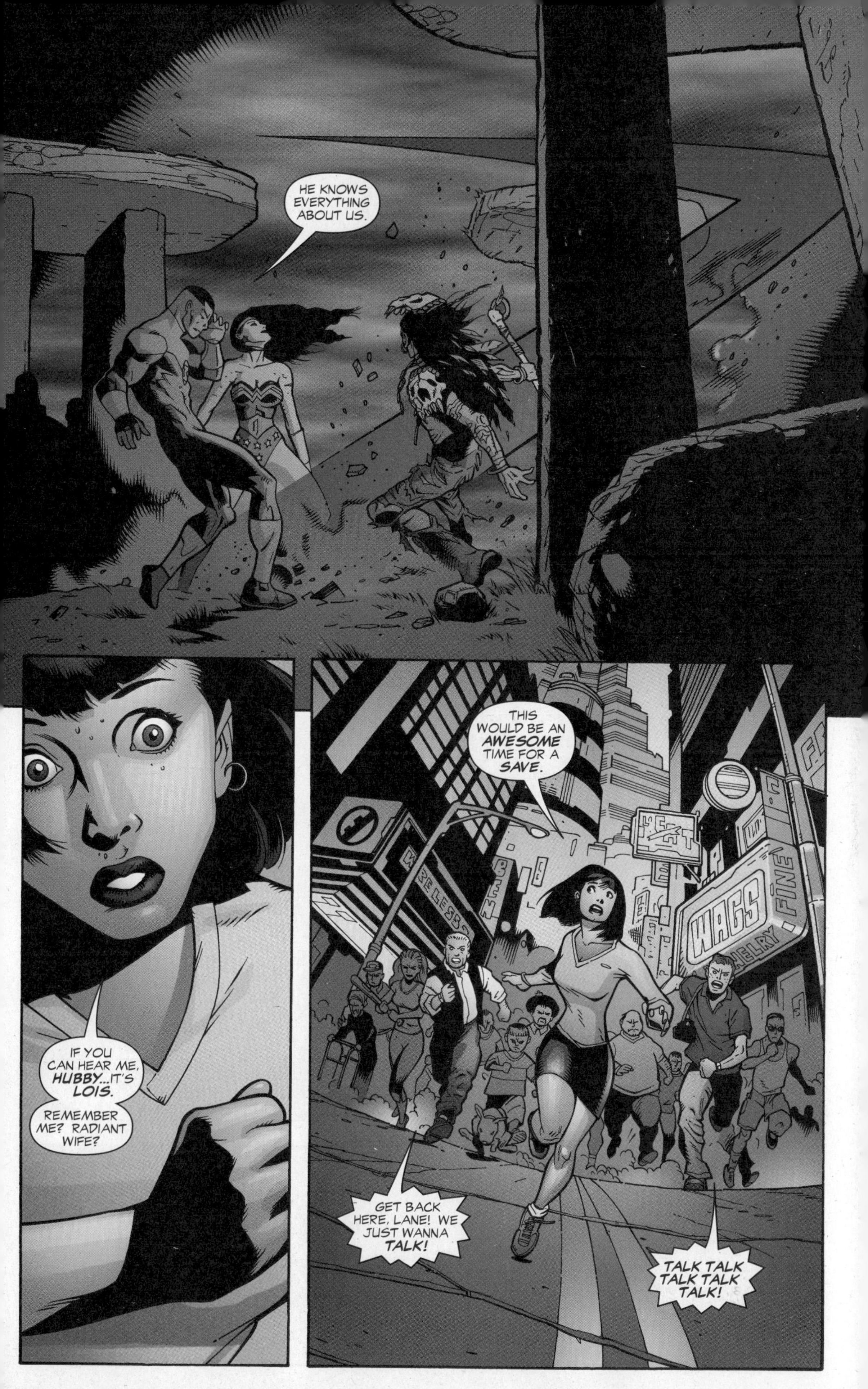
HE KNOWS EVERYTHING ABOUT US.
IF YOU CAN HEAR ME, HUBBY...IT'S LOIS.
REMEMBER ME? RADIANT WIFE?
THIS WOULD BE AN AWESOME TIME FOR A SAVE.
GET BACK HERE, LANE! WE JUST WANNA TALK!
TALK TALK TALK TALK TALK!
WAGS
FINE

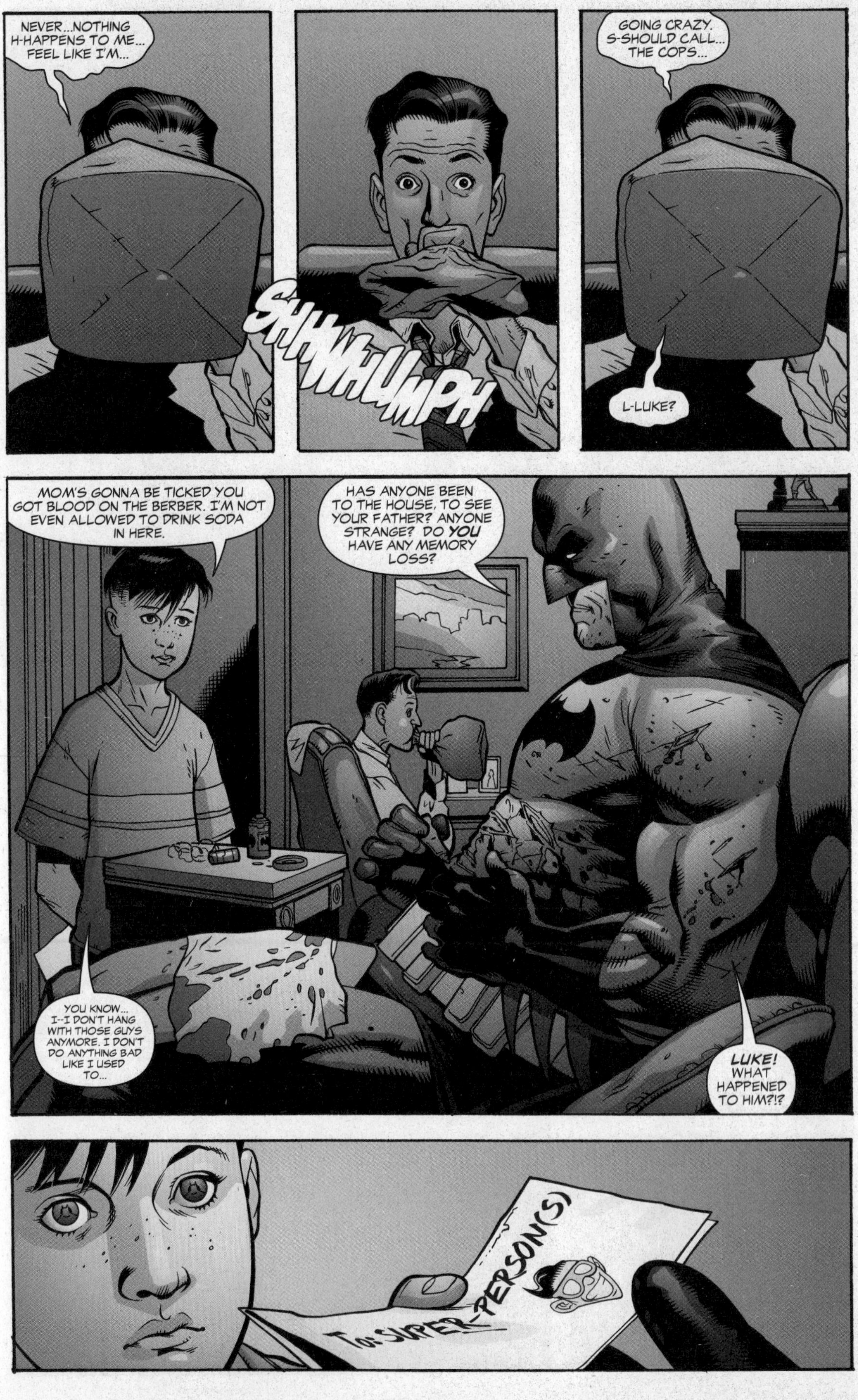

NEVER...NOTHING H-HAPPENS TO ME... FEEL LIKE I'M...
SHHWHUMPH
GOING CRAZY. S-SHOULD CALL... THE COPS...
L-LUKE?
MOM'S GONNA BE TICKED YOU GOT BLOOD ON THE BERBER. I'M NOT EVEN ALLOWED TO DRINK SODA IN HERE.
HAS ANYONE BEEN TO THE HOUSE, TO SEE YOUR FATHER? ANYONE STRANGE? DO *YOU* HAVE ANY MEMORY LOSS?
YOU KNOW... I--I DON'T HANG WITH THOSE GUYS ANYMORE. I DON'T DO ANYTHING BAD LIKE I USED TO...
LUKE! WHAT HAPPENED TO HIM?!?
To: SUPER-PERSON(S)

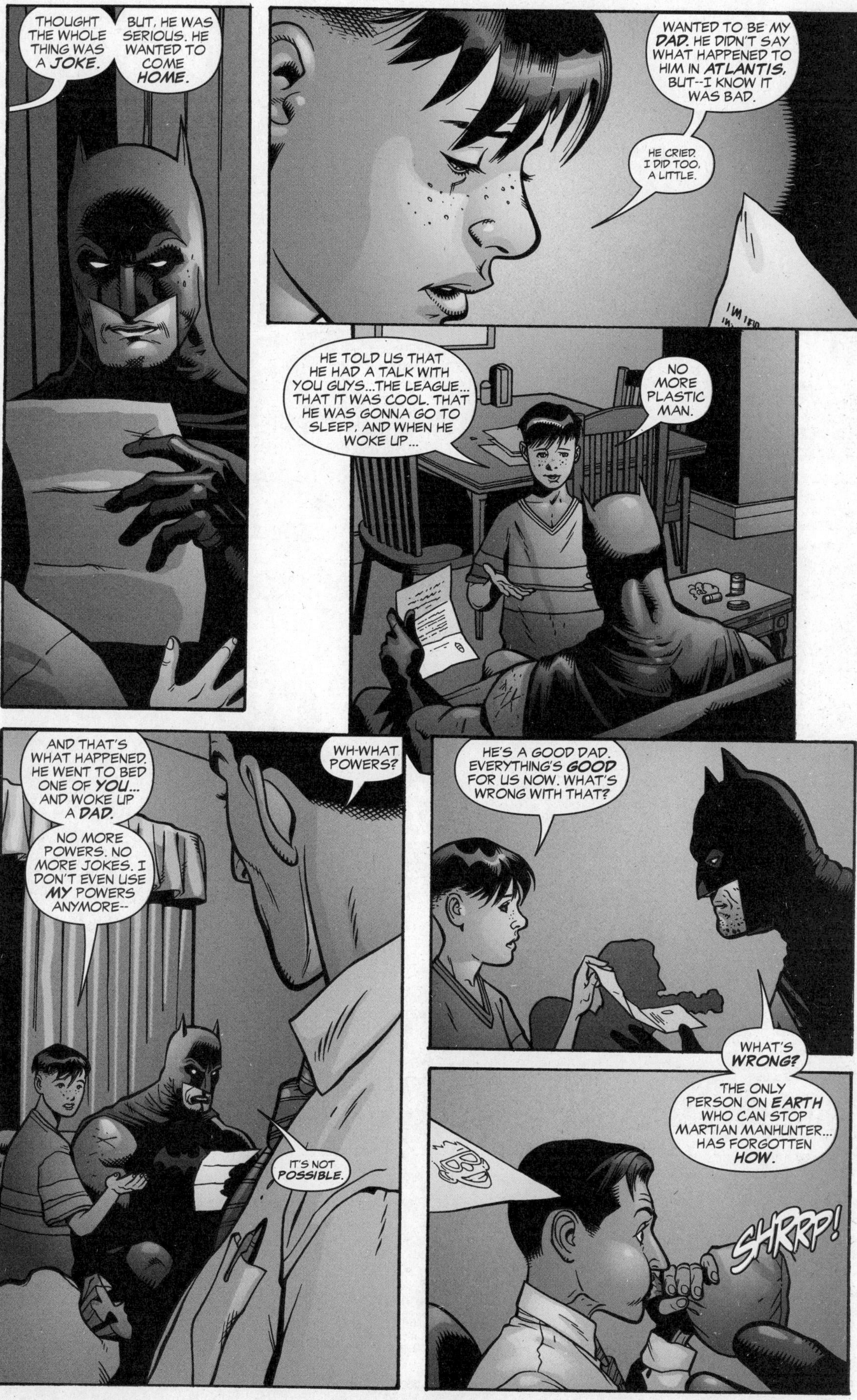
THOUGHT THE WHOLE THING WAS A JOKE.
BUT, HE WAS SERIOUS. HE WANTED TO COME HOME.
WANTED TO BE MY DAD. HE DIDN'T SAY WHAT HAPPENED TO HIM IN ATLANTIS, BUT--I KNOW IT WAS BAD.
HE CRIED. I DID TOO, A LITTLE.
HE TOLD US THAT HE HAD A TALK WITH YOU GUYS...THE LEAGUE... THAT IT WAS COOL. THAT HE WAS GONNA GO TO SLEEP, AND WHEN HE WOKE UP...
NO MORE PLASTIC MAN.
AND THAT'S WHAT HAPPENED. HE WENT TO BED ONE OF YOU... AND WOKE UP A DAD.
NO MORE POWERS. NO MORE JOKES. I DON'T EVEN USE MY POWERS ANYMORE--
WH-WHAT POWERS?
IT'S NOT POSSIBLE.
HE'S A GOOD DAD. EVERYTHING'S GOOD FOR US NOW. WHAT'S WRONG WITH THAT?
WHAT'S WRONG?
THE ONLY PERSON ON EARTH WHO CAN STOP MARTIAN MANHUNTER... HAS FORGOTTEN HOW.
SHRRP!

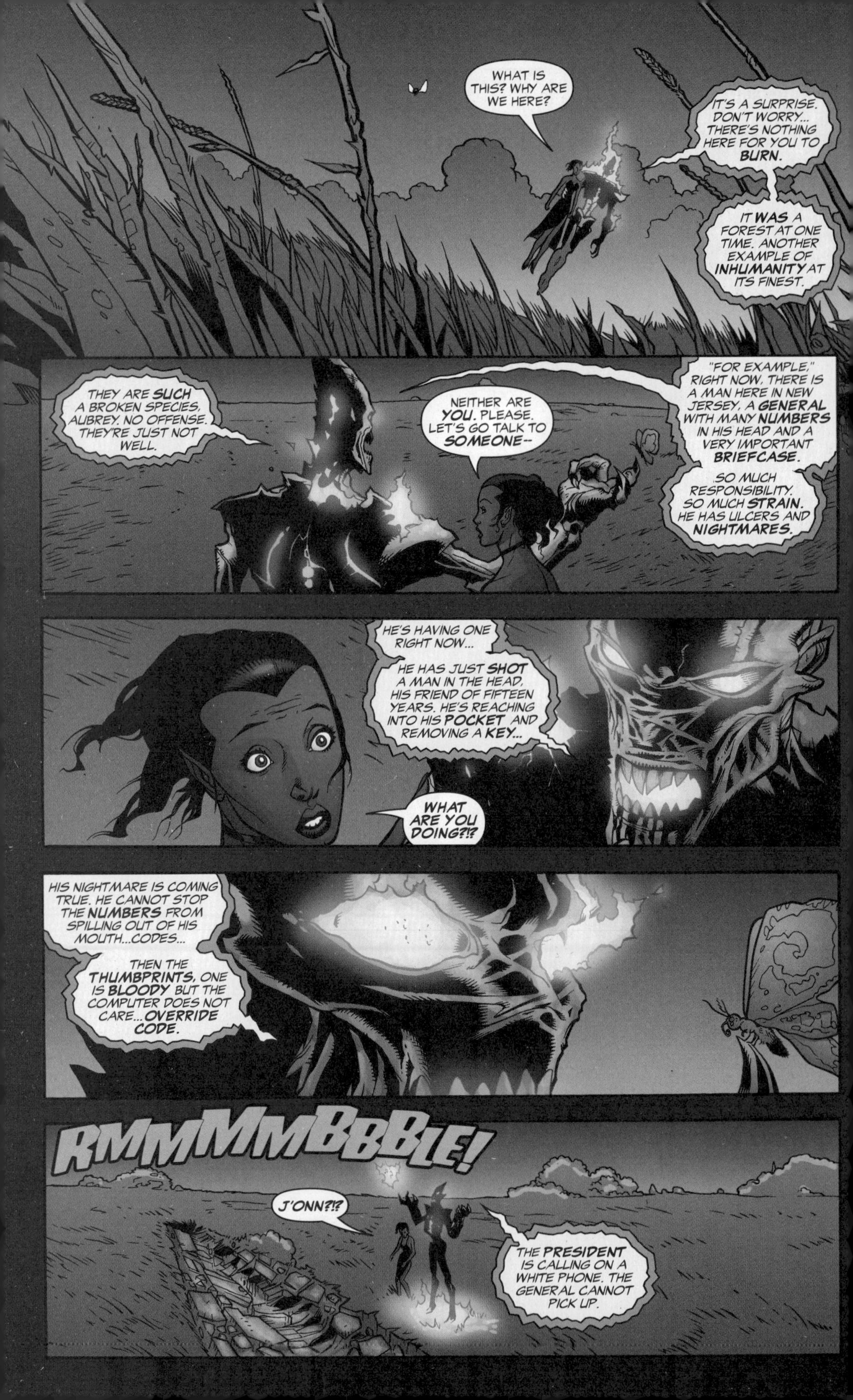
WHAT IS THIS? WHY ARE WE HERE?
IT'S A SURPRISE. DON'T WORRY... THERE'S NOTHING HERE FOR YOU TO **BURN**.
IT **WAS** A FOREST AT ONE TIME. ANOTHER EXAMPLE OF **INHUMANITY** AT ITS FINEST.
THEY ARE **SUCH** A BROKEN SPECIES, AUBREY. NO OFFENSE. THEY'RE JUST NOT WELL.
NEITHER ARE **YOU**. PLEASE. LET'S GO TALK TO **SOMEONE**--
"FOR EXAMPLE," RIGHT NOW, THERE IS A MAN HERE IN NEW JERSEY, A **GENERAL** WITH MANY **NUMBERS** IN HIS HEAD AND A VERY IMPORTANT **BRIEFCASE**.
SO MUCH RESPONSIBILITY. SO MUCH **STRAIN**. HE HAS ULCERS AND **NIGHTMARES**.
HE'S HAVING ONE RIGHT NOW...
HE HAS JUST **SHOT** A MAN IN THE **HEAD**, HIS FRIEND OF FIFTEEN YEARS. HE'S REACHING INTO HIS **POCKET** AND REMOVING A **KEY**...
WHAT ARE YOU DOING?!?
HIS NIGHTMARE IS COMING TRUE. HE CANNOT STOP THE **NUMBERS** FROM SPILLING OUT OF HIS MOUTH...CODES...
THEN THE **THUMBPRINTS**, ONE IS **BLOODY** BUT THE COMPUTER DOES NOT CARE...**OVERRIDE CODE**.
RMMMMMBBBLE!
J'ONN?!?
THE **PRESIDENT** IS CALLING ON A WHITE PHONE. THE GENERAL CANNOT PICK UP.

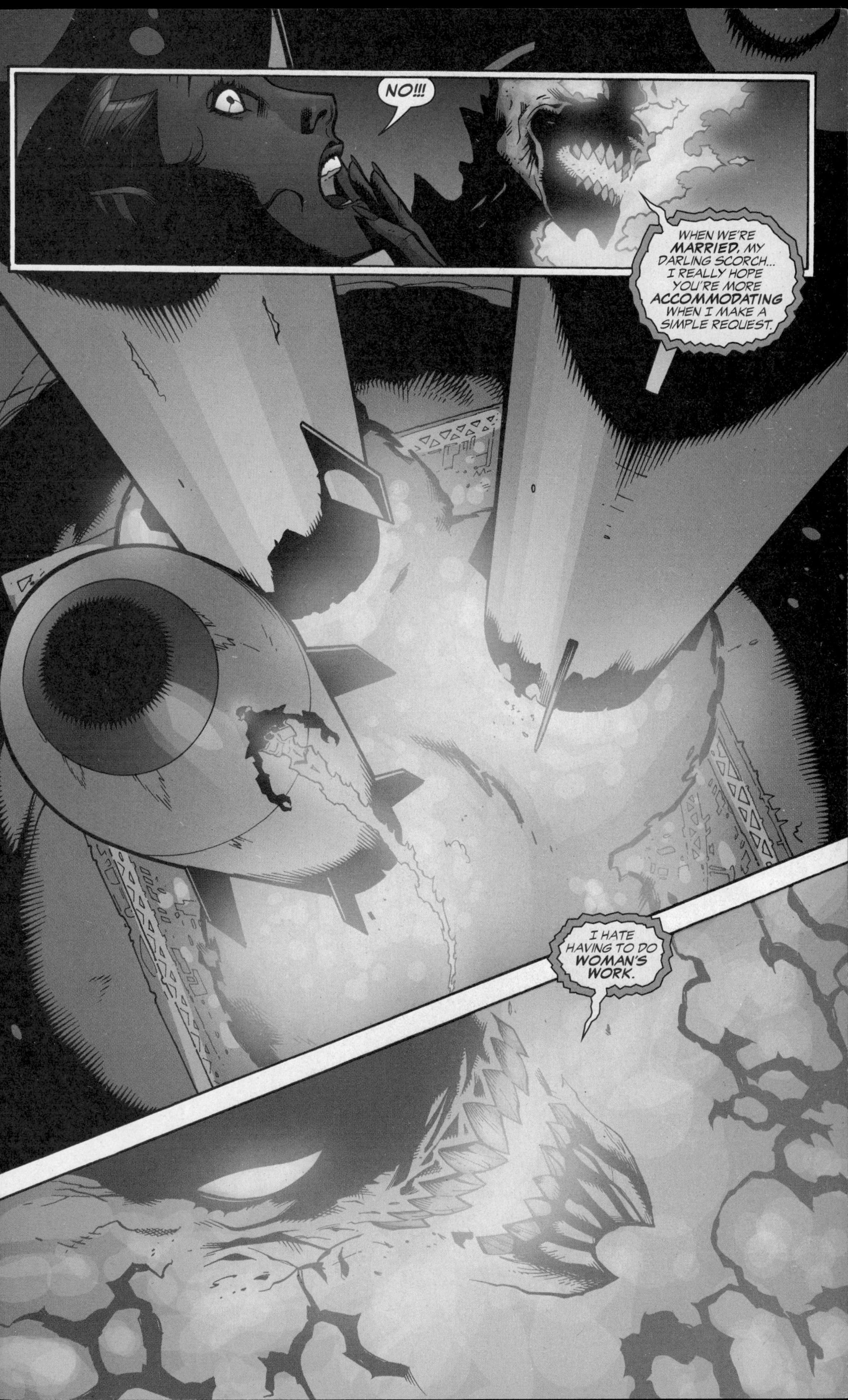
NO!!!
WHEN WE'RE MARRIED, MY DARLING SCORCH... I REALLY HOPE YOU'RE MORE ACCOMMODATING WHEN I MAKE A SIMPLE REQUEST.
I HATE HAVING TO DO WOMAN'S WORK.

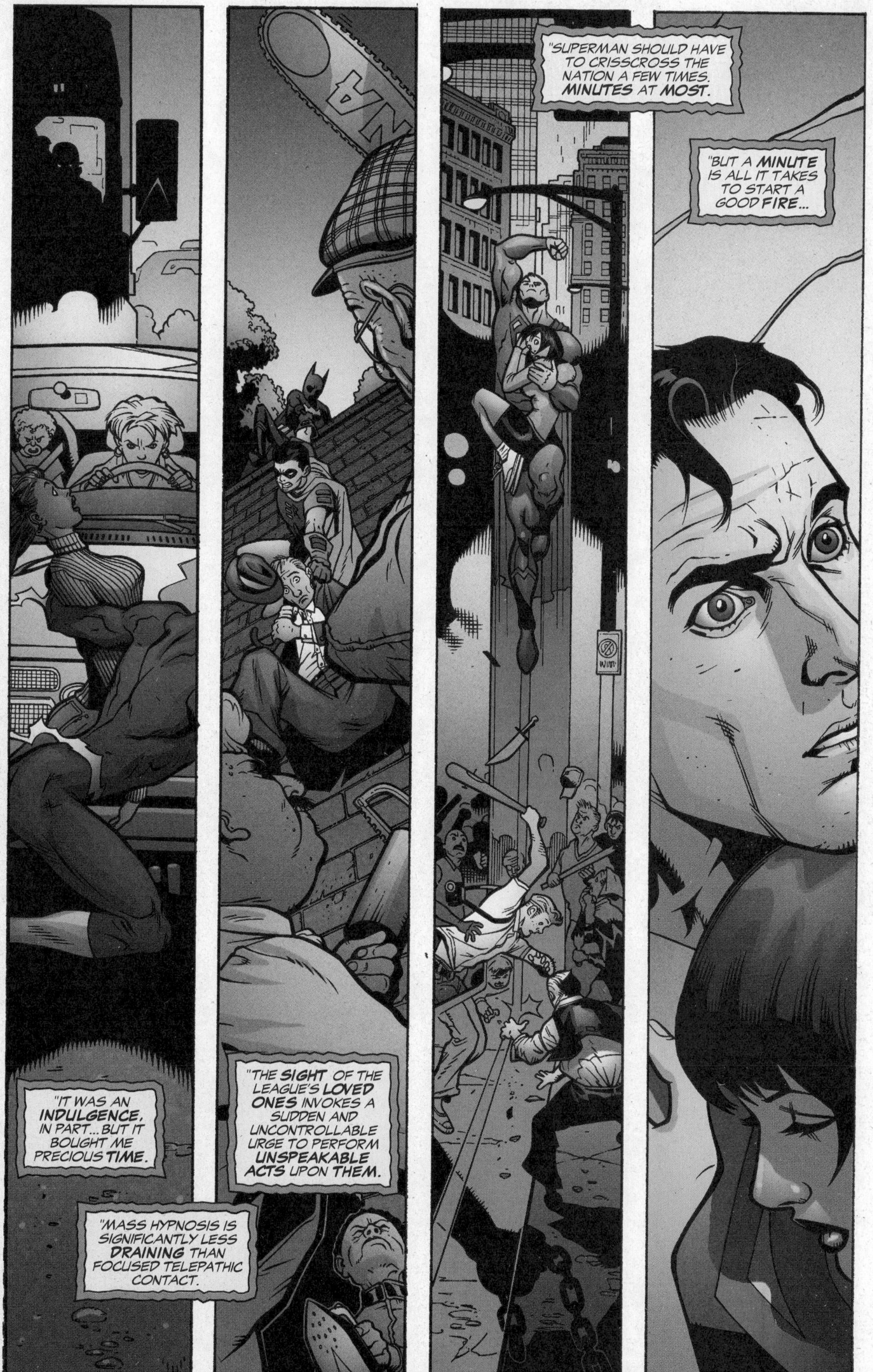
"IT WAS AN INDULGENCE, IN PART...BUT IT BOUGHT ME PRECIOUS TIME.
"MASS HYPNOSIS IS SIGNIFICANTLY LESS DRAINING THAN FOCUSED TELEPATHIC CONTACT.
"THE SIGHT OF THE LEAGUE'S LOVED ONES INVOKES A SUDDEN AND UNCONTROLLABLE URGE TO PERFORM UNSPEAKABLE ACTS UPON THEM.
"SUPERMAN SHOULD HAVE TO CRISSCROSS THE NATION A FEW TIMES. MINUTES AT MOST.
"BUT A MINUTE IS ALL IT TAKES TO START A GOOD FIRE...

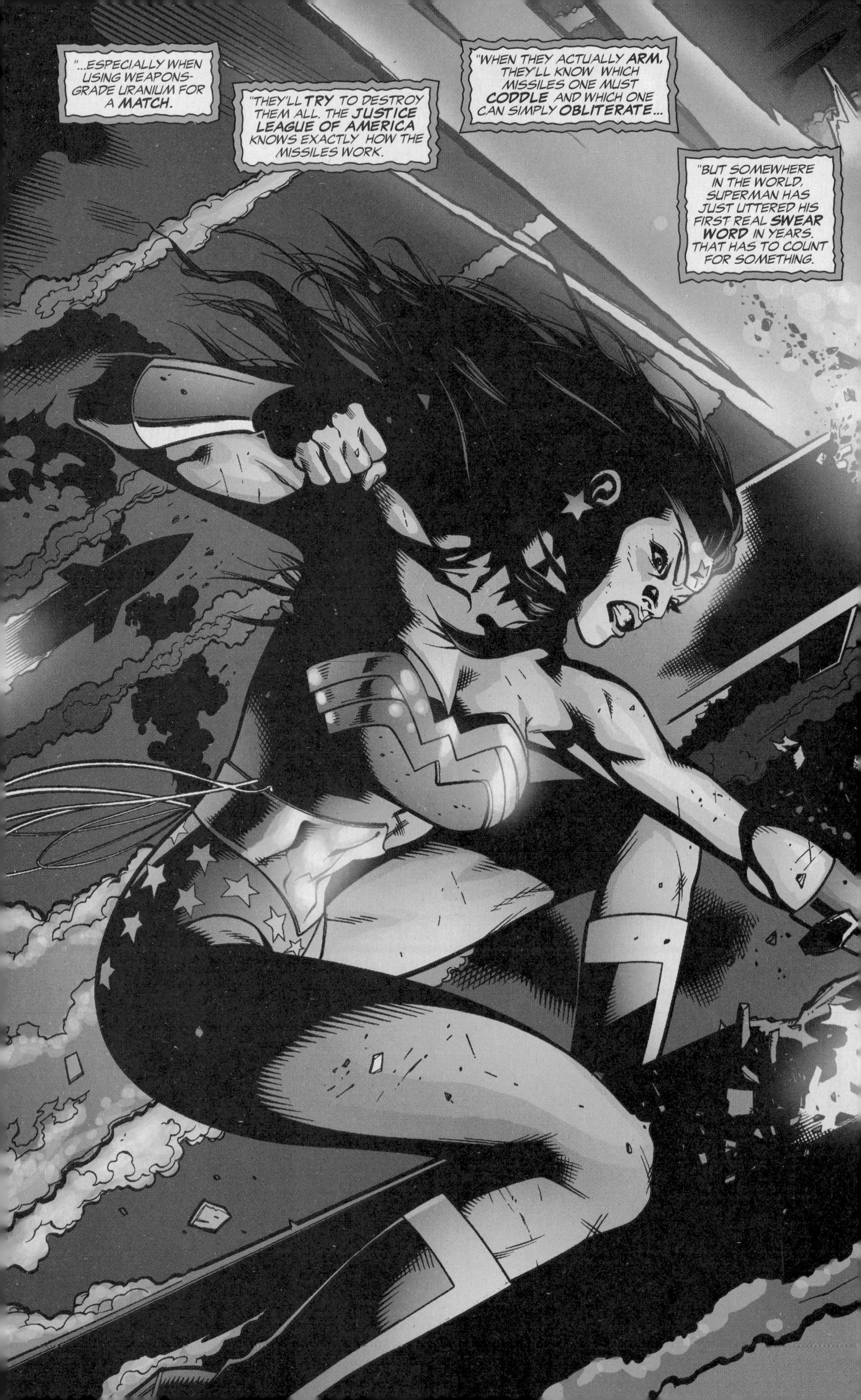
"...ESPECIALLY WHEN USING WEAPONS-GRADE URANIUM FOR A MATCH.
"THEY'LL TRY TO DESTROY THEM ALL. THE JUSTICE LEAGUE OF AMERICA KNOWS EXACTLY HOW THE MISSILES WORK.
"WHEN THEY ACTUALLY ARM, THEY'LL KNOW WHICH MISSILES ONE MUST CODDLE AND WHICH ONE CAN SIMPLY OBLITERATE...
"BUT SOMEWHERE IN THE WORLD, SUPERMAN HAS JUST UTTERED HIS FIRST REAL SWEAR WORD IN YEARS. THAT HAS TO COUNT FOR SOMETHING.

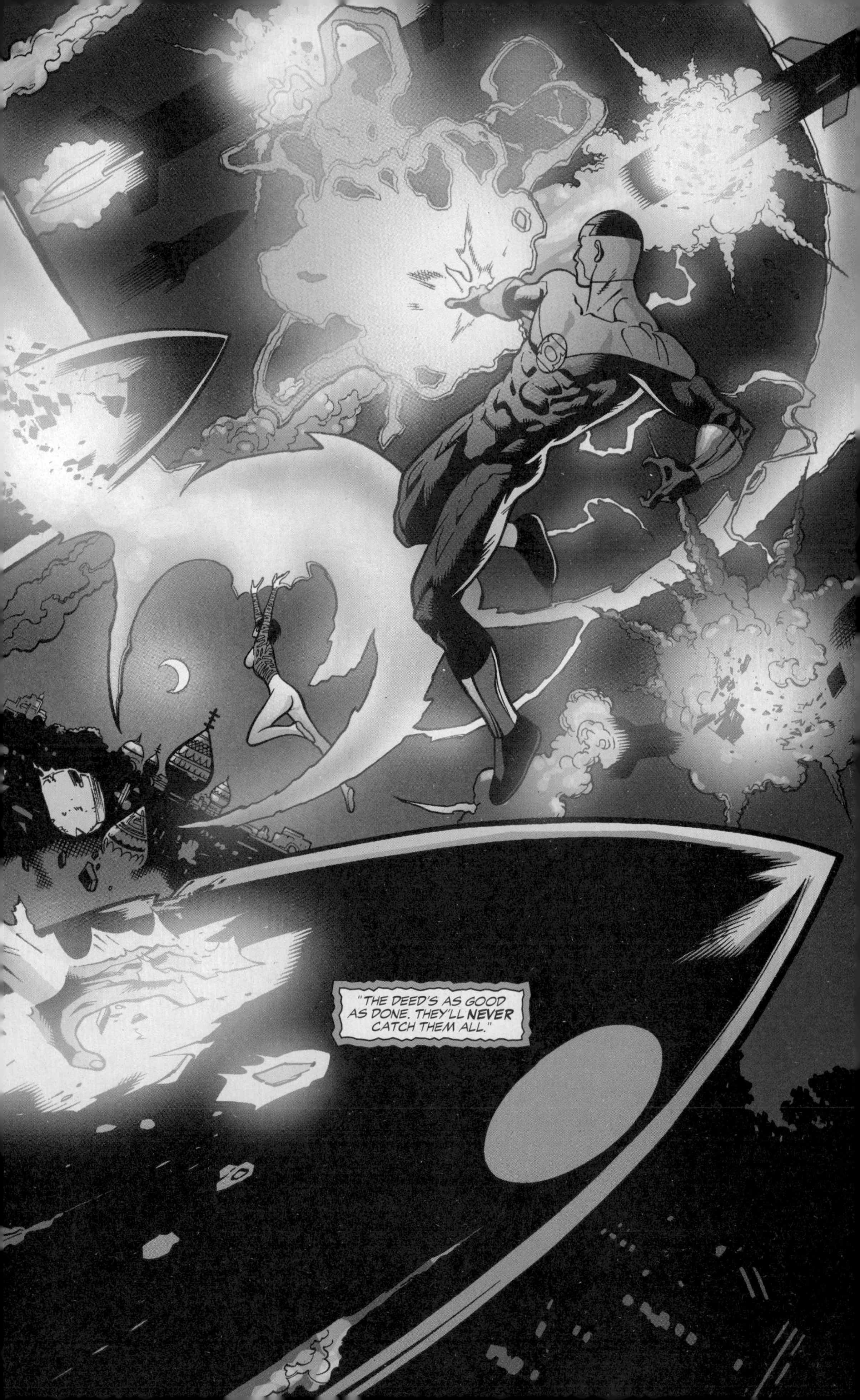
"THE DEED'S AS GOOD
AS DONE. THEY'LL **NEVER**
CATCH THEM ALL."

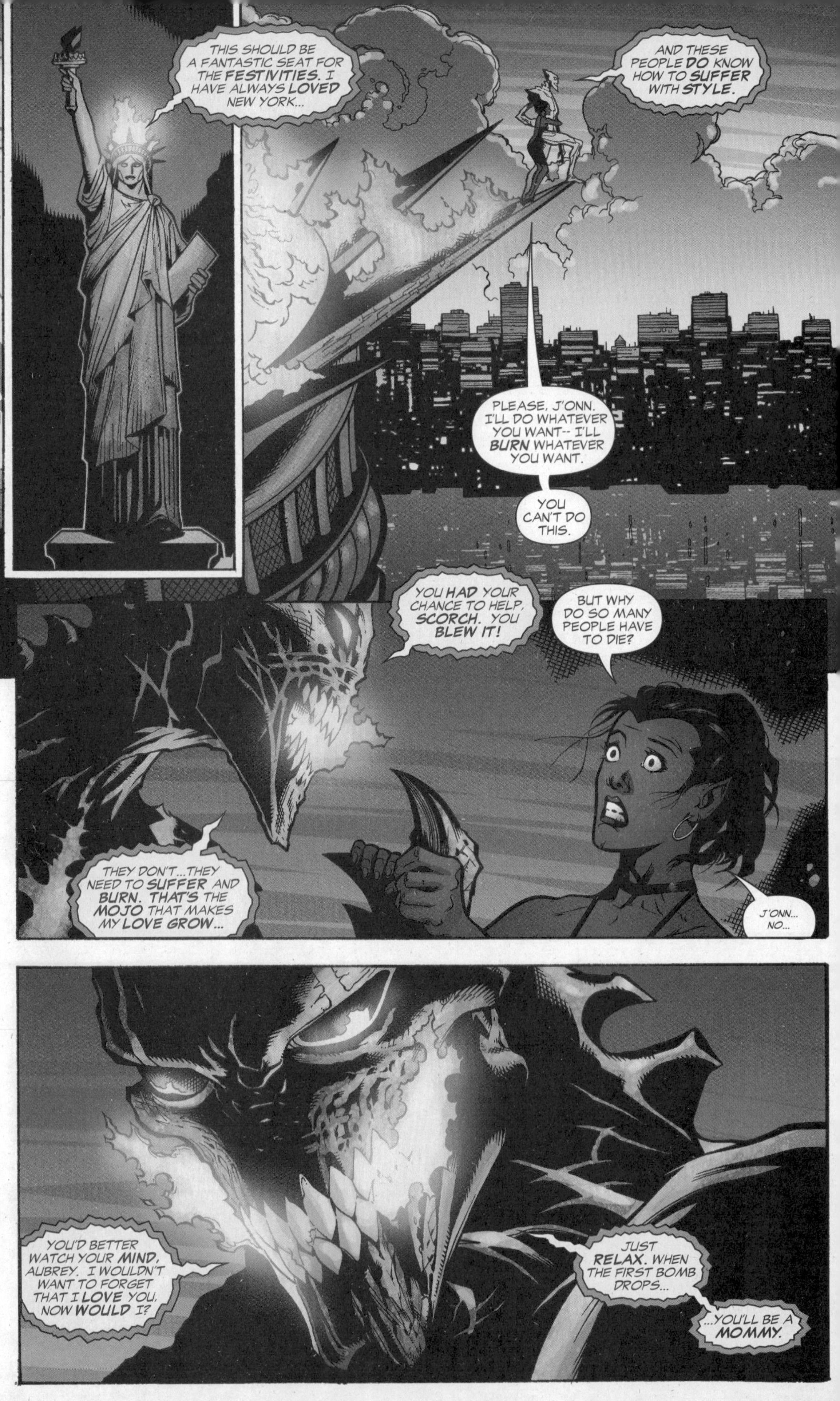
THIS SHOULD BE A FANTASTIC SEAT FOR THE FESTIVITIES. I HAVE ALWAYS LOVED NEW YORK...
AND THESE PEOPLE DO KNOW HOW TO SUFFER WITH STYLE.
PLEASE, J'ONN. I'LL DO WHATEVER YOU WANT-- I'LL BURN WHATEVER YOU WANT.
YOU CAN'T DO THIS.
YOU HAD YOUR CHANCE TO HELP, SCORCH. YOU BLEW IT!
BUT WHY DO SO MANY PEOPLE HAVE TO DIE?
THEY DON'T...THEY NEED TO SUFFER AND BURN. THAT'S THE MOJO THAT MAKES MY LOVE GROW...
J'ONN... NO...
YOU'D BETTER WATCH YOUR MIND, AUBREY. I WOULDN'T WANT TO FORGET THAT I LOVE YOU, NOW WOULD I?
JUST RELAX. WHEN THE FIRST BOMB DROPS...
...YOU'LL BE A MOMMY.

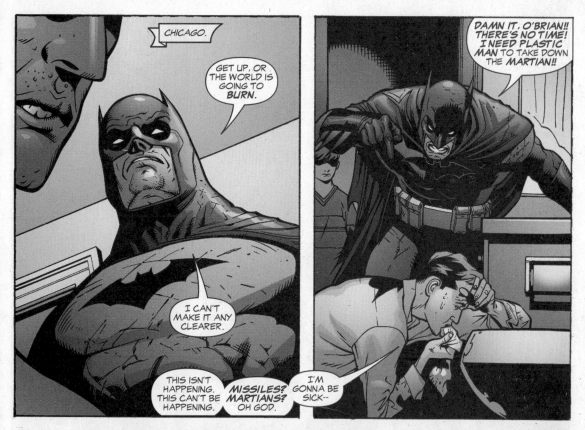

CHICAGO.

GET UP, OR THE WORLD IS GOING TO *BURN*.

I CAN'T MAKE IT ANY CLEARER.

DAMN IT, O'BRIAN!! THERE'S NO TIME!! I NEED PLASTIC MAN TO TAKE DOWN THE *MARTIAN*!!

THIS ISN'T HAPPENING. THIS CAN'T BE HAPPENING.

MISSILES? MARTIANS? OH GOD.

I'M GONNA BE SICK--

YOUR "VACATION" IS *OVER!*

I AM *NOT* PLASTIC MAN!!!

HE'S *NOT* UNDER MENTAL CONTROL, *LUKE*. HE *CAN'T* BE. THAT'S WHY HE'S MY "SECRET WEAPON."

IT MUST BE A FORM OF *HYPNOSIS.* VOLUNTARY. HE *WON'T* LET GO.

SO *SCARE* HIM! SCARE THE HELL OUTTA HIM! YOU DID IT TO *ME!*

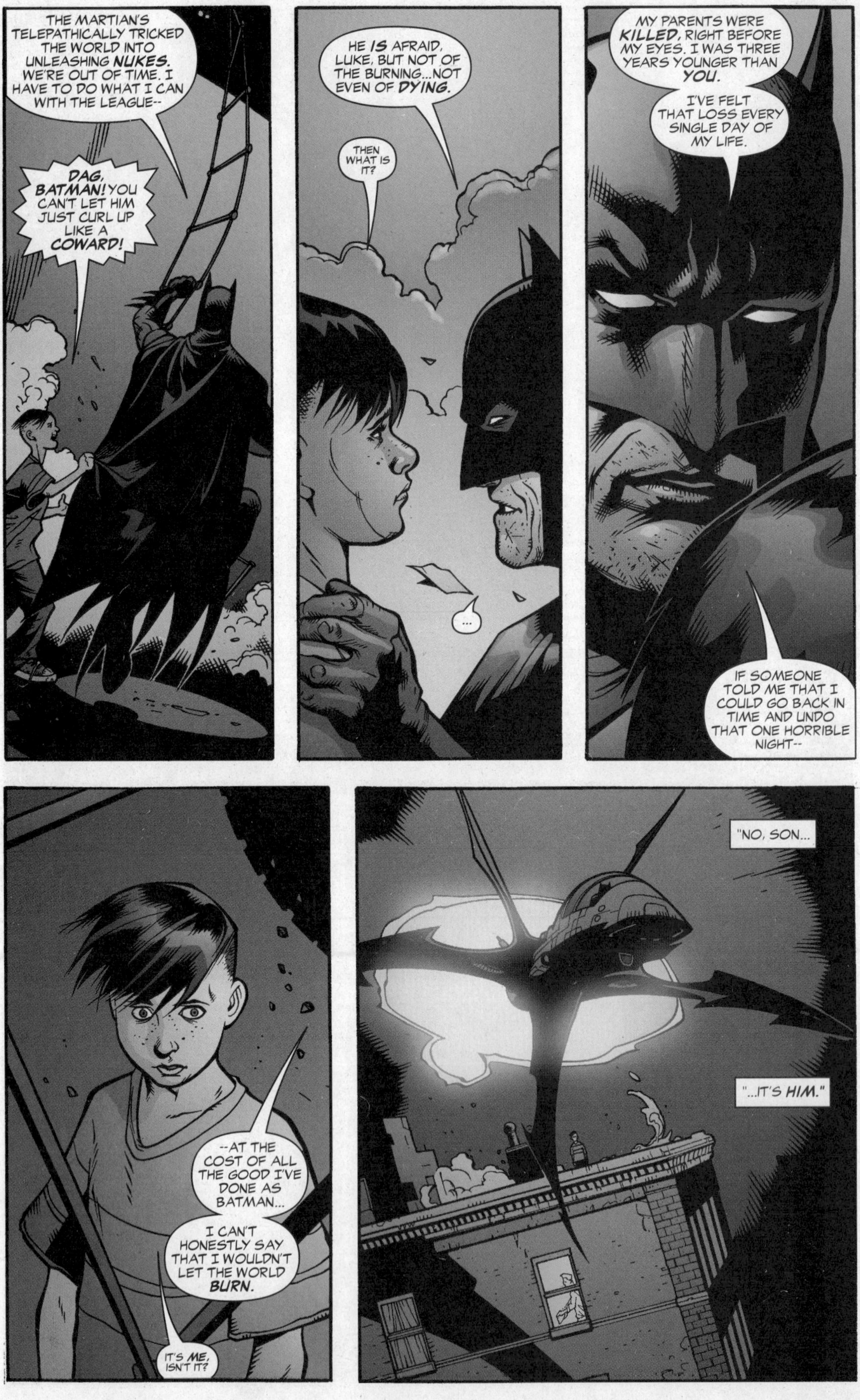
THE MARTIAN'S TELEPATHICALLY TRICKED THE WORLD INTO UNLEASHING NUKES. WE'RE OUT OF TIME. I HAVE TO DO WHAT I CAN WITH THE LEAGUE--
DAG, BATMAN! YOU CAN'T LET HIM JUST CURL UP LIKE A COWARD!
HE IS AFRAID, LUKE, BUT NOT OF THE BURNING...NOT EVEN OF DYING.
THEN WHAT IS IT?
...
MY PARENTS WERE KILLED, RIGHT BEFORE MY EYES. I WAS THREE YEARS YOUNGER THAN YOU.
I'VE FELT THAT LOSS EVERY SINGLE DAY OF MY LIFE.
IF SOMEONE TOLD ME THAT I COULD GO BACK IN TIME AND UNDO THAT ONE HORRIBLE NIGHT--
--AT THE COST OF ALL THE GOOD I'VE DONE AS BATMAN...
I CAN'T HONESTLY SAY THAT I WOULDN'T LET THE WORLD BURN.
IT'S ME, ISN'T IT?
"NO, SON...
"...IT'S HIM."

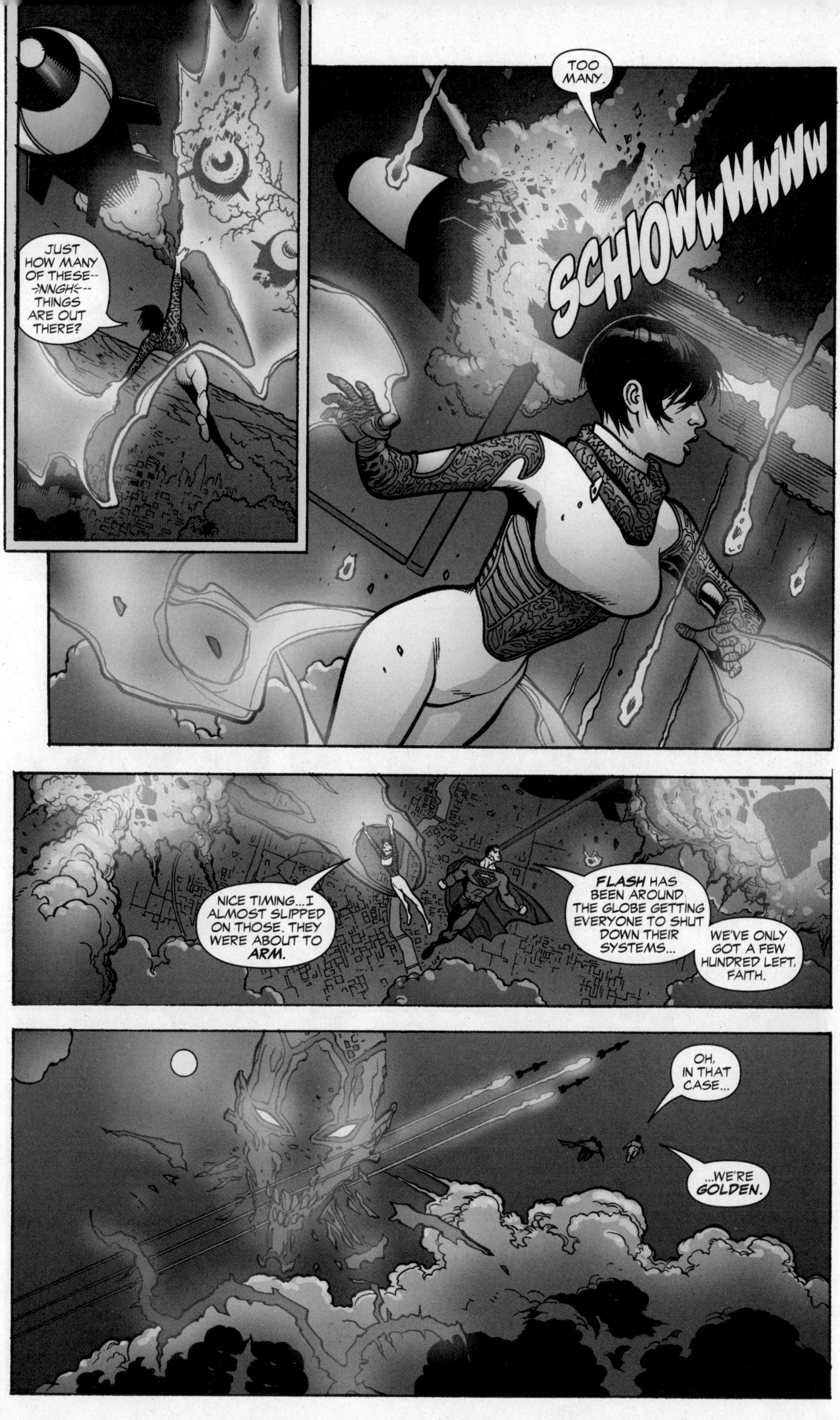
JUST HOW MANY OF THESE-- -NNGH- -- THINGS ARE OUT THERE?
TOO MANY.
SCHIOWwWwWw
NICE TIMING...I ALMOST SLIPPED ON THOSE. THEY WERE ABOUT TO ARM.
FLASH HAS BEEN AROUND THE GLOBE GETTING EVERYONE TO SHUT DOWN THEIR SYSTEMS...
WE'VE ONLY GOT A FEW HUNDRED LEFT, FAITH.
OH, IN THAT CASE...
...WE'RE GOLDEN.

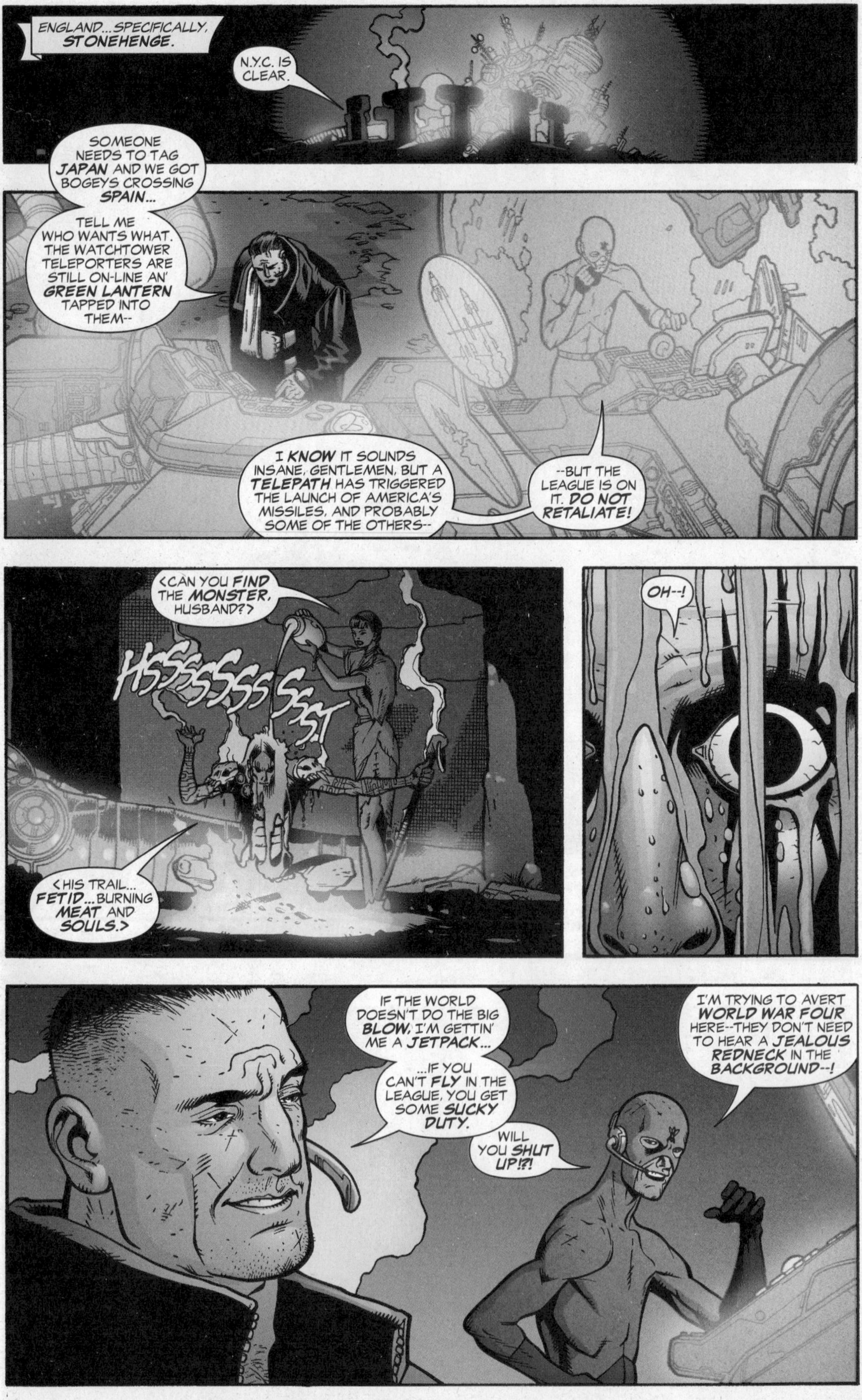
ENGLAND...SPECIFICALLY, STONEHENGE.
N.Y.C. IS CLEAR.
SOMEONE NEEDS TO TAG JAPAN AND WE GOT BOGEYS CROSSING SPAIN...
TELL ME WHO WANTS WHAT. THE WATCHTOWER TELEPORTERS ARE STILL ON-LINE AN' GREEN LANTERN TAPPED INTO THEM--
I KNOW IT SOUNDS INSANE, GENTLEMEN, BUT A TELEPATH HAS TRIGGERED THE LAUNCH OF AMERICA'S MISSILES, AND PROBABLY SOME OF THE OTHERS--
--BUT THE LEAGUE IS ON IT. DO NOT RETALIATE!
<CAN YOU FIND THE MONSTER, HUSBAND?>
HSSSSSSSSSST
<HIS TRAIL... FETID...BURNING MEAT AND SOULS.>
OH--!
IF THE WORLD DOESN'T DO THE BIG BLOW, I'M GETTIN' ME A JETPACK...
...IF YOU CAN'T FLY IN THE LEAGUE, YOU GET SOME SUCKY DUTY.
WILL YOU SHUT UP!?!
I'M TRYING TO AVERT WORLD WAR FOUR HERE--THEY DON'T NEED TO HEAR A JEALOUS REDNECK IN THE BACKGROUND--!

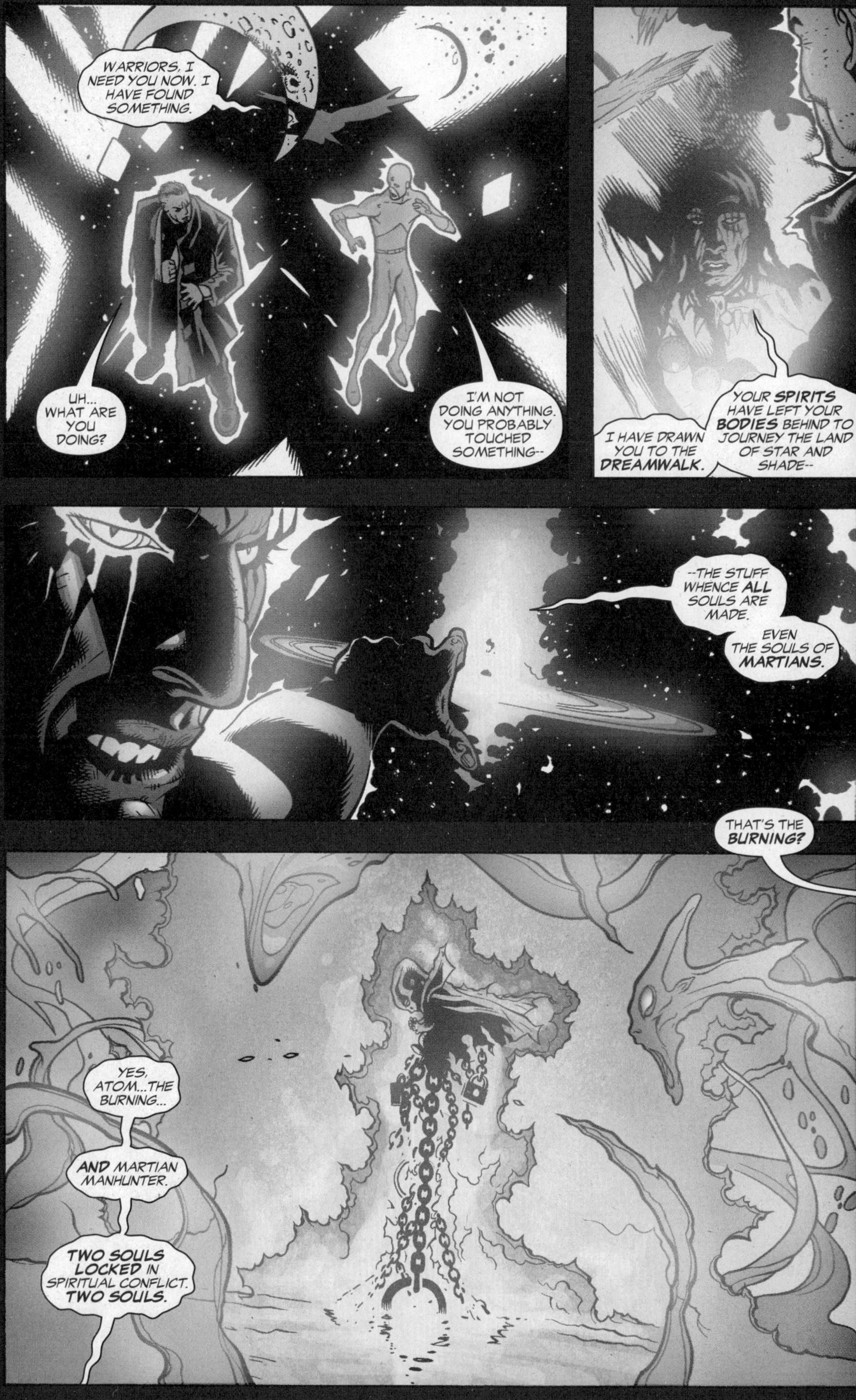
WARRIORS, I NEED YOU NOW. I HAVE FOUND SOMETHING.
UH... WHAT ARE YOU DOING?
I'M NOT DOING ANYTHING. YOU PROBABLY TOUCHED SOMETHING--
I HAVE DRAWN YOU TO THE DREAMWALK.
YOUR SPIRITS HAVE LEFT YOUR BODIES BEHIND TO JOURNEY THE LAND OF STAR AND SHADE--
--THE STUFF WHENCE ALL SOULS ARE MADE.
EVEN THE SOULS OF MARTIANS.
THAT'S THE BURNING?
YES, ATOM...THE BURNING...
AND MARTIAN MANHUNTER.
TWO SOULS LOCKED IN SPIRITUAL CONFLICT. TWO SOULS.

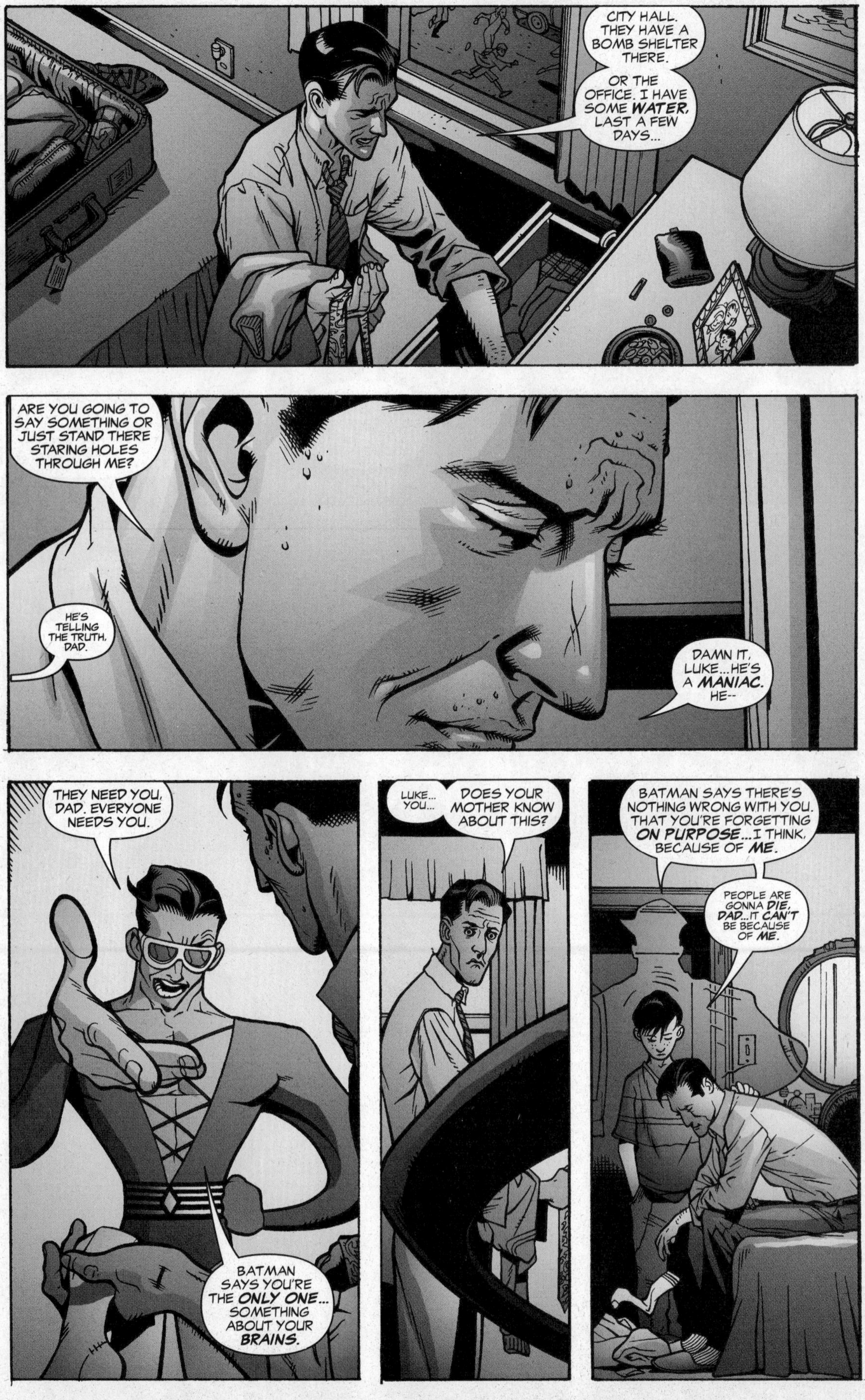
CITY HALL. THEY HAVE A BOMB SHELTER THERE.
OR THE OFFICE. I HAVE SOME WATER, LAST A FEW DAYS...
ARE YOU GOING TO SAY SOMETHING OR JUST STAND THERE STARING HOLES THROUGH ME?
HE'S TELLING THE TRUTH, DAD.
DAMN IT, LUKE...HE'S A MANIAC. HE--
THEY NEED YOU, DAD. EVERYONE NEEDS YOU.
BATMAN SAYS YOU'RE THE ONLY ONE... SOMETHING ABOUT YOUR BRAINS.
LUKE... YOU...
DOES YOUR MOTHER KNOW ABOUT THIS?
BATMAN SAYS THERE'S NOTHING WRONG WITH YOU. THAT YOU'RE FORGETTING ON PURPOSE...I THINK, BECAUSE OF ME.
PEOPLE ARE GONNA DIE, DAD...IT CAN'T BE BECAUSE OF ME.

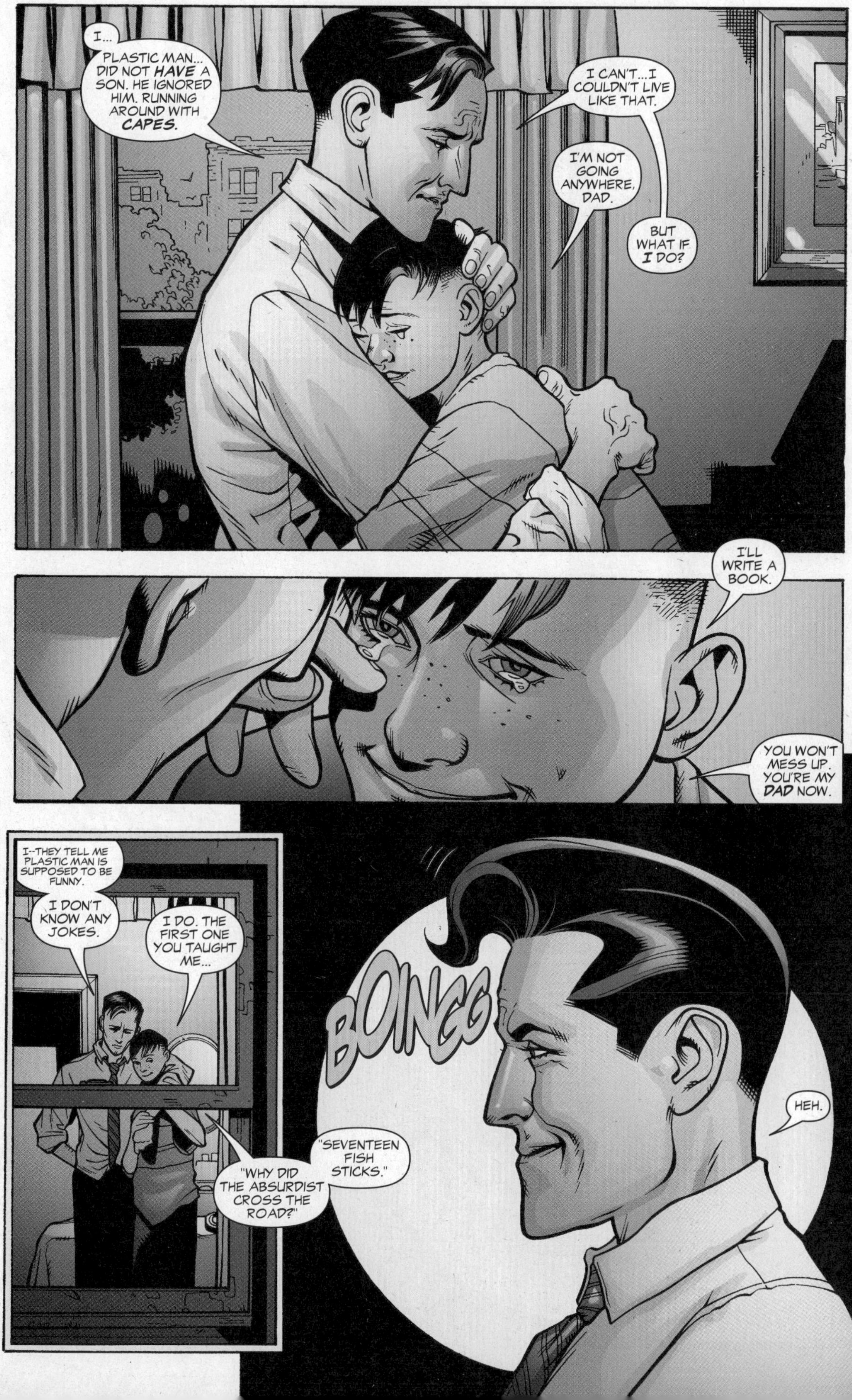
I...
PLASTIC MAN... DID NOT HAVE A SON. HE IGNORED HIM. RUNNING AROUND WITH CAPES.
I CAN'T...I COULDN'T LIVE LIKE THAT.
I'M NOT GOING ANYWHERE, DAD.
BUT WHAT IF I DO?
I'LL WRITE A BOOK.
YOU WON'T MESS UP. YOU'RE MY DAD NOW.
I--THEY TELL ME PLASTIC MAN IS SUPPOSED TO BE FUNNY.
I DON'T KNOW ANY JOKES.
I DO. THE FIRST ONE YOU TAUGHT ME...
"WHY DID THE ABSURDIST CROSS THE ROAD?"
"SEVENTEEN FISH STICKS."
BOINGG
HEH.

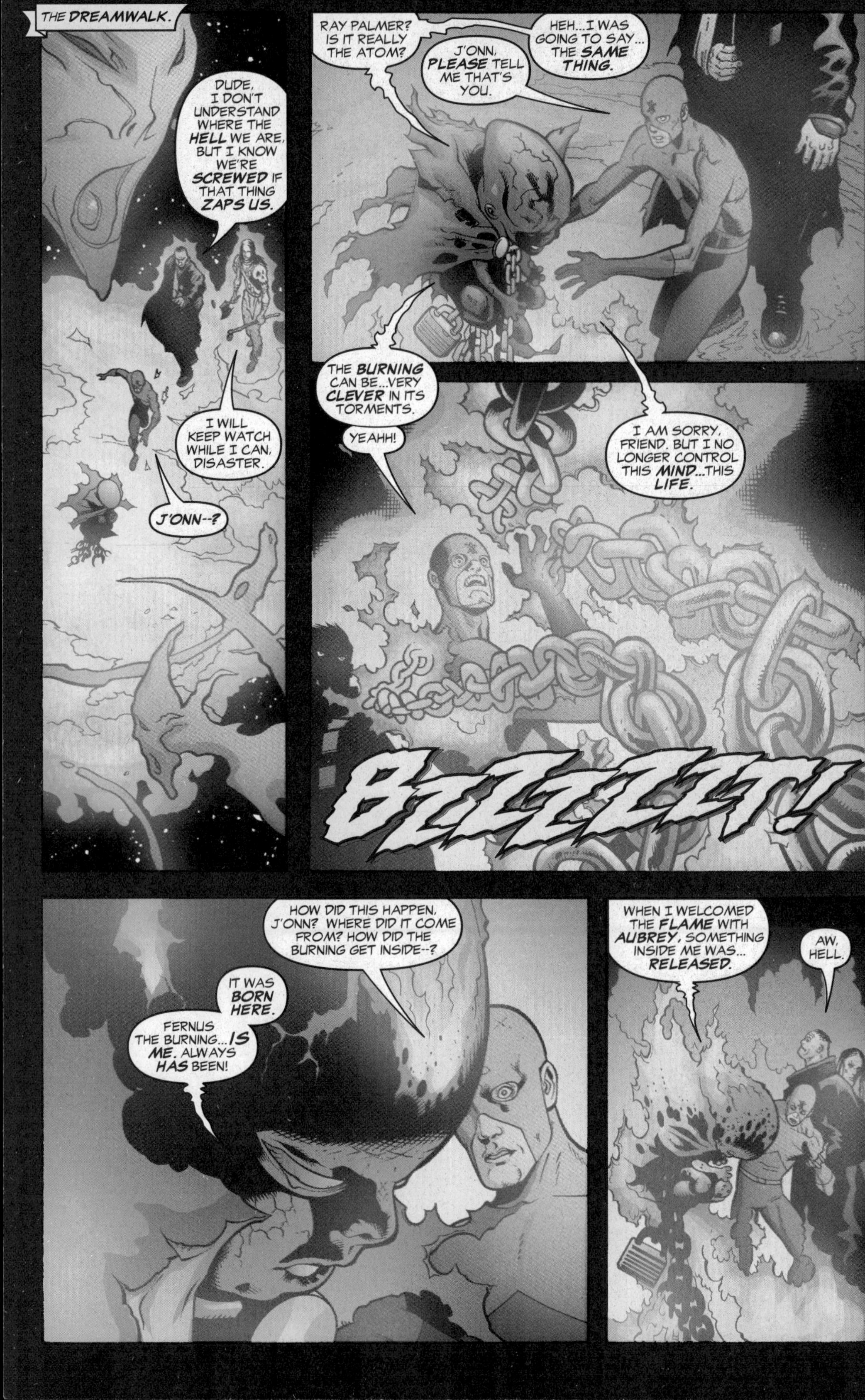
THE DREAMWALK.
DUDE, I DON'T UNDERSTAND WHERE THE HELL WE ARE, BUT I KNOW WE'RE SCREWED IF THAT THING ZAPS US.
I WILL KEEP WATCH WHILE I CAN, DISASTER.
J'ONN--?
RAY PALMER? IS IT REALLY THE ATOM?
J'ONN, PLEASE TELL ME THAT'S YOU.
HEH...I WAS GOING TO SAY... THE SAME THING.
THE BURNING CAN BE...VERY CLEVER IN ITS TORMENTS.
YEAHH!
I AM SORRY, FRIEND. BUT I NO LONGER CONTROL THIS MIND...THIS LIFE.
BZZZZZT!
HOW DID THIS HAPPEN, J'ONN? WHERE DID IT COME FROM? HOW DID THE BURNING GET INSIDE--?
IT WAS BORN HERE.
FERNUS THE BURNING...IS ME. ALWAYS HAS BEEN!
WHEN I WELCOMED THE FLAME WITH AUBREY, SOMETHING INSIDE ME WAS... RELEASED.
AW, HELL.

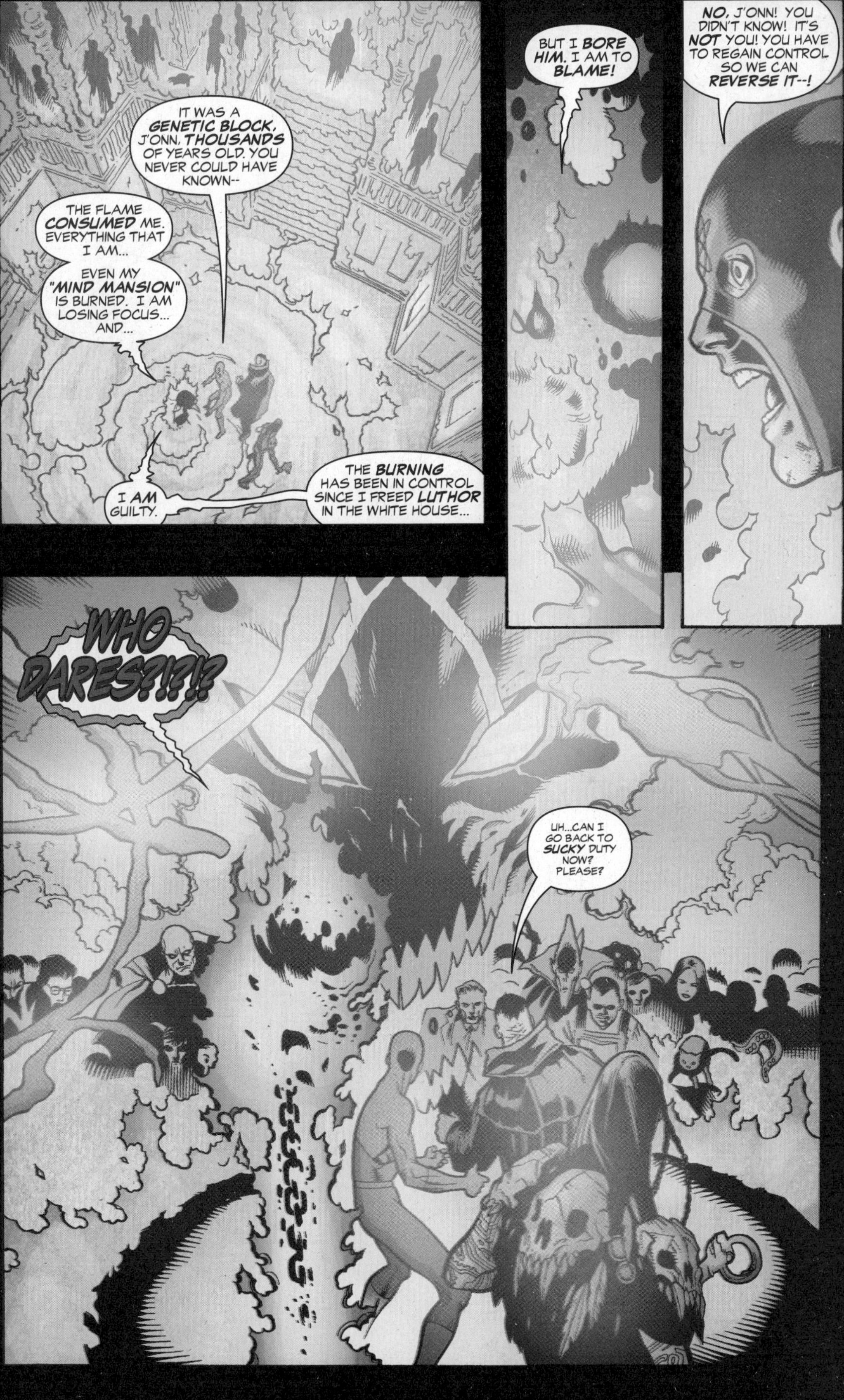
IT WAS A GENETIC BLOCK, J'ONN, THOUSANDS OF YEARS OLD. YOU NEVER COULD HAVE KNOWN--
THE FLAME CONSUMED ME. EVERYTHING THAT I AM...
EVEN MY "MIND MANSION" IS BURNED. I AM LOSING FOCUS... AND...
THE BURNING HAS BEEN IN CONTROL SINCE I FREED LUTHOR IN THE WHITE HOUSE...
I AM GUILTY.
BUT I BORE HIM. I AM TO BLAME!
NO, J'ONN! YOU DIDN'T KNOW! IT'S NOT YOU! YOU HAVE TO REGAIN CONTROL SO WE CAN REVERSE IT--!
WHO DARES?!?!?
UH...CAN I GO BACK TO SUCKY DUTY NOW? PLEASE?

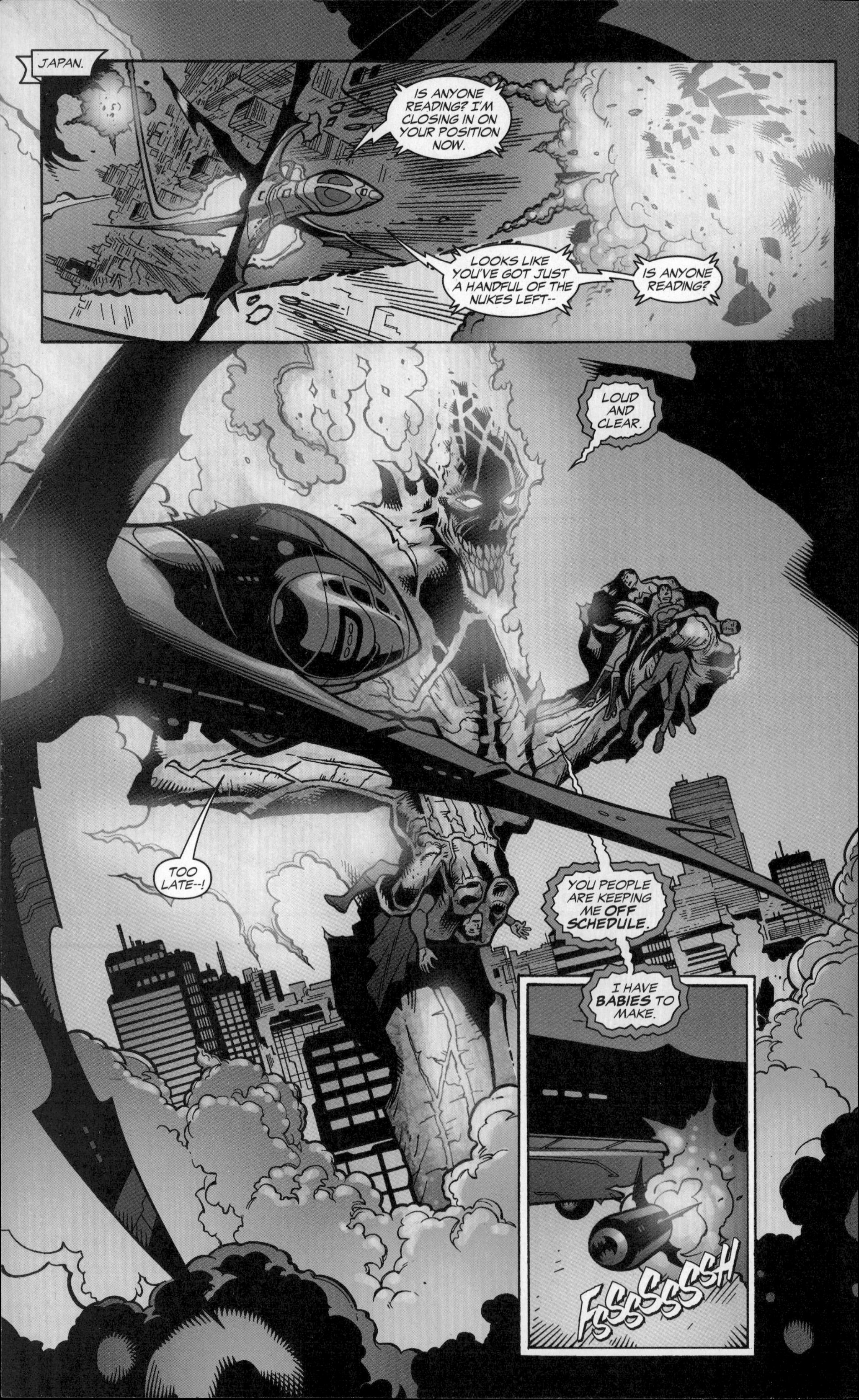
JAPAN.
IS ANYONE READING? I'M CLOSING IN ON YOUR POSITION NOW.
LOOKS LIKE YOU'VE GOT JUST A HANDFUL OF THE NUKES LEFT--
IS ANYONE READING?
LOUD AND CLEAR.
TOO LATE--!
YOU PEOPLE ARE KEEPING ME OFF SCHEDULE.
I HAVE BABIES TO MAKE.
FSSSSSSSSH

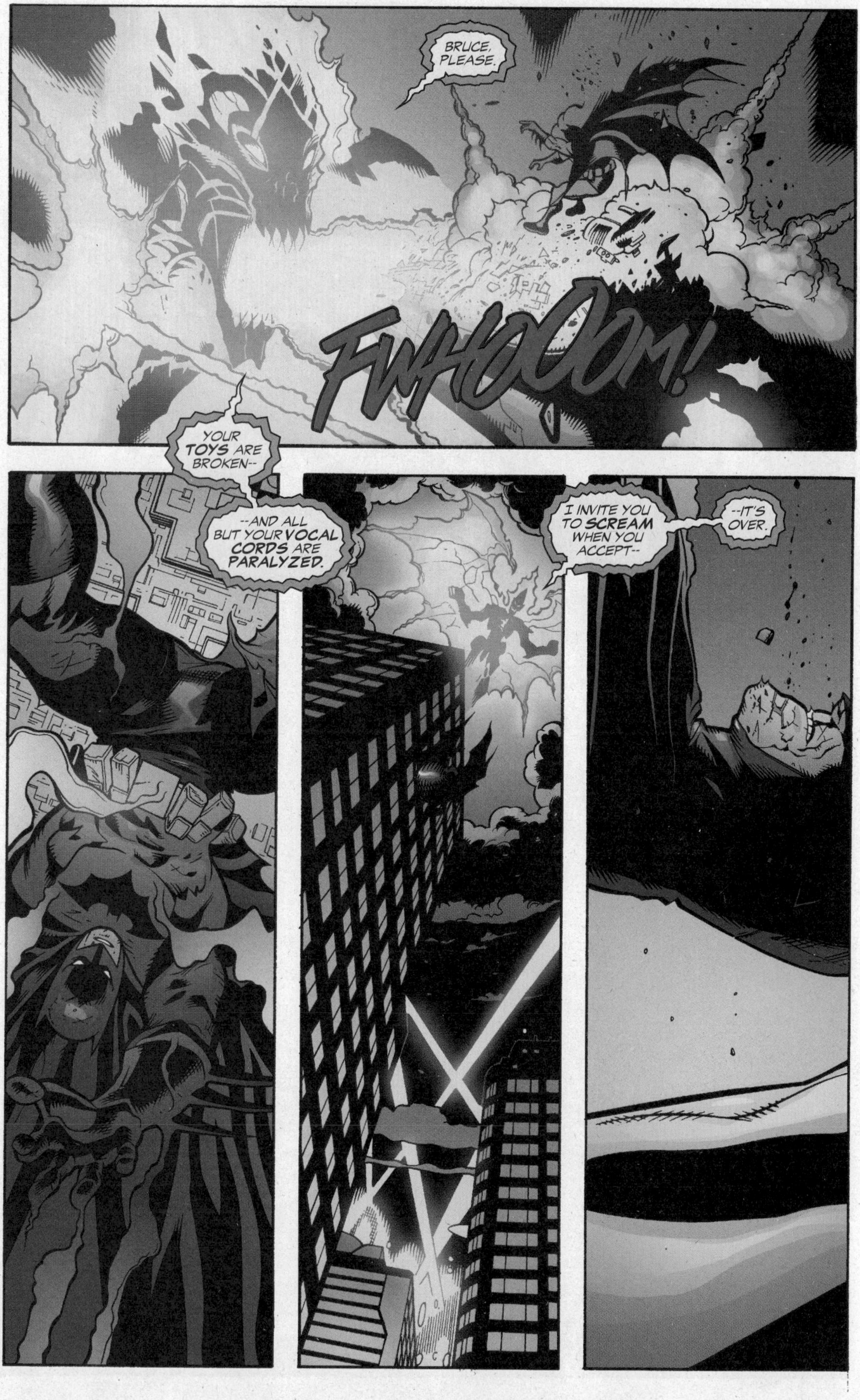

BRUCE, PLEASE.
FWHOOOM!
YOUR TOYS ARE BROKEN--
--AND ALL BUT YOUR VOCAL CORDS ARE PARALYZED.
I INVITE YOU TO SCREAM WHEN YOU ACCEPT--
--IT'S OVER.

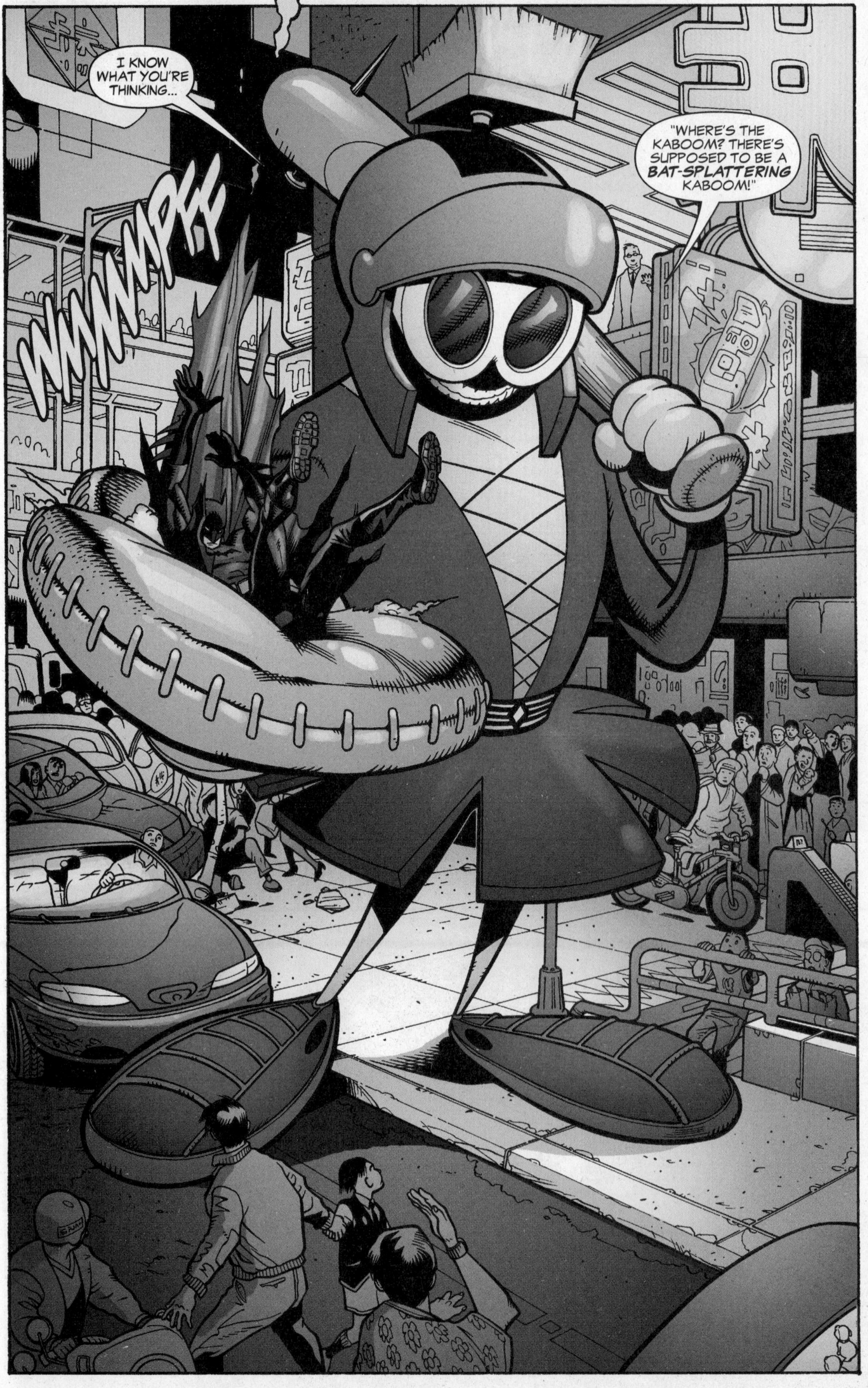
I KNOW WHAT YOU'RE THINKING...
"WHERE'S THE KABOOM? THERE'S SUPPOSED TO BE A **BAT-SPLATTERING** KABOOM!"
WMMPFF

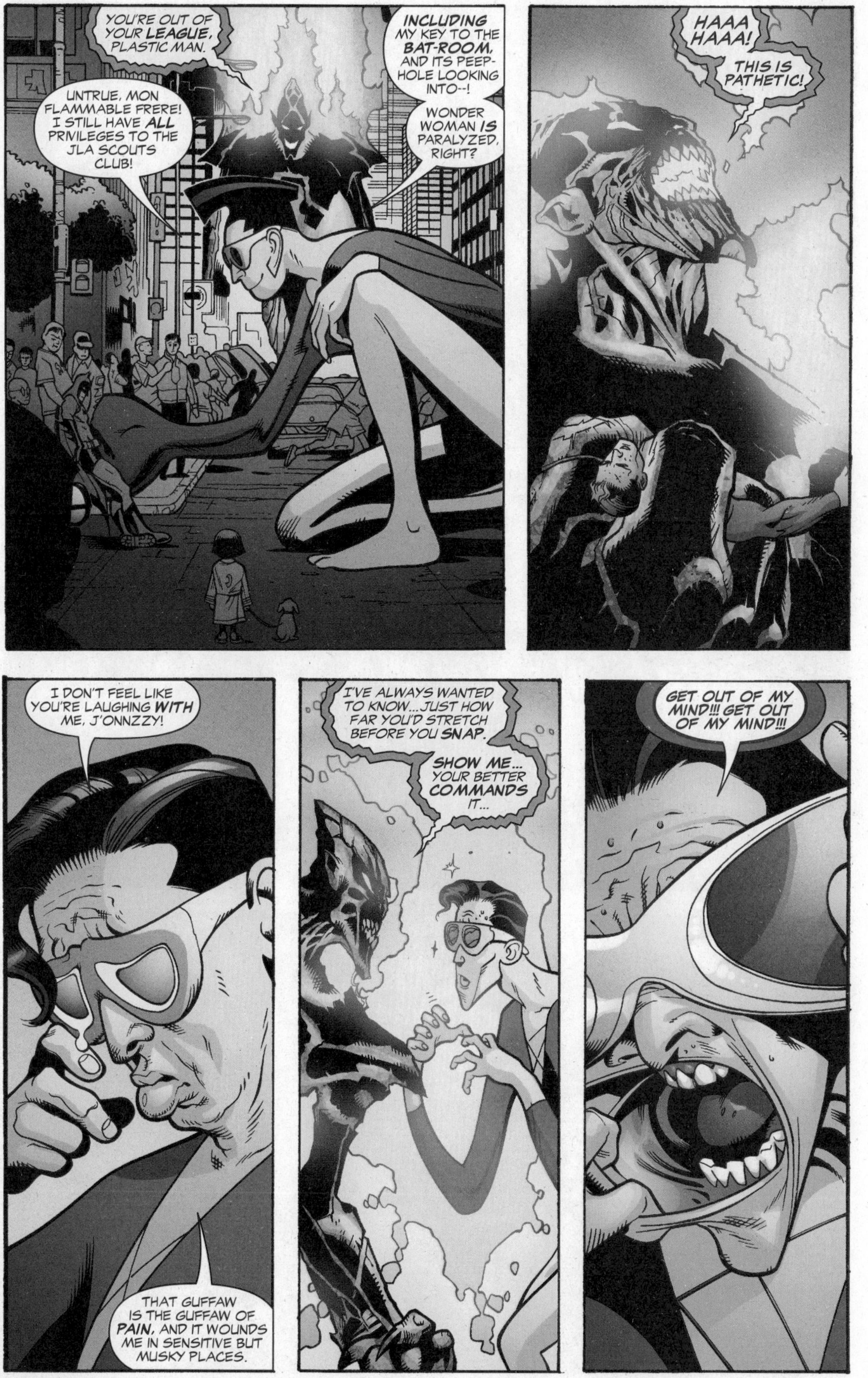
YOU'RE OUT OF YOUR LEAGUE, PLASTIC MAN.
UNTRUE, MON FLAMMABLE FRERE! I STILL HAVE ALL PRIVILEGES TO THE JLA SCOUTS CLUB!
INCLUDING MY KEY TO THE BAT-ROOM, AND ITS PEEP-HOLE LOOKING INTO--!
WONDER WOMAN IS PARALYZED, RIGHT?
HAAA HAAA!
THIS IS PATHETIC!
I DON'T FEEL LIKE YOU'RE LAUGHING WITH ME, J'ONNZZY!
THAT GUFFAW IS THE GUFFAW OF PAIN, AND IT WOUNDS ME IN SENSITIVE BUT MUSKY PLACES.
I'VE ALWAYS WANTED TO KNOW... JUST HOW FAR YOU'D STRETCH BEFORE YOU SNAP.
SHOW ME... YOUR BETTER COMMANDS IT...
GET OUT OF MY MIND!!! GET OUT OF MY MIND!!!

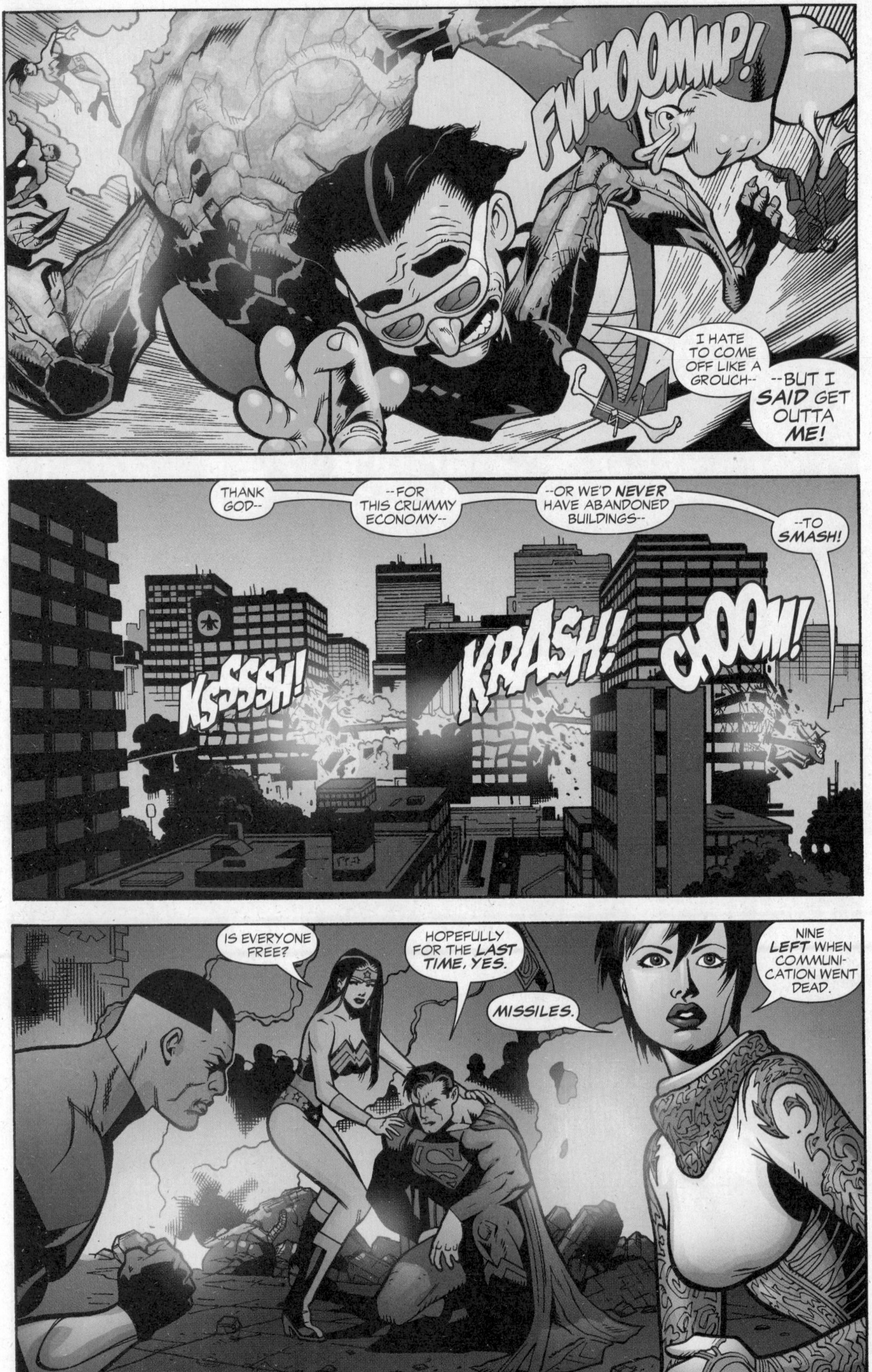
FWHOOMMP!
I HATE TO COME OFF LIKE A GROUCH--
--BUT I SAID GET OUTTA ME!
THANK GOD--
--FOR THIS CRUMMY ECONOMY--
--OR WE'D NEVER HAVE ABANDONED BUILDINGS--
--TO SMASH!
KSSSSH!
KRASH!
CHOOM!
IS EVERYONE FREE?
HOPEFULLY FOR THE LAST TIME, YES.
MISSILES.
NINE LEFT WHEN COMMUNI-CATION WENT DEAD.

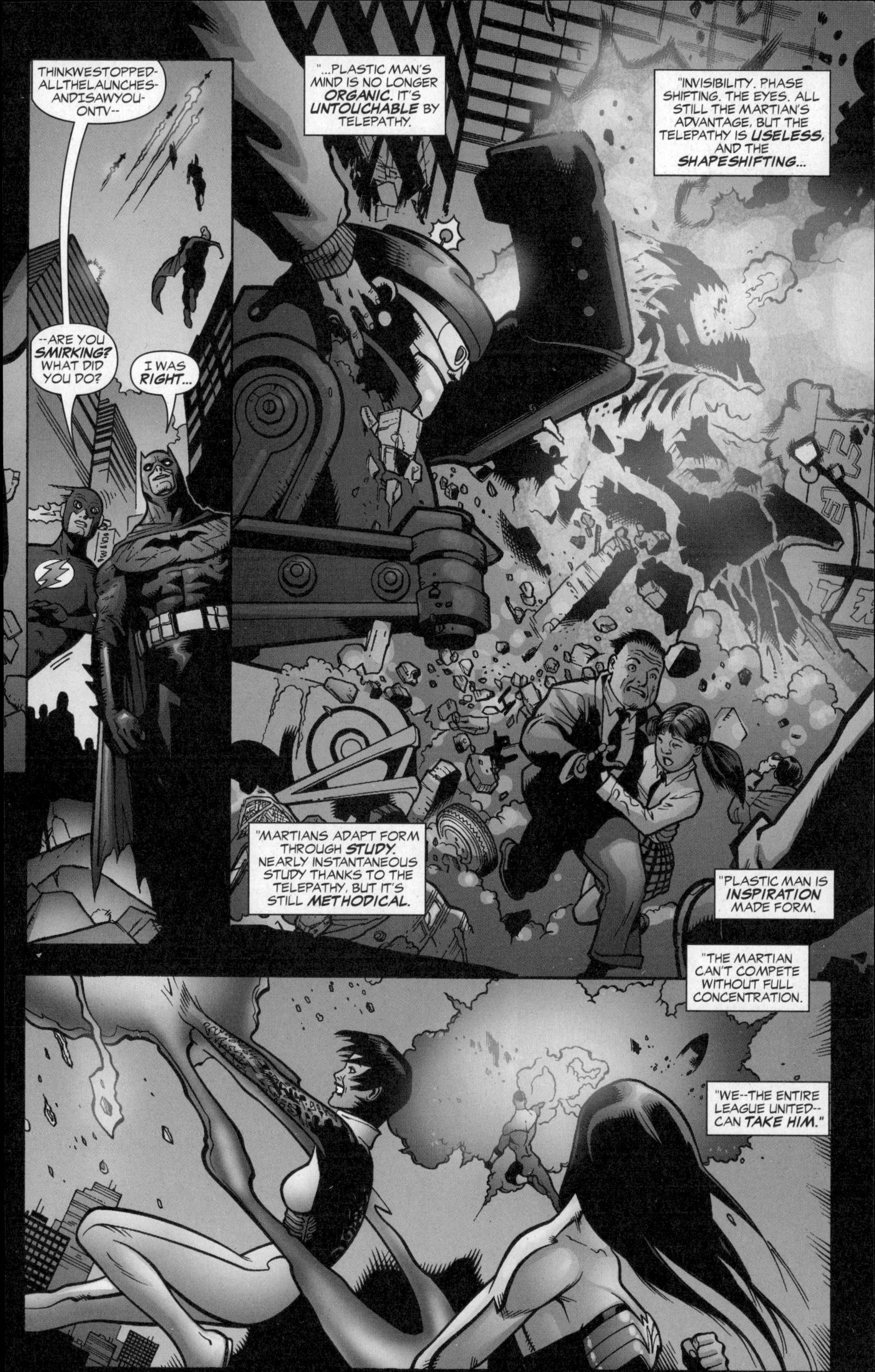
THINKWESTOPPED-ALLTHELAUNCHES-ANDISAWYOU-ONTV--
--ARE YOU SMIRKING? WHAT DID YOU DO?
I WAS RIGHT...
"...PLASTIC MAN'S MIND IS NO LONGER ORGANIC. IT'S UNTOUCHABLE BY TELEPATHY.
"INVISIBILITY. PHASE SHIFTING. THE EYES. ALL STILL THE MARTIAN'S ADVANTAGE, BUT THE TELEPATHY IS USELESS, AND THE SHAPESHIFTING...
"MARTIANS ADAPT FORM THROUGH STUDY. NEARLY INSTANTANEOUS STUDY THANKS TO THE TELEPATHY, BUT IT'S STILL METHODICAL.
"PLASTIC MAN IS INSPIRATION MADE FORM.
"THE MARTIAN CAN'T COMPETE WITHOUT FULL CONCENTRATION.
"WE--THE ENTIRE LEAGUE UNITED--CAN TAKE HIM."

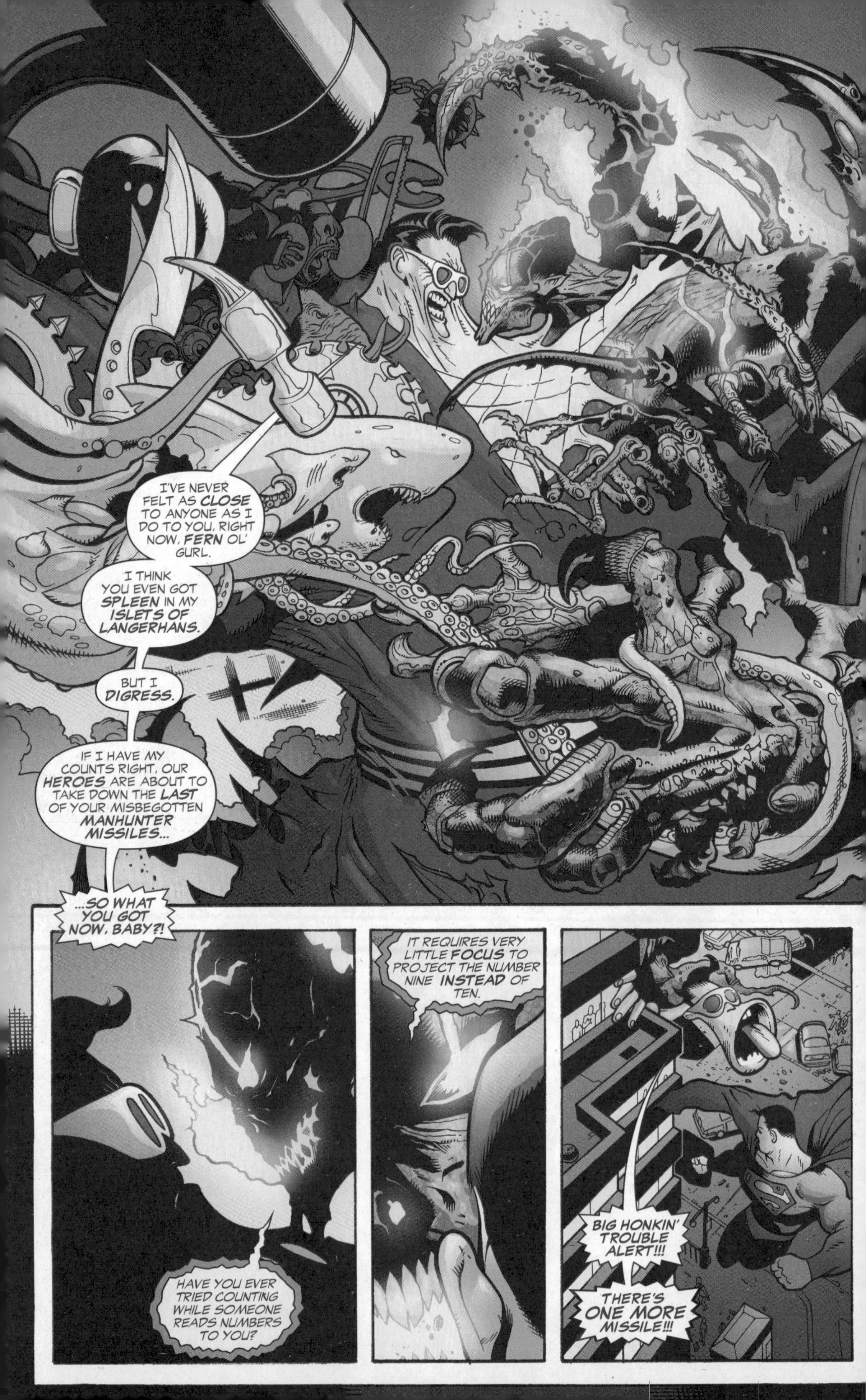
I'VE NEVER FELT AS CLOSE TO ANYONE AS I DO TO YOU, RIGHT NOW, FERN OL' GURL.
I THINK YOU EVEN GOT SPLEEN IN MY ISLETS OF LANGERHANS.
BUT I DIGRESS.
IF I HAVE MY COUNTS RIGHT, OUR HEROES ARE ABOUT TO TAKE DOWN THE LAST OF YOUR MISBEGOTTEN MANHUNTER MISSILES...
...SO WHAT YOU GOT NOW, BABY?!
HAVE YOU EVER TRIED COUNTING WHILE SOMEONE READS NUMBERS TO YOU?
IT REQUIRES VERY LITTLE FOCUS TO PROJECT THE NUMBER NINE INSTEAD OF TEN.
BIG HONKIN' TROUBLE ALERT!!!
THERE'S ONE MORE MISSILE!!!

FSSSSSSSSSSSH

FFSSSSSSHHH

≥NNNGH!≤

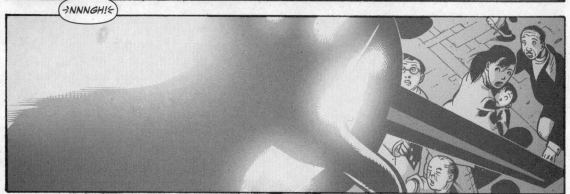

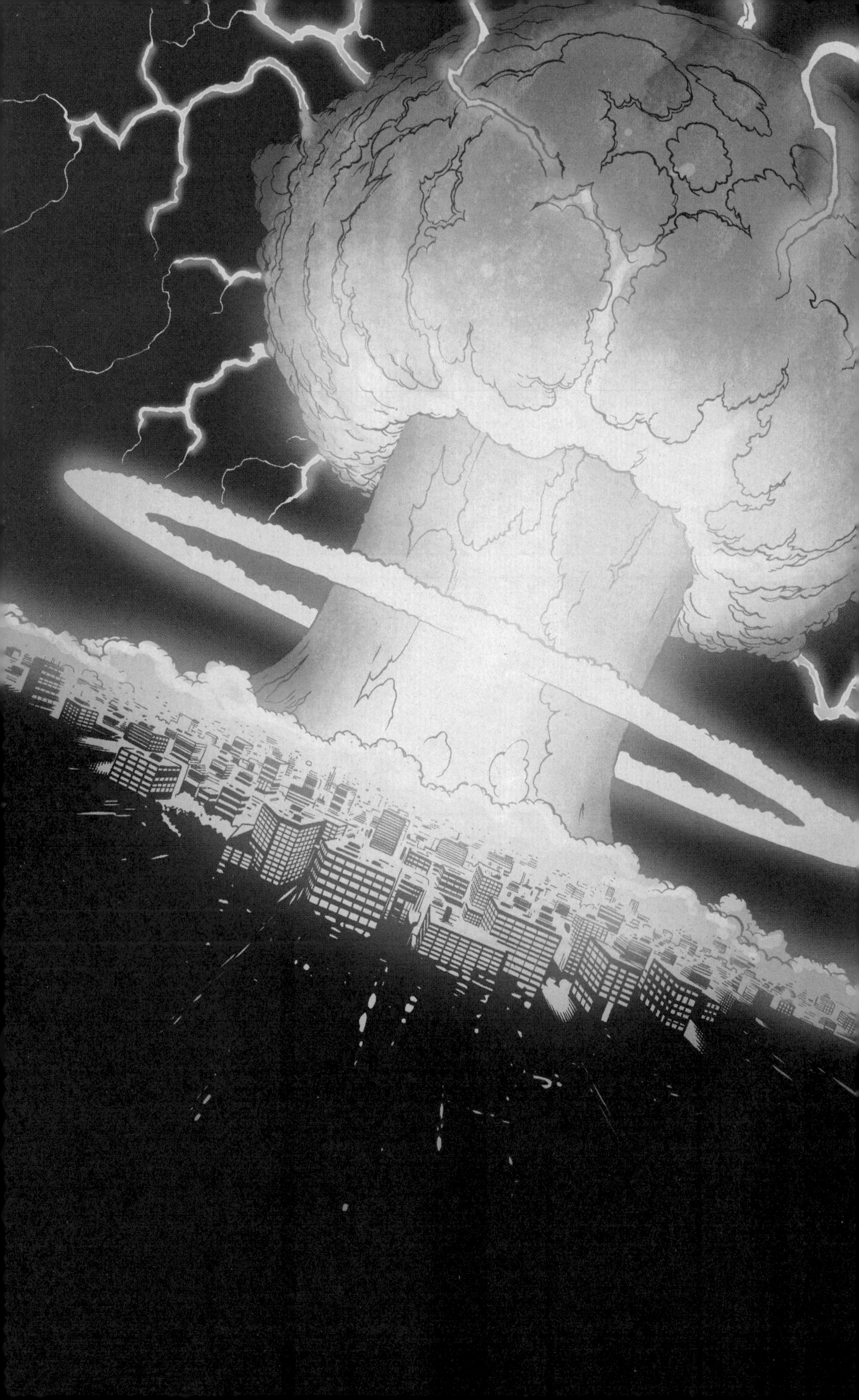

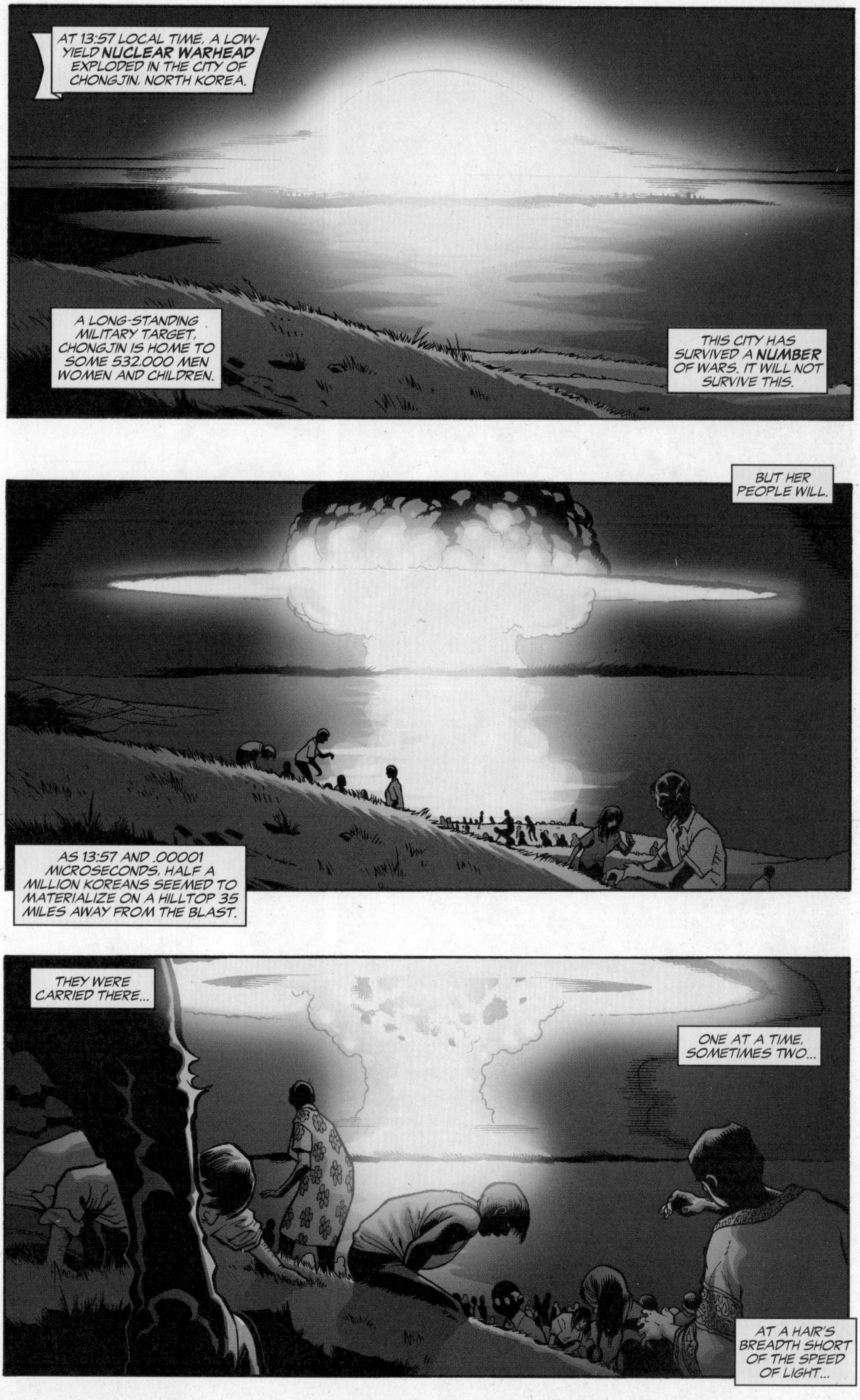
AT 13:57 LOCAL TIME, A LOW-YIELD NUCLEAR WARHEAD EXPLODED IN THE CITY OF CHONGJIN, NORTH KOREA.
A LONG-STANDING MILITARY TARGET, CHONGJIN IS HOME TO SOME 532,000 MEN WOMEN AND CHILDREN.
THIS CITY HAS SURVIVED A NUMBER OF WARS. IT WILL NOT SURVIVE THIS.
BUT HER PEOPLE WILL.
AS 13:57 AND .00001 MICROSECONDS, HALF A MILLION KOREANS SEEMED TO MATERIALIZE ON A HILLTOP 35 MILES AWAY FROM THE BLAST.
THEY WERE CARRIED THERE...
ONE AT A TIME, SOMETIMES TWO...
AT A HAIR'S BREADTH SHORT OF THE SPEED OF LIGHT...

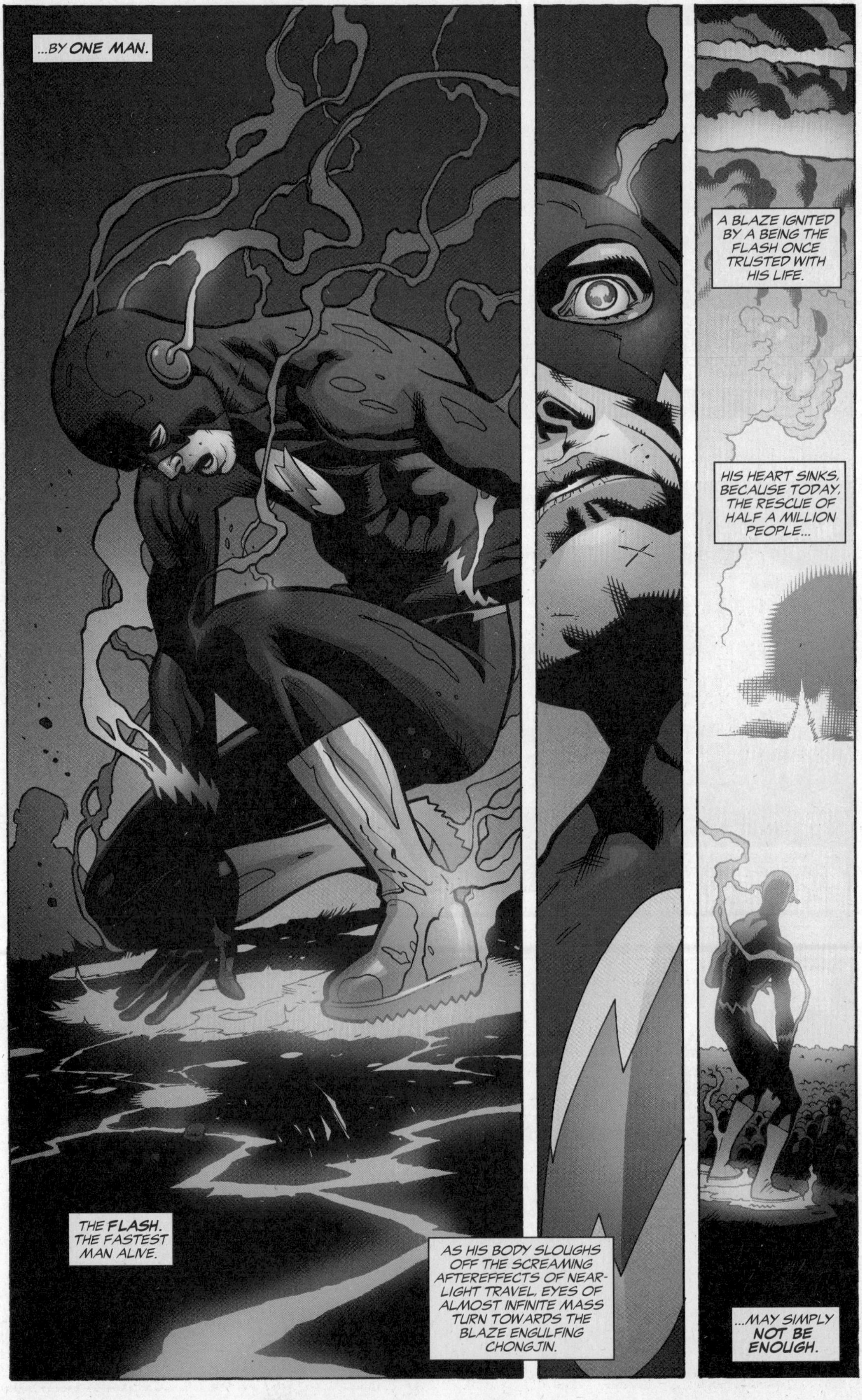
...BY ONE MAN.
THE FLASH. THE FASTEST MAN ALIVE.
AS HIS BODY SLOUGHS OFF THE SCREAMING AFTEREFFECTS OF NEAR-LIGHT TRAVEL, EYES OF ALMOST INFINITE MASS TURN TOWARDS THE BLAZE ENGULFING CHONGJIN.
A BLAZE IGNITED BY A BEING THE FLASH ONCE TRUSTED WITH HIS LIFE.
HIS HEART SINKS, BECAUSE TODAY, THE RESCUE OF HALF A MILLION PEOPLE...
...MAY SIMPLY NOT BE ENOUGH.

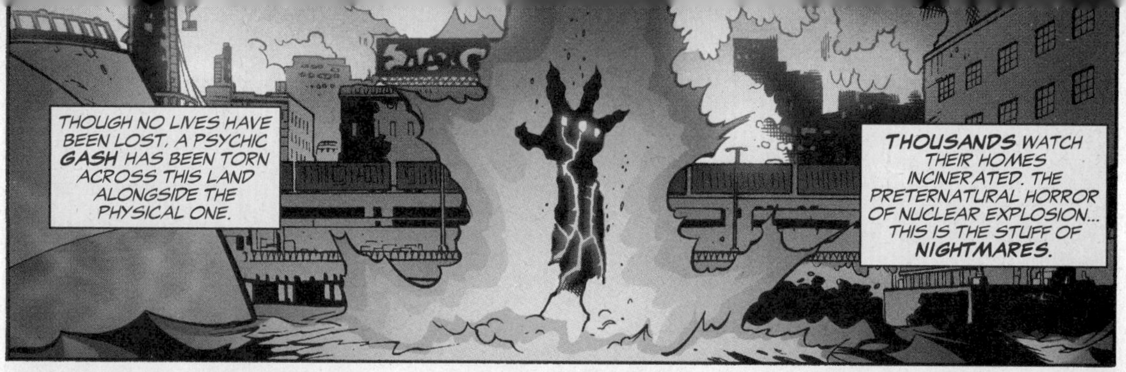
THOUGH NO LIVES HAVE BEEN LOST, A PSYCHIC GASH HAS BEEN TORN ACROSS THIS LAND ALONGSIDE THE PHYSICAL ONE.
THOUSANDS WATCH THEIR HOMES INCINERATED. THE PRETERNATURAL HORROR OF NUCLEAR EXPLOSION... THIS IS THE STUFF OF NIGHTMARES.

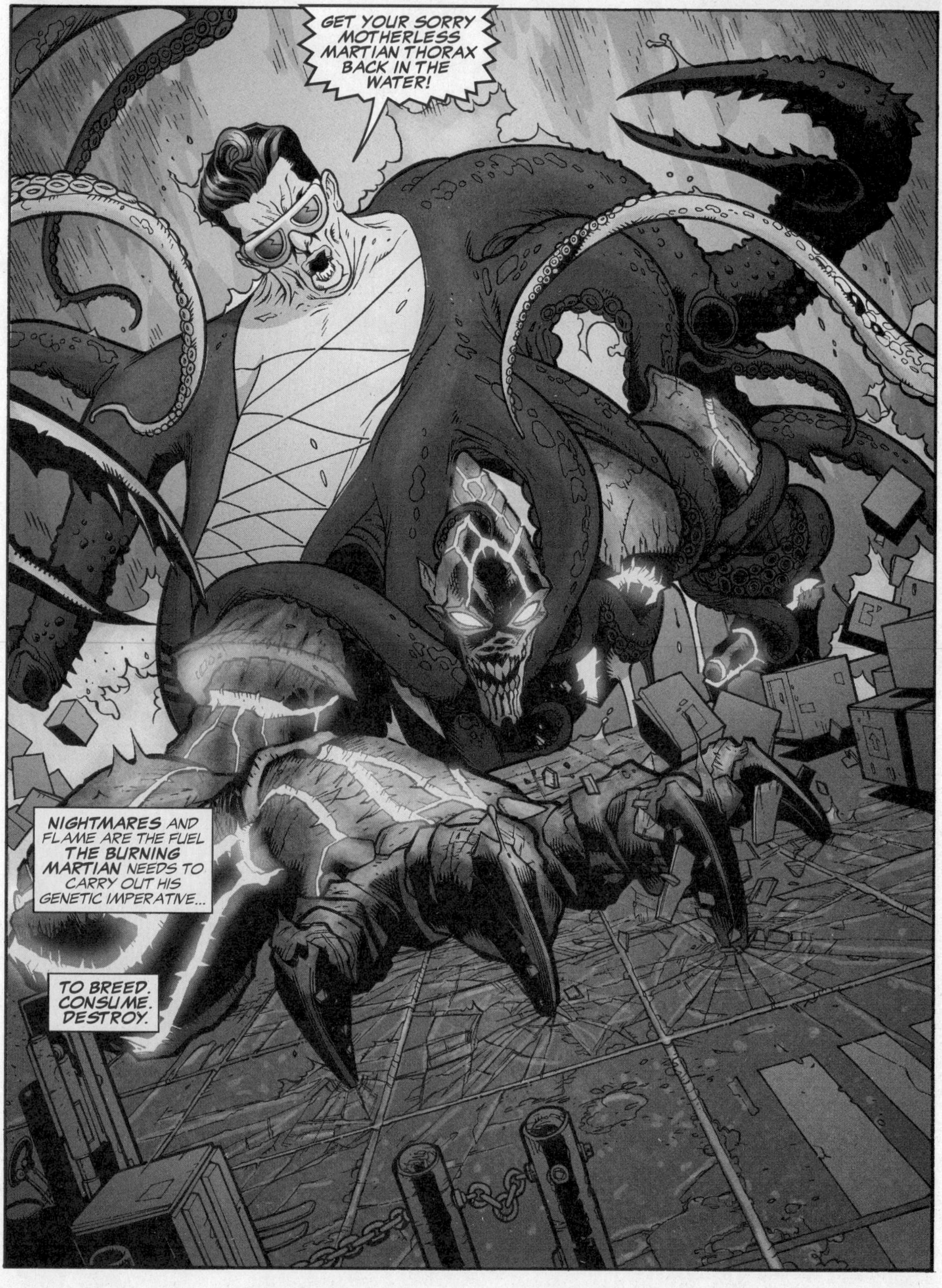
GET YOUR SORRY MOTHERLESS MARTIAN THORAX BACK IN THE WATER!
NIGHTMARES AND FLAME ARE THE FUEL THE BURNING MARTIAN NEEDS TO CARRY OUT HIS GENETIC IMPERATIVE...
TO BREED. CONSUME. DESTROY.

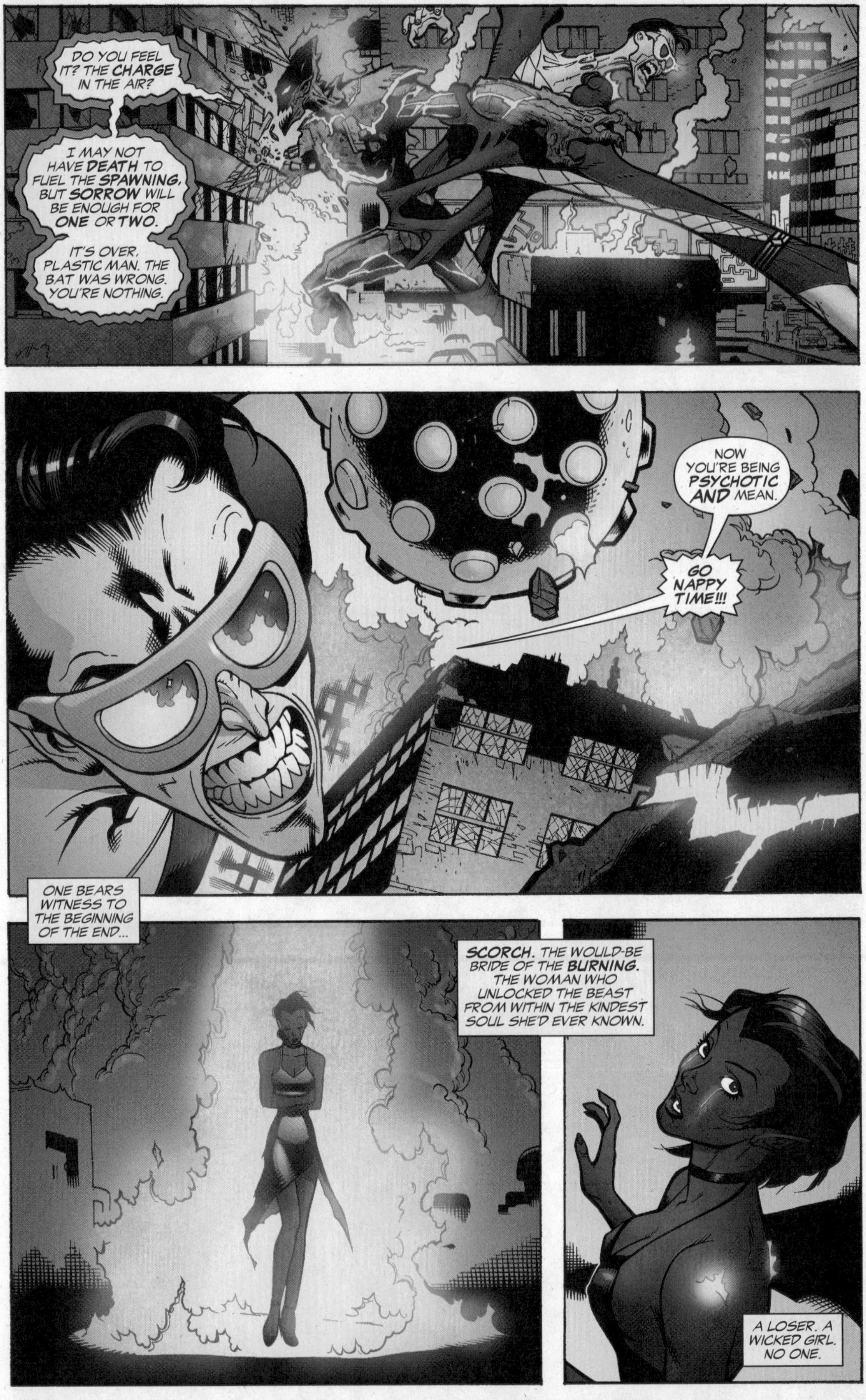
DO YOU FEEL IT? THE CHARGE IN THE AIR?
I MAY NOT HAVE DEATH TO FUEL THE SPAWNING, BUT SORROW WILL BE ENOUGH FOR ONE OR TWO.
IT'S OVER, PLASTIC MAN. THE BAT WAS WRONG. YOU'RE NOTHING.
NOW YOU'RE BEING PSYCHOTIC AND MEAN.
GO NAPPY TIME!!!
ONE BEARS WITNESS TO THE BEGINNING OF THE END...
SCORCH. THE WOULD-BE BRIDE OF THE BURNING. THE WOMAN WHO UNLOCKED THE BEAST FROM WITHIN THE KINDEST SOUL SHE'D EVER KNOWN.
A LOSER. A WICKED GIRL. NO ONE.

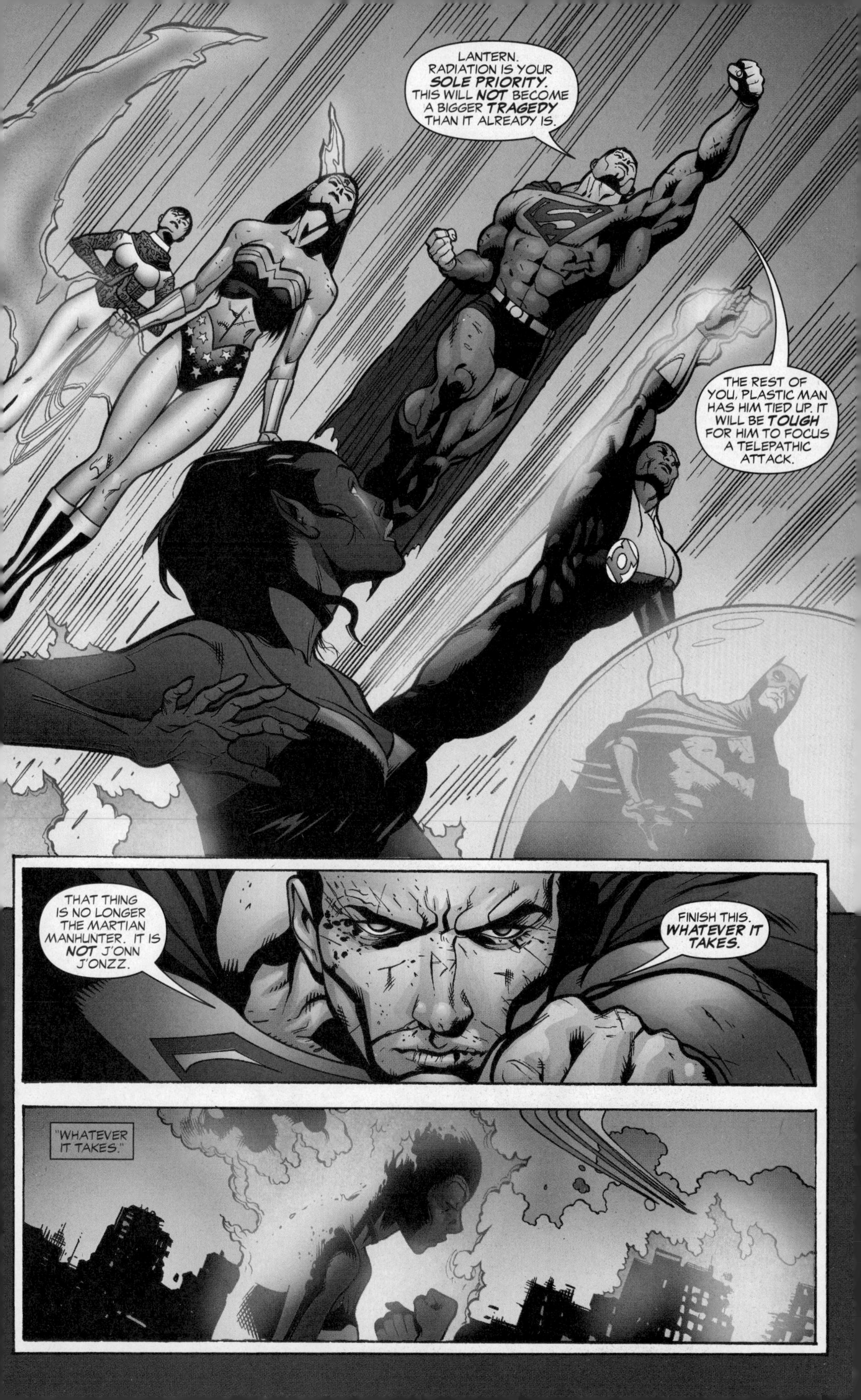
LANTERN. RADIATION IS YOUR SOLE PRIORITY. THIS WILL NOT BECOME A BIGGER TRAGEDY THAN IT ALREADY IS.
THE REST OF YOU, PLASTIC MAN HAS HIM TIED UP. IT WILL BE TOUGH FOR HIM TO FOCUS A TELEPATHIC ATTACK.
THAT THING IS NO LONGER THE MARTIAN MANHUNTER. IT IS NOT J'ONN J'ONZZ.
FINISH THIS. WHATEVER IT TAKES.
"WHATEVER IT TAKES."

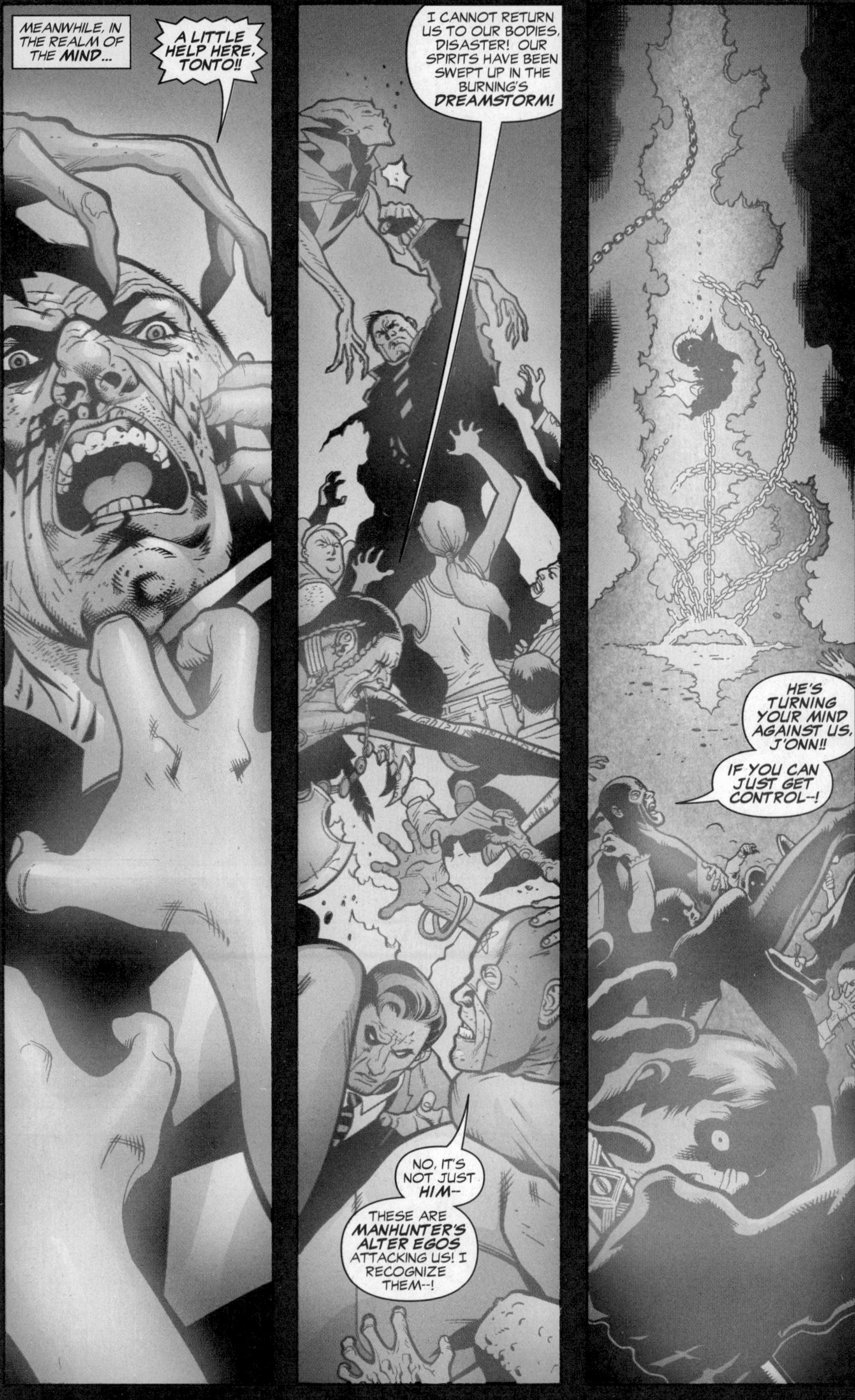

MEANWHILE, IN THE REALM OF THE MIND...
A LITTLE HELP HERE, TONTO!!
I CANNOT RETURN US TO OUR BODIES, DISASTER! OUR SPIRITS HAVE BEEN SWEPT UP IN THE BURNING'S DREAMSTORM!
NO, IT'S NOT JUST HIM--
THESE ARE MANHUNTER'S ALTER EGOS ATTACKING US! I RECOGNIZE THEM--!
HE'S TURNING YOUR MIND AGAINST US, J'ONN!!
IF YOU CAN JUST GET CONTROL--!

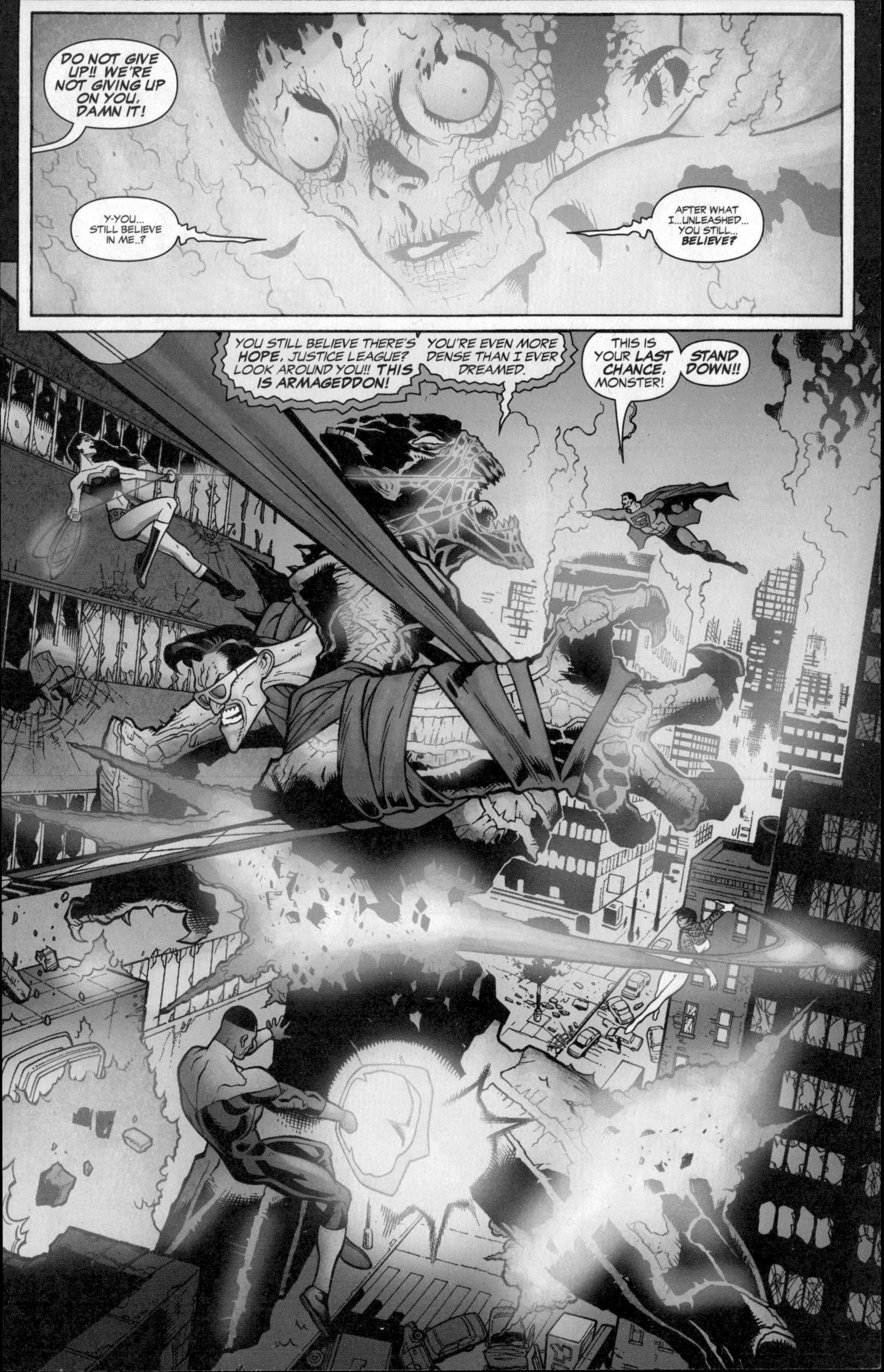
DO NOT GIVE UP!! WE'RE NOT GIVING UP ON YOU, DAMN IT!
Y-YOU... STILL BELIEVE IN ME..?
AFTER WHAT I...UNLEASHED... YOU STILL... BELIEVE?
YOU STILL BELIEVE THERE'S HOPE, JUSTICE LEAGUE? LOOK AROUND YOU!! THIS IS ARMAGEDDON!
YOU'RE EVEN MORE DENSE THAN I EVER DREAMED.
THIS IS YOUR LAST CHANCE, MONSTER!
STAND DOWN!!

CAPITAL IDEA, SUPERMAN.

NOW, IF YOU'RE QUITE THROUGH...

KRAKT!

I'M *DONE*, GANG. MISSILES USED UP MY T.K., I'M PRETTY MUCH DOWN TO THROWING ROCKS.

WHAT DO WE DO NOW?

I...

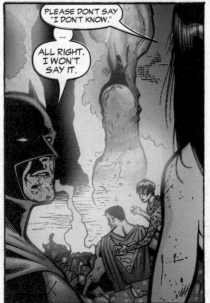

PLEASE DON'T SAY "I DON'T KNOW."

... ALL RIGHT, I WON'T SAY IT.

HRRAAAAAAGH!!

H-HEY, YOU GUYS?

W-WANNA SEE SOMETHING COOL?

FFFFSH!

WHERE IS MY FIRE?!?!

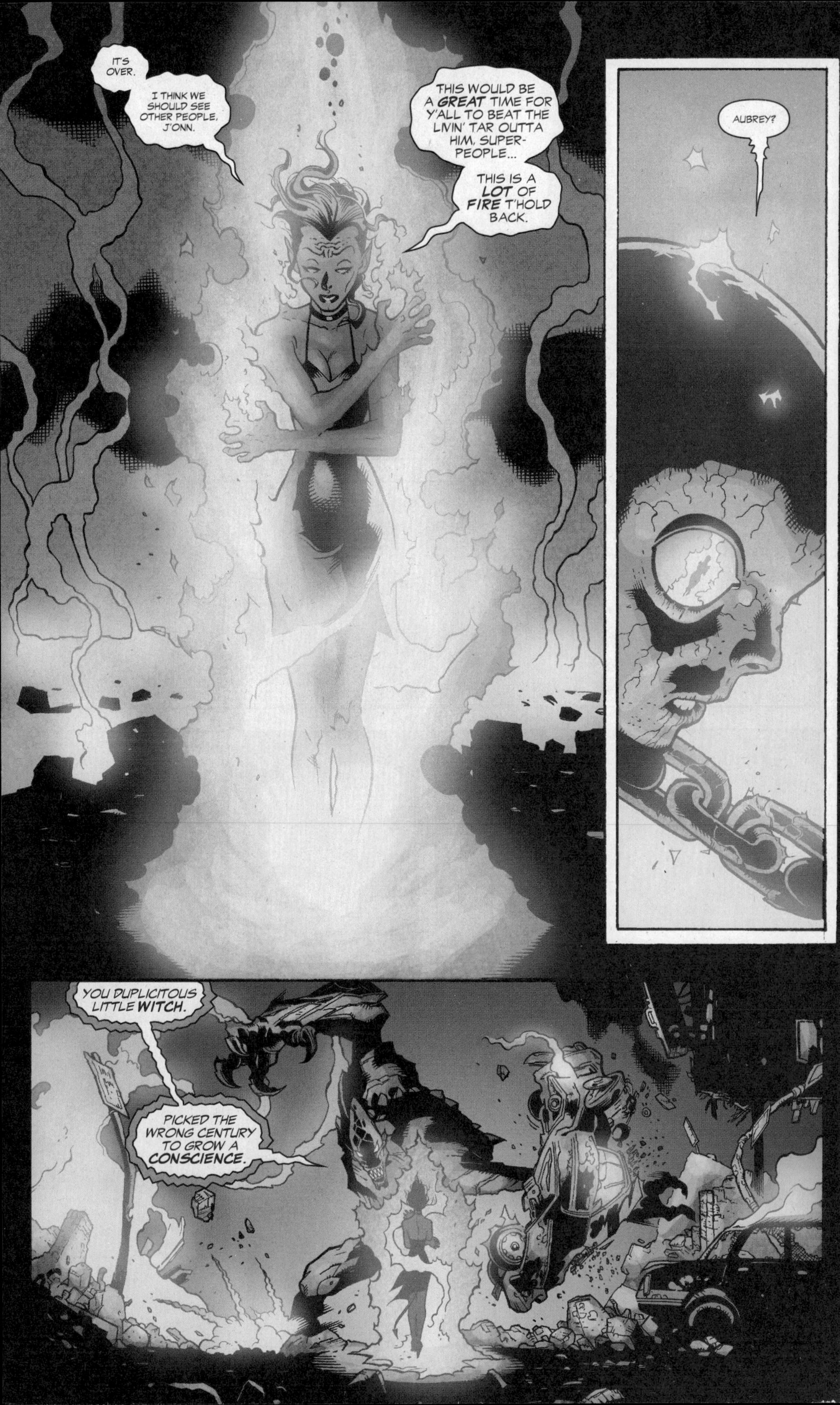
IT'S OVER.
I THINK WE SHOULD SEE OTHER PEOPLE, J'ONN.
THIS WOULD BE A GREAT TIME FOR Y'ALL TO BEAT THE LIVIN' TAR OUTTA HIM, SUPER-PEOPLE...
THIS IS A LOT OF FIRE T'HOLD BACK.
AUBREY?
YOU DUPLICITOUS LITTLE WITCH.
PICKED THE WRONG CENTURY TO GROW A CONSCIENCE.

LEAVE NOTHING STANDING, PEOPLE!

THE HALF-GHOSTS--THEY WEAKEN!

HE'S DOING IT...

YOU'RE DOING IT!! TAKE CONTROL, J'ONN!

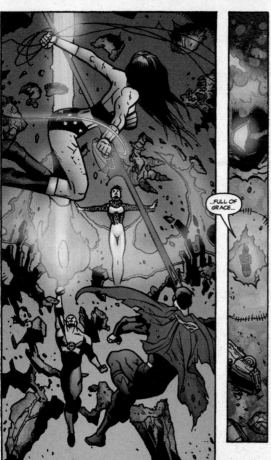

...FULL OF GRACE...

...THE LORD IS WITH THEE, BLESSED ART THOU...

HSSSSSSSSSSSSK

FORGIVE ME.

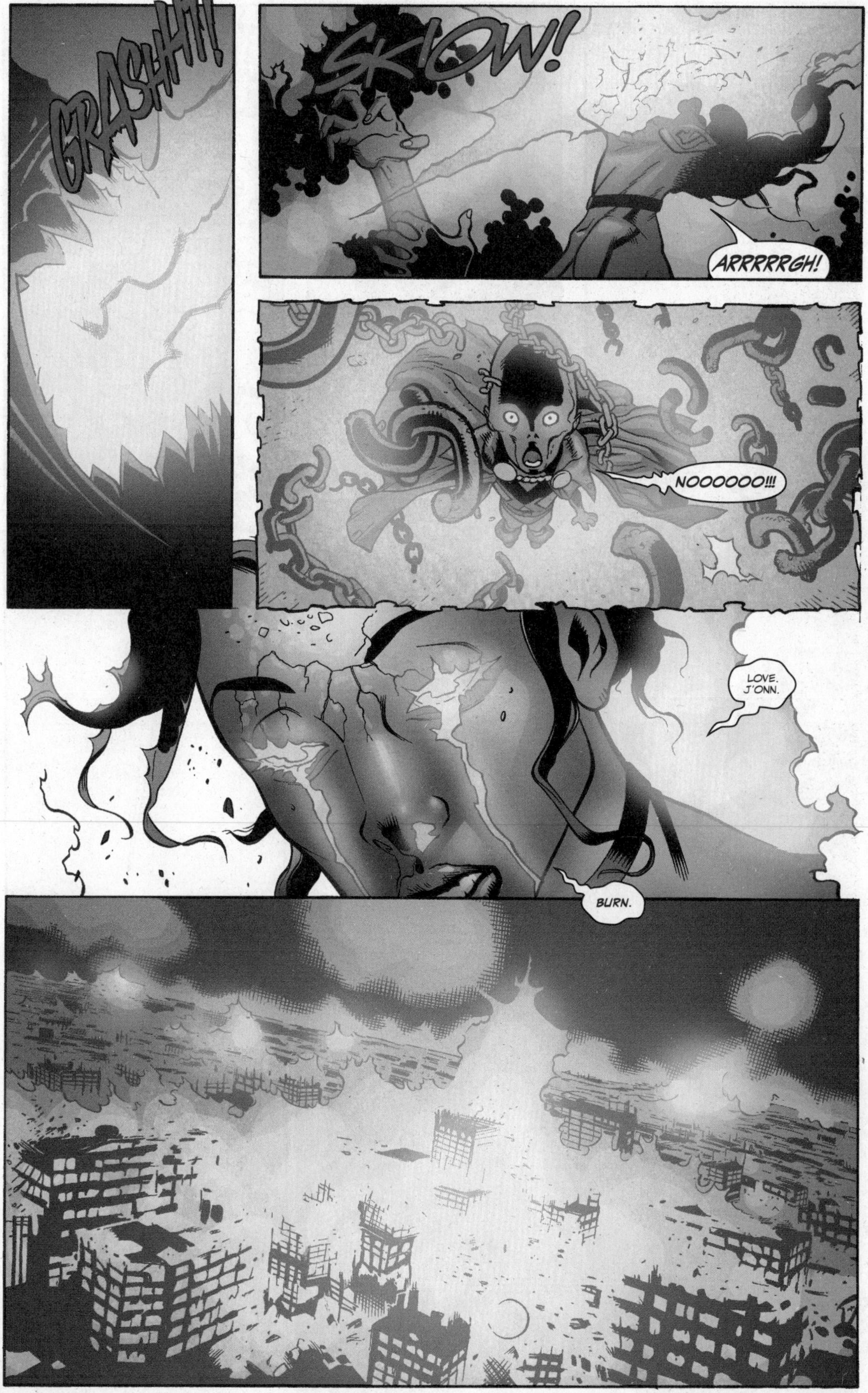
CRASHHT!
SKIOW!
ARRRRRGH!
NOOOOOO!!!
LOVE. J'ONN.
BURN.

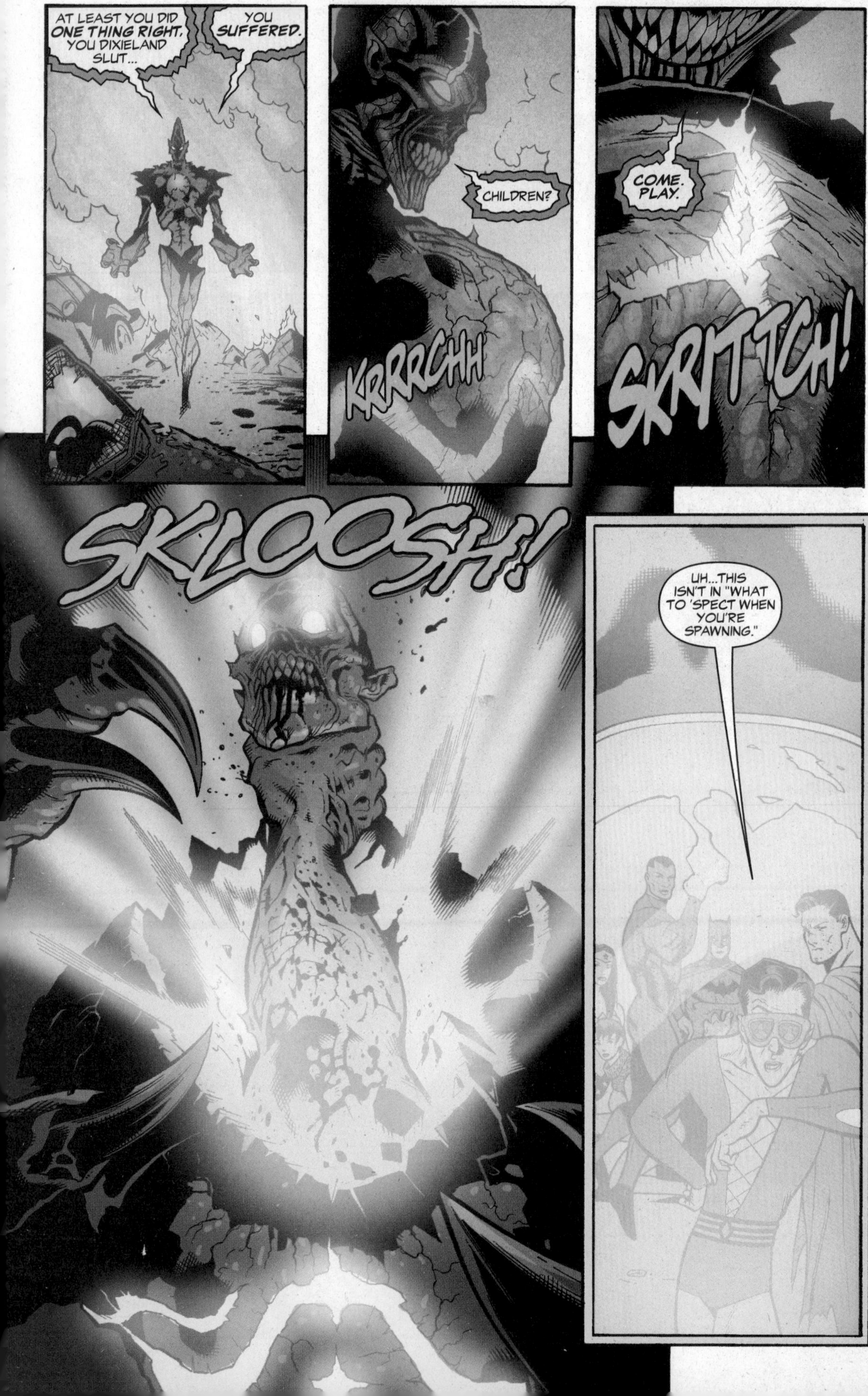
AT LEAST YOU DID ONE THING RIGHT, YOU DIXIELAND SLUT...
YOU SUFFERED.
CHILDREN?
KRRRCHH
COME. PLAY.
SKRITTCH!
SKLOOSH!
UH...THIS ISN'T IN "WHAT TO 'SPECT WHEN YOU'RE SPAWNING."

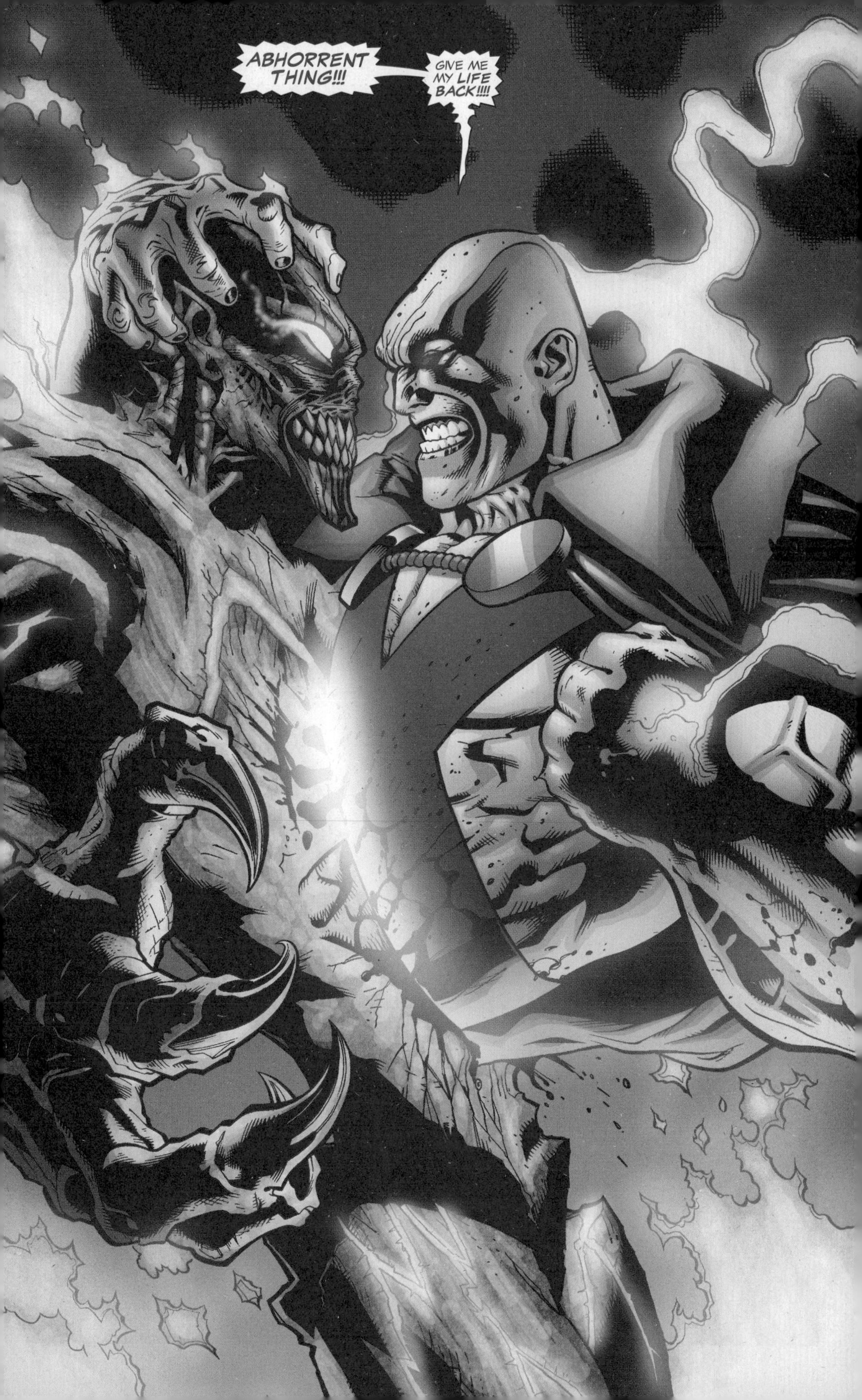
ABHORRENT THING!!!
GIVE ME MY LIFE BACK!!!!

THE PSYCHIC REALM IS ONCE AGAIN *MY OWN.* THANK YOU...FOR BELIEVING.

NOW, *GO...* SOMETHING *TERRIBLE* HAS HAPPENED.

WHAT HAPPENED!? WHERE?!

I TAKE IT ALL BACK. I WANT PERMANENT *MONITOR* DUTY.

WE RETURN TO THE EARTH. PREPARE.

GOOD LORD. I'D JUST WRAPPED THE *RADIATION* WHEN THE *FLAMES* WENT OUT...I *ALMOST* THOUGHT WE'D *WON.*

GIVE ME GOOD NEWS, FAITH. *PLEASE.*

I--

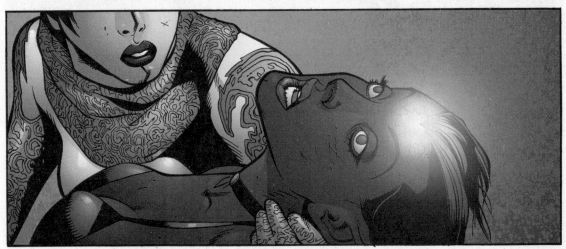

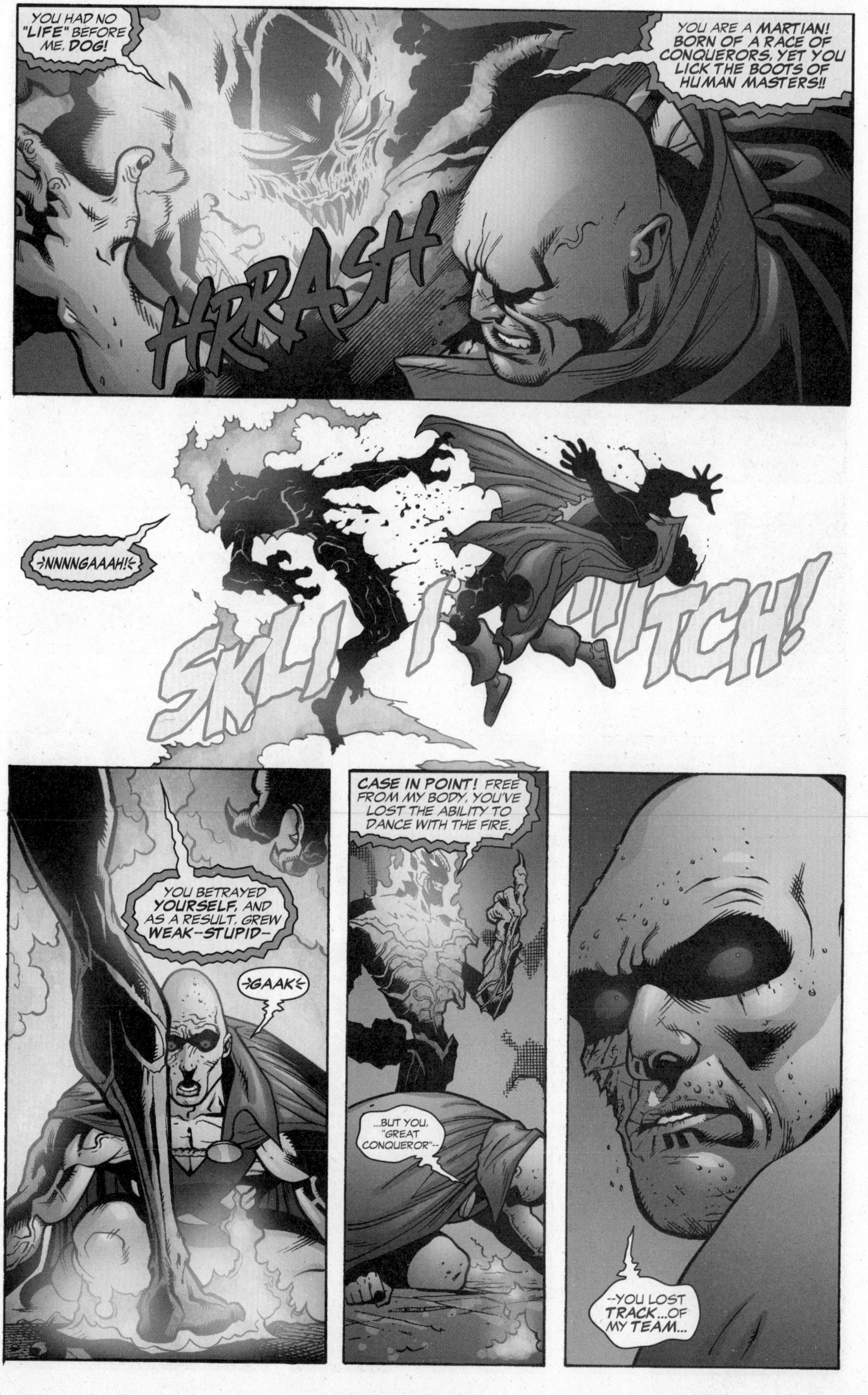

YOU HAD NO "LIFE" BEFORE ME, DOG!
YOU ARE A MARTIAN! BORN OF A RACE OF CONQUERORS, YET YOU LICK THE BOOTS OF HUMAN MASTERS!!
HRRASH
NNNNGAAAH!
YOU BETRAYED YOURSELF, AND AS A RESULT, GREW WEAK--STUPID--
GAAK
CASE IN POINT! FREE FROM MY BODY, YOU'VE LOST THE ABILITY TO DANCE WITH THE FIRE.
...BUT YOU, "GREAT CONQUEROR"--
--YOU LOST TRACK...OF MY TEAM...

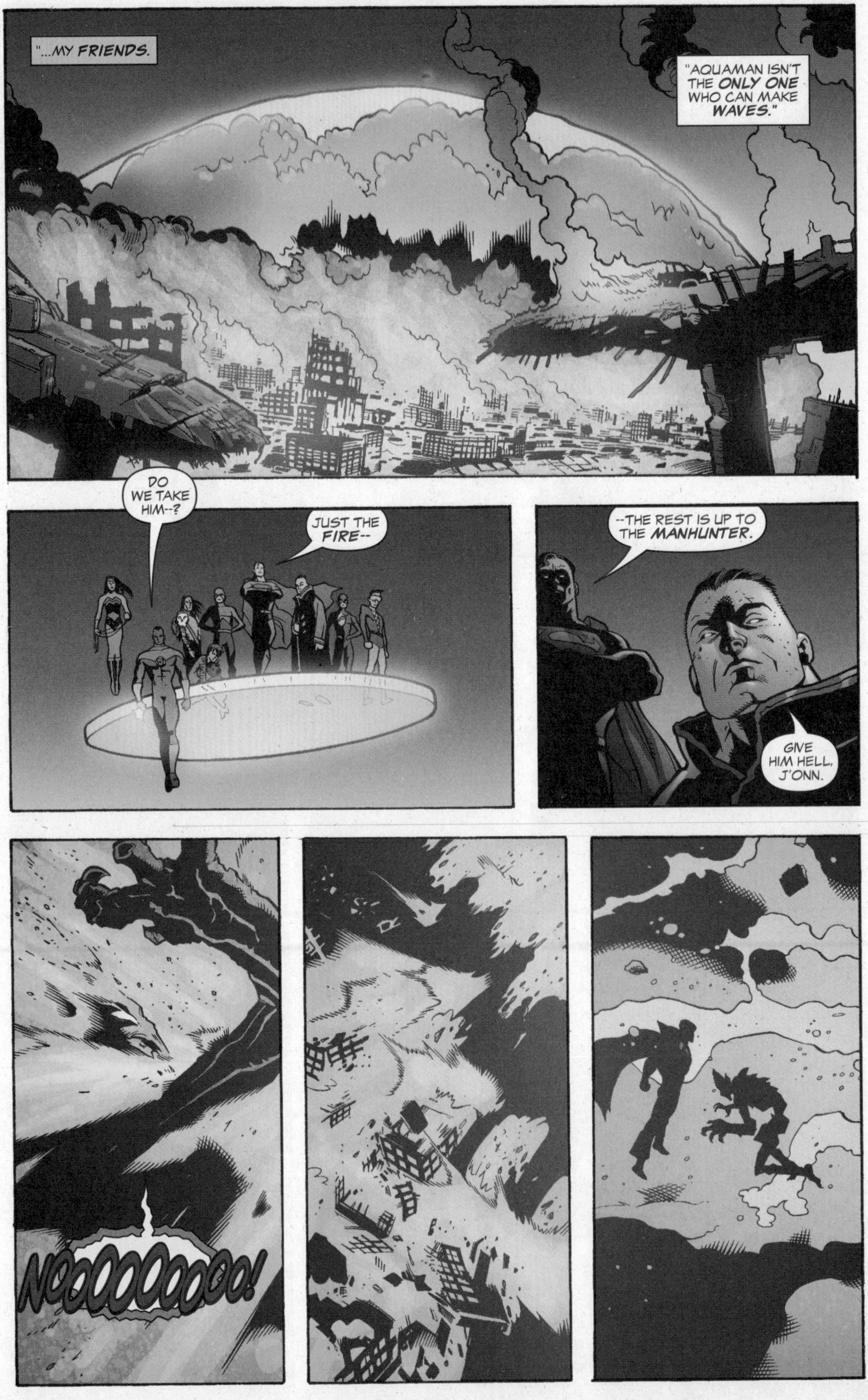
"...MY FRIENDS.
"AQUAMAN ISN'T THE ONLY ONE WHO CAN MAKE WAVES."
DO WE TAKE HIM--?
JUST THE FIRE--
--THE REST IS UP TO THE MANHUNTER.
GIVE HIM HELL, J'ONN.
NOOOOOOOOOO!

KEEP THAT **RIGHTEOUS STENCH** IN YOUR OWN MIND, J'ONZZ.

WHATEVER I AM COMES FROM **YOU**. YOU **MADE** ME!

I KNOW, FERNUS...

AND SO SHALL I **UNMAKE** YOU.

YOU CANNOT UNMAKE WHAT YOU ARE. I AM YOUR EVERY ANGER AND FOUL THOUGHT MADE **FLESH**!

AS YOU **LIVE**-- SO SHALL I, AND ONE DAY--

--I WILL BREED.

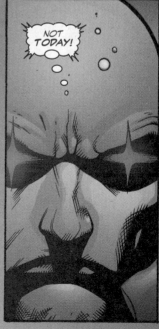

NOT TODAY!

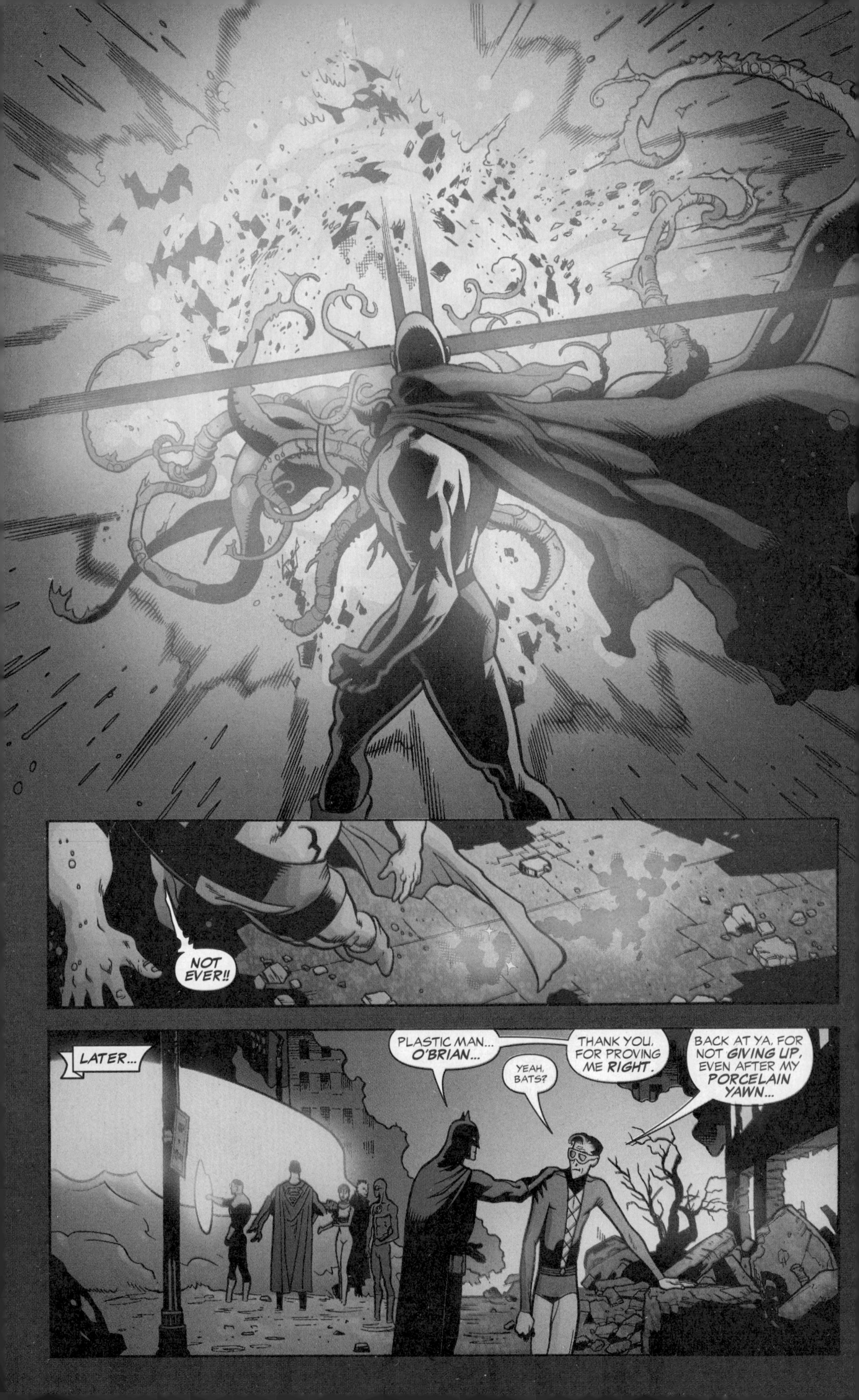
NOT EVER!!
LATER...
PLASTIC MAN... O'BRIAN...
YEAH, BATS?
THANK YOU, FOR PROVING ME RIGHT.
BACK AT YA, FOR NOT GIVING UP, EVEN AFTER MY PORCELAIN YAWN...

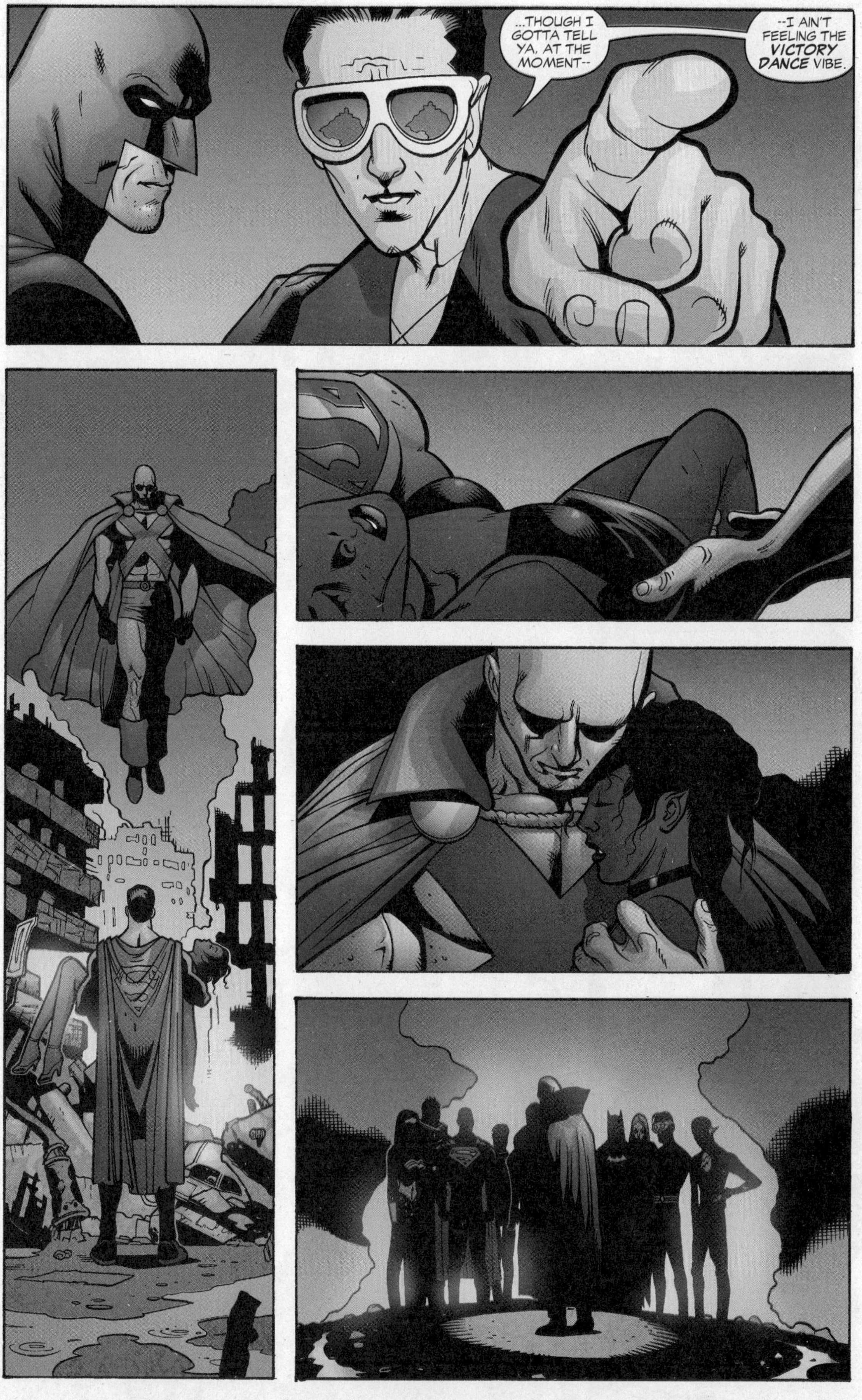
...THOUGH I GOTTA TELL YA, AT THE MOMENT--
--I AIN'T FEELING THE VICTORY DANCE VIBE.

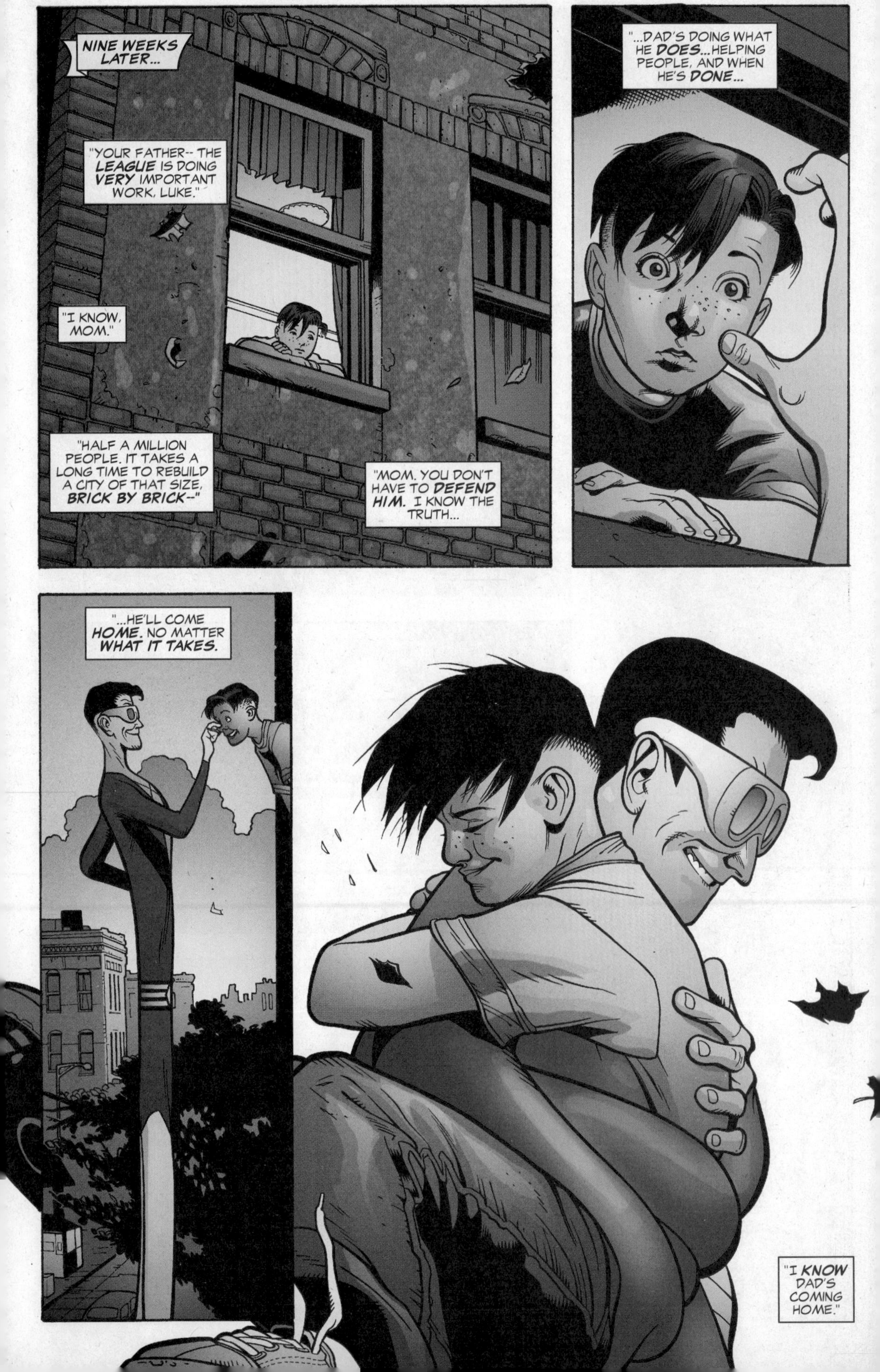
NINE WEEKS LATER...
"YOUR FATHER-- THE LEAGUE IS DOING VERY IMPORTANT WORK, LUKE."
"I KNOW, MOM."
"HALF A MILLION PEOPLE. IT TAKES A LONG TIME TO REBUILD A CITY OF THAT SIZE, BRICK BY BRICK--"
"MOM. YOU DON'T HAVE TO DEFEND HIM. I KNOW THE TRUTH...
"...DAD'S DOING WHAT HE DOES...HELPING PEOPLE, AND WHEN HE'S DONE...
"...HE'LL COME HOME. NO MATTER WHAT IT TAKES.
"I KNOW DAD'S COMING HOME."

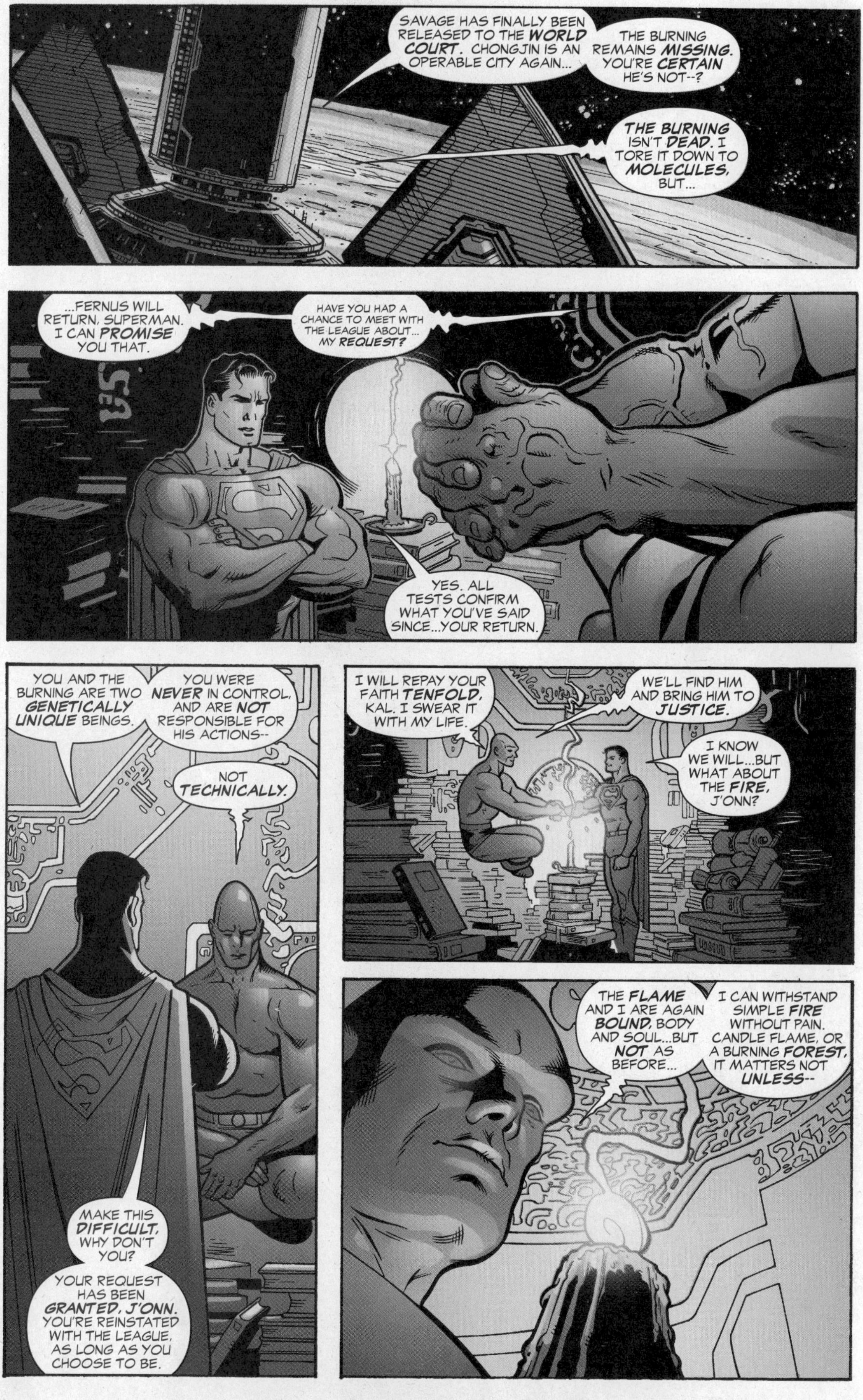
SAVAGE HAS FINALLY BEEN RELEASED TO THE WORLD COURT. CHONGJIN IS AN OPERABLE CITY AGAIN...
THE BURNING REMAINS MISSING. YOU'RE CERTAIN HE'S NOT--?
THE BURNING ISN'T DEAD. I TORE IT DOWN TO MOLECULES, BUT...
...FERNUS WILL RETURN, SUPERMAN. I CAN PROMISE YOU THAT.
HAVE YOU HAD A CHANCE TO MEET WITH THE LEAGUE ABOUT... MY REQUEST?
YES. ALL TESTS CONFIRM WHAT YOU'VE SAID SINCE...YOUR RETURN.
YOU AND THE BURNING ARE TWO GENETICALLY UNIQUE BEINGS.
YOU WERE NEVER IN CONTROL, AND ARE NOT RESPONSIBLE FOR HIS ACTIONS--
NOT TECHNICALLY.
MAKE THIS DIFFICULT, WHY DON'T YOU?
YOUR REQUEST HAS BEEN GRANTED, J'ONN. YOU'RE REINSTATED WITH THE LEAGUE, AS LONG AS YOU CHOOSE TO BE.
I WILL REPAY YOUR FAITH TENFOLD, KAL. I SWEAR IT WITH MY LIFE.
WE'LL FIND HIM AND BRING HIM TO JUSTICE.
I KNOW WE WILL...BUT WHAT ABOUT THE FIRE, J'ONN?
THE FLAME AND I ARE AGAIN BOUND, BODY AND SOUL...BUT NOT AS BEFORE...
I CAN WITHSTAND SIMPLE FIRE WITHOUT PAIN. CANDLE FLAME, OR A BURNING FOREST, IT MATTERS NOT UNLESS--

-- THEY ARE FLAMES OF *PSYCHIC SIGNIFICANCE.* FLAMES OF *SUFFERING,* AS THE BURNING CREATED...FLAMES OF *PASSION,* AS AN *ARSONIST* MIGHT CREATE...

PFFFT

FLAMES OF *LOVE.* THOSE... THOSE MOST OF ALL. I CANNOT BEAR.

FINALLY GOT MY *CLEAN BILL* FROM *BATMAN.* I CAN GO BACK TO BEING *FIRESTORM.*

J'ONN TOLD US THAT WHAT YOU SAW DURING YOUR ATTACK WAS A MERELY A MALICIOUS *ILLUSION* TO AMUSE THE BURNING, BUT YOU KNOW *BATMAN...*

THOROUGH. MANHUNTER GONNA BE OKAY?

I THINK SO...

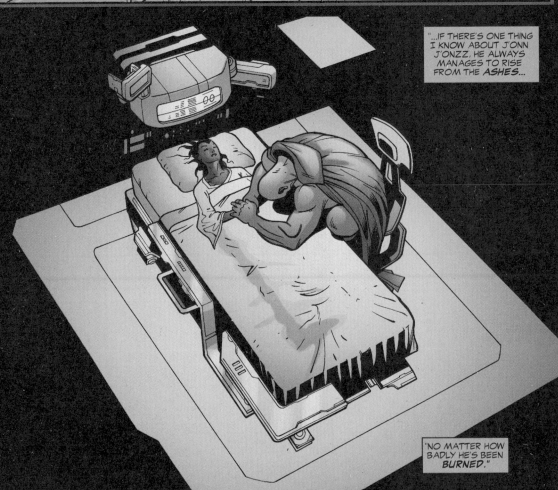

"...IF THERE'S ONE THING I KNOW ABOUT J'ONN J'ONZZ, HE ALWAYS MANAGES TO RISE FROM THE *ASHES...*

"NO MATTER HOW BADLY HE'S BEEN *BURNED.*"

THE END

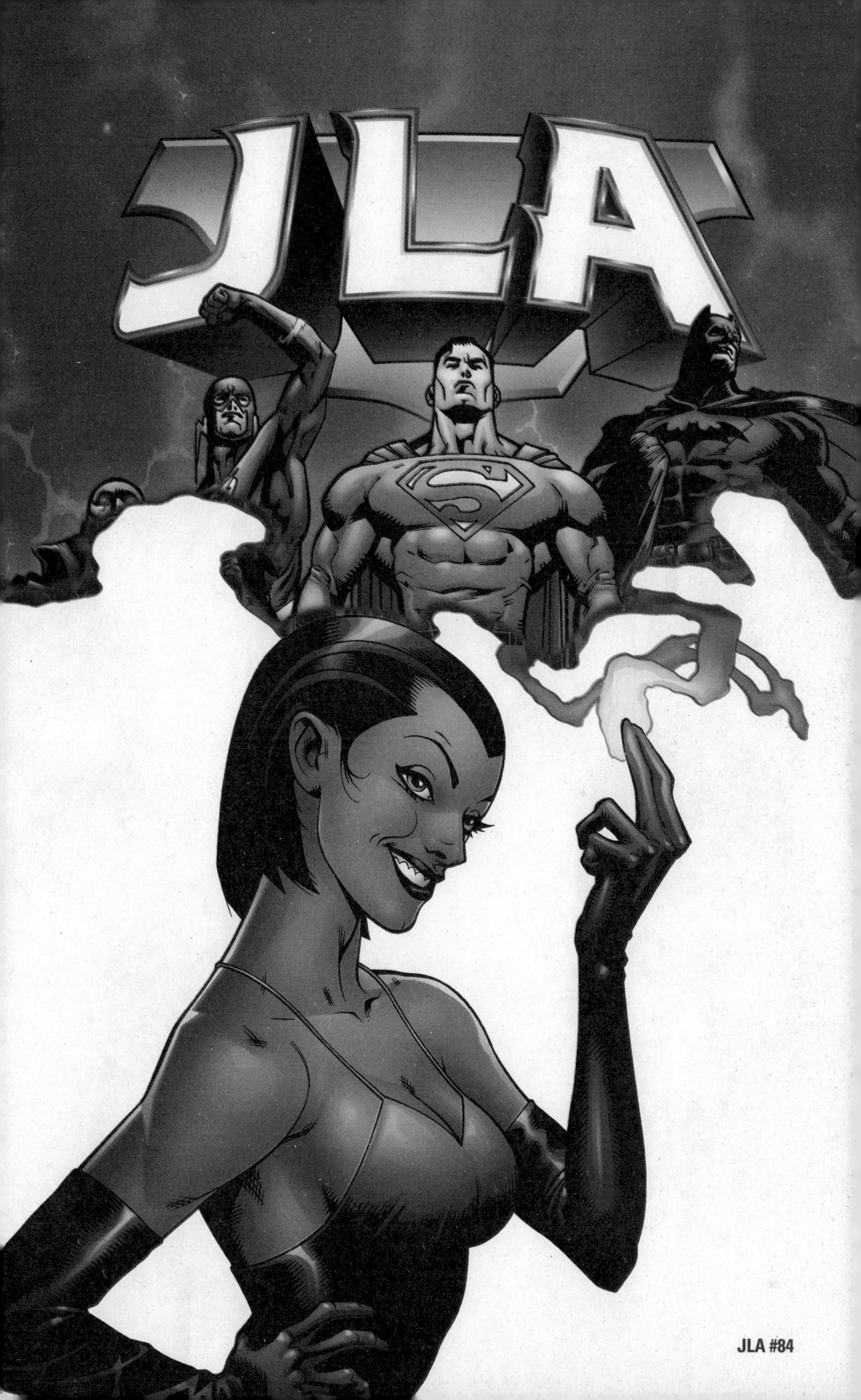
JLA

JLA #84

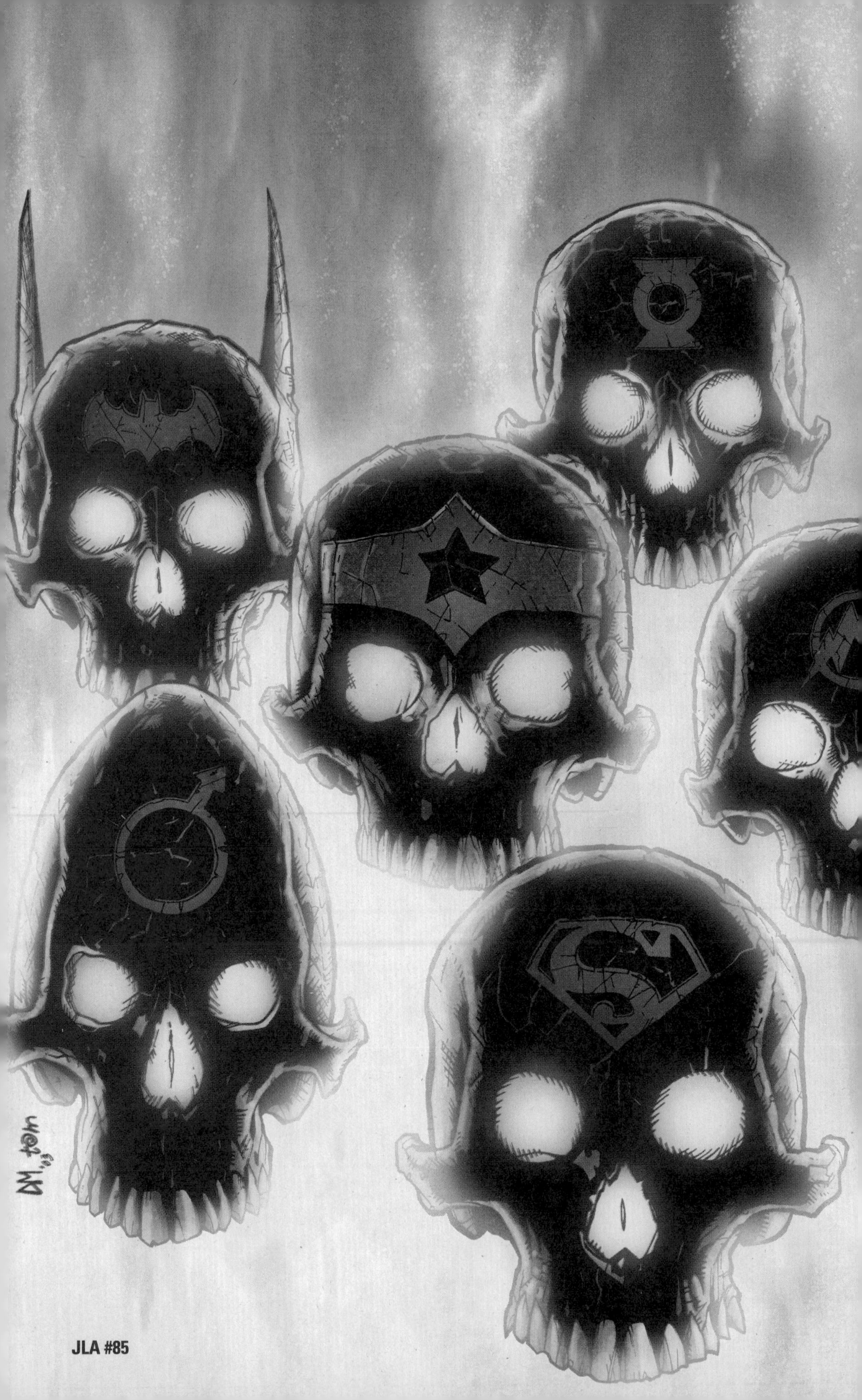

JLA #85

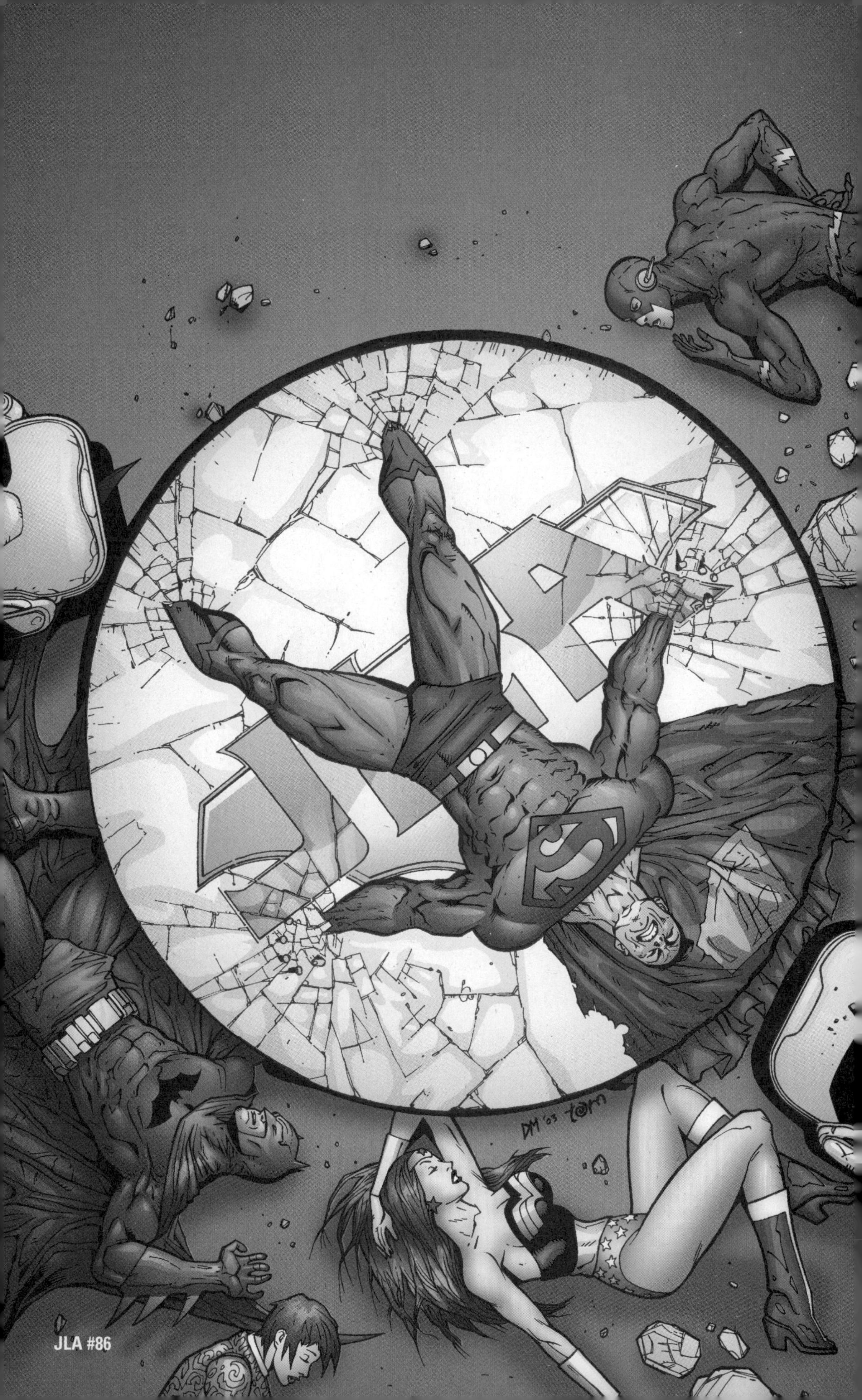

JLA #86

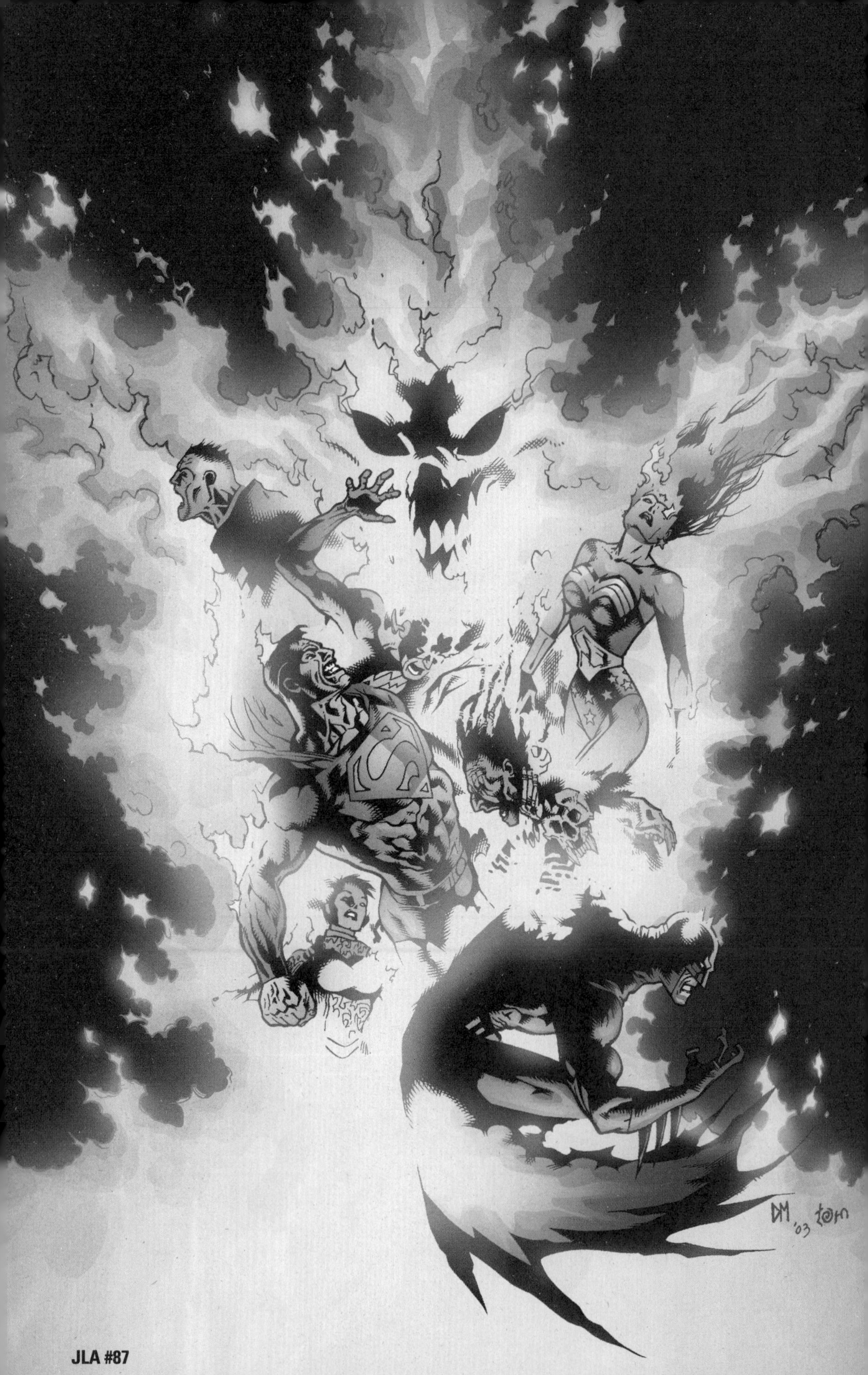

JLA #87

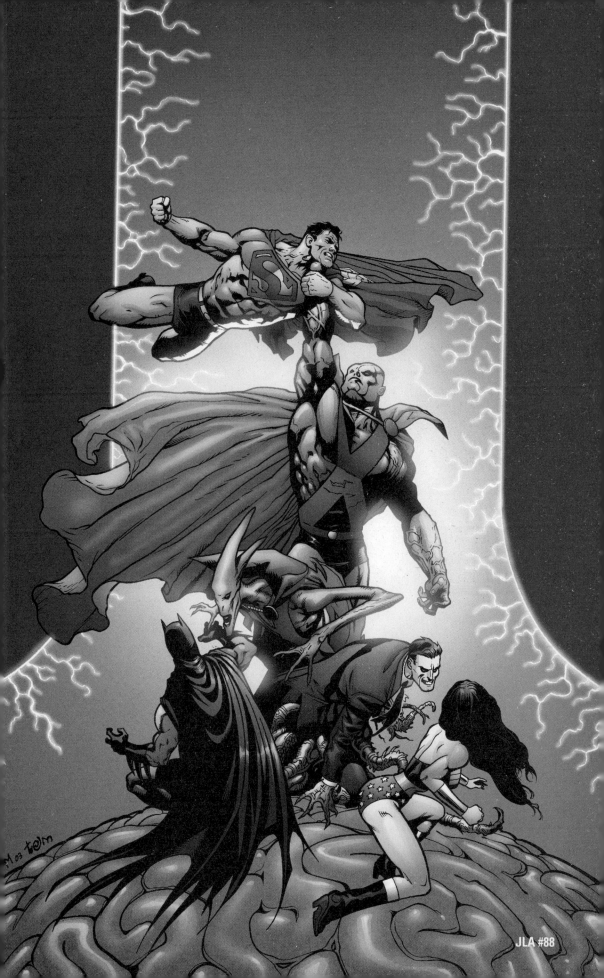

JLA #88

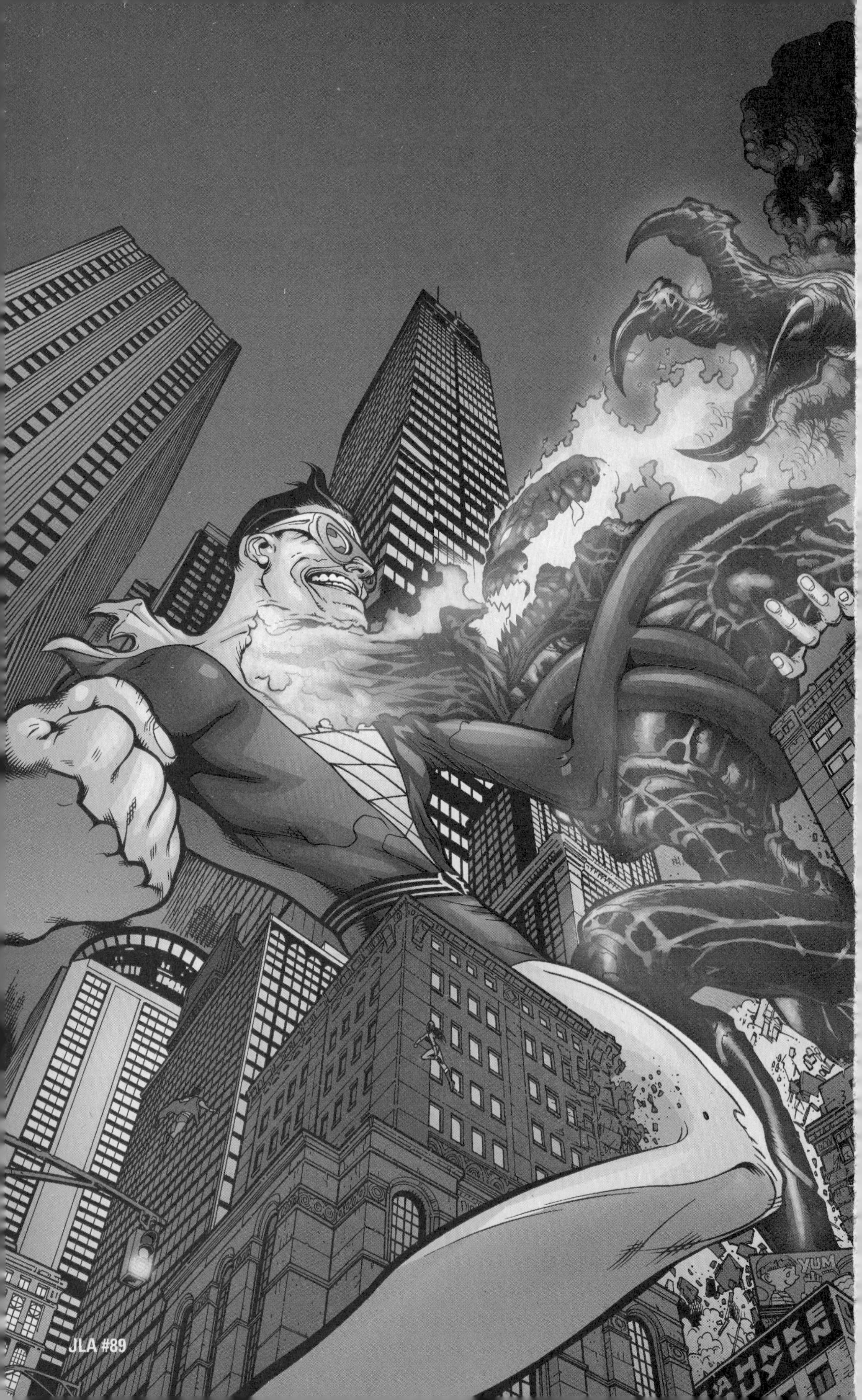
YUM

JLA #89